MURRAY'S
ENCYCLOPEDIA
OF
SOUTHERN GOSPEL MUSIC

Murray, David Bruce, 1966-

David Bruce Murray's Illustrated Encyclopedia of Southern Gospel Music

David Bruce Murray

For all the
fans of
Southern Gospel

Introduction

This book is an encyclopedia of Southern Gospel music. From all I've been able to gather, it's the only book of its kind that collects historical Southern Gospel data and categorizes it alphabetically.

This book is not meant to be a balanced look at the genre, however. I intentionally included some obscure entries for trivia buffs such as the **Brown's Berry Four** and a little known movie titled *Sing A Song For Heaven's Sake*. Popular groups haven't necessarily been treated equally either. For example, the **Statesmen Quartet** entry is much longer than the **Stamps Quartet** or the **Blackwood Brothers** entries. Some critics will likely say these entries should be equal in scope, but the point of this encyclopedia is not to proportionately represent groups based on their popularity.

The point of this work is to pass on to readers the results of my historical research. When my research led me to quite a bit more information about **Jack Toney** than it did about **Jim Hamill**, for example, I didn't feel like I should intentionally reduce the Toney entry so as to be consistent with the shorter length of the Hamill entry. I hope no one is offended by the lack of balance, because balance was never my intention in the first place.

The encyclopedia format of this book should allow you to use it as a reference work, but you can also read it from cover to cover. There's some redundancy from entry to entry where personalities overlap. This is intentional to aid the reader in mentally connecting the dots as they read through the material.

Every effort has been made to get all the facts correct in this book, but there's bound to be a few errors that slipped by. Corrections and additional information are welcome and may be directed to my attention via my website at www.musicscribe.com or by email to dbmurray@musicscribe.com. I hope to publish a greatly expanded second edition of this book a few years.

David Bruce Murray, October 6, 2005

Abernathy, Lee Roy
(Aug. 13, 1913 - 1993)

Lee Roy Abernathy was born into a sharecropping family that frequently relocated during his teen years. He began singing at the age of five in his father's group, the Atco Quartet, and learned to play piano by the time he was 14. In addition to sitting under shape note instructors like James Vaughan and Adger Pace, Abernathy studied at the Conservatory of Music in Atlanta, GA.

Abernathy wrote a number of gospel classics including "He's A Personal Savior," "A Newborn Feeling," "Wonderful Time Up There (Gospel Boogie)" and a parody of that song called "Terrible Time Down There." He was also noted as a Southern Gospel music instructor, particularly for his "Modern Gospel Piano Course By Mail." Along with Dwight Brock, Abernathy was one of the first to play "turnaround" type introductions on songs. He was responsible for printing the first gospel sheet music and boasted of thousands of piano students taught with his *Modern Gospel Piano Course by Mail*. He also served as a vocal coach to individuals such as London Parris who went on to have great success in the industry.

He wrote a book in 1948 simply entitled *IT*. The book is a collection of his songs and his commentaries about quartet life. It was designed to be a handbook for gospel musicians. It is a highly sought collector's item today.

Abernathy was also well known as a performer. He pulled stints with the Rangers and the Homeland Harmony Quartet. Abernathy and Carroll "Shorty" Bradford also performed together as the Happy Two, billed as a "two man quartet." The Happy Two were an unusual group. Their program focused on corny humor and drew from songs that had interesting parts that intertwined with each other. When they sang, they sounded almost like a quartet. Both singers had extensive vocal ranges, and this added to their appeal. At one time, a $500 diamond ring was offered to anyone that could sing as high and as low as Bradford. They excelled at novelty tunes. One of their recordings, "Shorty's Banjo," features Bradford playing "Cripple Creek" on the piano. He makes the piano sound remarkably like a 5-string banjo.

The expertise of these two gentlemen led them to form a new quartet in the early 1950s called the Miracle Men. A former comrade from the Homeland Harmony Quartet, Aycel Soward, joined the pair to sing bass. Earl Terry was the first tenor and Idus Spivey filled out the quartet at the baritone. When the Miracle Men were on a program, you could rest assured that they would be singing songs that no other group on the program would sing. This was because Abernathy was a prolific songwriter. Often, the group would sing five-part music with Abernathy providing the fifth vocal part. Abernathy and Bradford only kept the Miracle Men together for about a year before returning to their popular two-man format.

In addition to gospel music, politics also had an attraction for Abernathy. He composed songs for Franklin Roosevelt's 1936 campaign and was a candidate for governor of Georgia in 1958.

Abernathy continued to teach piano and voice lessons to many famous gospel musicians until his death in 1993. The SGMA Hall of Fame and the Georgia Music Hall of Fame have inducted him into their respective halls. In later years, he continued to travel on a part time basis with various quartets as a vocal coach and pianist. In 1983, a recording titled *Command Performance* paid tribute to the songs of Abernathy, with performances by the Rex Nelon Singers, Gold City, the Singing Americans, the Hemphills and others.
---John Crenshaw contributed to this entry.

Abner, James Buford
(Nov. 10, 1917-)
Buford Abner was best known for his work with the Swanee River Boys, a frequently featured group on the *Saturday Night Barn Dance* on radio station WSB in Atlanta. The group also released a number of radio transcriptions. Abner sang lead and managed the group until he retired in the early 1970s. The SGMA Hall of Fame inducted him in 2002.

Buford Abner has garnered his share of honors. The University of Florida recognized his accomplishments, presenting him with a copy of Stephen Foster's handwritten manuscript of the song "Way Down Upon the Suwanee River" Buford Abner was also an inductee into the Southern Gospel Music Association Hall of Fame in 2002, and was presented with a Living Legend Award at the 2003 Grand Ole Gospel Reunion. That evening, he joined with three other legends (Mosie Lister, Glen Allred, and Fred Daniel) to delight the crowd with a couple of songs in the old Swanee River Boys style.
---John Crenshaw contributed to this entry.

Aikin, Jesse
See: **Shape Note Method (Solfege)** and *Christian Minstrel*

Allen, Duane
Duane Allen sang lead for the popular Prophets quartet in the early 1960s, but is best remembered for his 40-year stint with the Oak Ridge Boys. With Allen at lead, the group was recognized as one of the top gospel quartets on the circuit until 1975 when they left gospel music to pursue a successful career in Country music. In 2001, Allen and the Oaks returned to gospel music when they signed with Spring Hill, one of the larger gospel record labels. Allen chose the songs and sang lead for an all gospel project titled

From The Heart. Another all gospel recording by the Oaks called *Common Threads* was released in 2005.

Allen, Joseph

Joseph Allen sang tenor for the original Vaughan Quartet in 1910. In 1917, he traveled with a unique group called the Vaughan Saxophone Quartet. This group sang songs in the expected Vaughan quartet style, but they also performed four part sax instrumentals.

All Night Sings

The Stamps-Baxter School Of Music promoted the first event to be billed as an "All Night Sing" in 1938 at the conclusion of a singing school they had sponsored in Dallas. It became an annual event that lasted into the 1950s. In 1948, Wally Fowler began hosting an all night singing event at the Ryman Auditorium in Nashvilee and broadcasting it over WSM radio. The popularity of the event caught on and was duplicated at venues across the country by Fowler and other concert promoters.

Allred, Glennan "Glen"
(Jun. 19, 1934-)

Glen Allred was born in Monroe, Tennessee. He joined the Oak Ridge Quartet when he was 16 to play guitar and sing baritone. He moved to the Gospel Melody Quartet in 1952, and has sung with that group (since re-named the Florida Boys) for over 50 years. Allred was recognized for his 50 plus years in gospel music in 2001 when he was inducted into the SGMA Hall of Fame.

America Sings

Produced by Jerry Goff, *America Sings* was a gospel show that aired on television from 1967 to 1972. The half hour program featured the Thrasher Brothers and Goff as recurring musical acts and helped to cement their respective careers as recognized Southern Gospel artists.

Andrus, Sherman

After singing with Andrae Crouch and The Disciples, Sherman Andrus was hired to sing for the Imperials in 1972. The Imperials were in the midst of a shift from traditional Southern Gospel to a more contemporary gospel style when Andrus joined them. Racial tensions were so tense at the time that Larry Gatlin sometimes filled in for Andrus at certain events, though Gatlin never recorded with the Imperials. In 1976, Andrus and Terry Blackwood left the Imperials to form a contemporary group called Andrus, Blackwood, and Company.

In 2004, the 1972-1976 version of the Imperials consisting of Andrus, Armond Morales, Jim Murray and Terry Blackwood recorded a CD along with the Stamps Quartet called *The Gospel Side Of Elvis*. Their live performance of "Swing Low, Sweet Chariot" at the 2004 National Quartet Convention featuring Andrus on a solo is included on a video project titled *Remembering The Greats*.

Arnold, Robert S.
(1905-)
Robert S. Arnold sang with the Carr Quartet in the 1920s. He started his National Music Company in 1937, and published shape note songbooks for 60 years.

Bagwell, Wendell Lee "Wendy"
(1925 - 1996)
After serving as a United States Marine, Wendy Bagwell formed the Sunliters in 1953 with Jan Buckner and Jerri Morrison. Their first major hit was a sentimental song called "Pearl Buttons." Over the next 40 years, the group released more than 60 recordings, and never changed the original lineup. The group is best remembered for their 1970 release titled *Here Come The Rattlesnakes*. The title track featured Bagwell's hilarious comedy routine about the Sunliters singing a date for a church that handled snakes in their worship services. It was the number one "song" on the *Singing News* chart from November 1970 to January 1971.

Bagwell was later hired to be a spokesman for Stanback brand headache powders in a television ad campaign. He became nationally known for his signature catch phrase "and that's a fact with my hand up." Some of his other comedy routines included "Ralph Bennett's Volkswagen," "Me, Old Ronnie, and the Monkey," and "Pickin' Up Paw Paws." Bagwell passed away in 1996 and was posthumously inducted into the SGMA Hall Of Fame in 1997.

A PARTIAL WENDY BAGWELL AND THE SUNLITERS DISCOGRAPHY: *This, That & The Other* (1970), *And That's A Fact With My Hand Up* (1986), *What's That Name?* (1988)

Bartlett, Eugene Monroe
(1884 - 1941)

E. M. Bartlett was a noted songwriter of hymns and Southern Gospel songs. In 1918, he became a founding partner in the Hartford Music Company. Like many music publishers of the day, Hartford began sponsoring traveling quartets who in turn promoted their products. In 1926, Albert E. Brumley joined the company and Bartlett served as his mentor.

In his career, Bartlett wrote a number of songs that are now Southern Gospel standards including "Everybody Will Be Happy Over There" and "Just a Little While to Stay Here." Bartlett also wrote the occasional novelty song, including "Take An Old Cold Tater And Wait" (later popularized by Little Jimmy Dickens). His best-known work was one of the last songs he wrote, the classic hymn "Victory In Jesus." It was written in 1939 just two years prior to his death in 1941. Bartlet's name was added to the SGMA Hall Of Fame in 2000.

Baxter, Clarice Howard
(1898 - 1972)

Clarice Baxter was the first woman in Gospel music circles to serve as president of a publishing company. Prior to achieving that status, Baxter was first exposed to Gospel music through singing schools in her native Georgia. In 1918, she became active in the music publishing industry alongside her husband J. R. Baxter, first at the A. J. Showalter Company and later with the company her husband co-owned with V. O. Stamps, the Stamps-Baxter Music and Printing Company. After her husband passed away in 1960, she assumed the duties that had previously been his. Her title was President and General Manager. Baxter's induction into the SGMA Hall Of Fame took place in 1997.

Baxter, **Jesse** Randall, Jr.
(1887 - 1960)

Inducted into the SGMA Hall Of Fame in 1997 along with his wife, J. R. Baxter first became involved in music publishing at the A. J. Showalter Company. In 1926, Baxter and V. O. Stamps launched the Stamps-Baxter Music and Printing Company, which ultimately grew to be the most prolific publisher of shaped note hymnbooks in the United States. In addition to publishing, Stamps-Baxter formed a school of music and sponsored numerous quartets who in turned sold Stamps-Baxter products to their audiences.

Beasley, Lester George "Les"
(1928 -)
Les Beasley joined the Gospel Melody Quartet in 1953 to sing lead and became the group's manager in 1958 following J. G. Whitfield's retirement. One mark Whitfield made on the group before his departure was changing their name to the Florida Boys.

Beasley has also promoted a number of Southern Gospel related business ventures over the years. He was a co-producer of *The Gospel Singing Jubilee*, a well-known television program that was syndicated during the 1960s and 1970s. Beasley continues to manage and perform with the Florida Boys today as their bass guitar player and emcee.

He is also a past president of the Gospel Music Association, and has held several leadership positions with the National Quartet Convention. He was inducted into the SGMA Hall Of Fame in 1997.

Bibletone Records
Dating back to the early 1950s, Bibletone Records was one of the first labels to be established exclusively for Gospel recording artists.

Bill Gaither Trio
Formed in the early 1960s as a family group consisting of siblings Bill, Danny, and Mary Ann Gaither, the Bill Gaither Trio quickly rose in popularity. After Mary Ann married, Bill's wife Gloria joined the group. The couple became a strong songwriting team. The trio was so successful their recording *Alleluia* (1968) sold over 250,000 units. In the 1970s, they were frequent guests at Billy Graham's crusades. The Gaither Trio's songs generally succeeded due to message driven lyrics rather than showy performance techniques. Their inspirational ballads include songs written by the Gaithers like "He Touched Me" and "The King Is Coming," which were frequently recorded by Southern Gospel groups of all types.

By the time Danny Gaither left the group, Bill and Gloria had begun to tour with an entourage of performers. Although Bill formed the all male Gaither Vocal Band in 1980, the trio continued to perform as well, typically with one of the Vocal Band members filling the lead singer role. The last recordings made by the trio featured Michael English at lead.

A PARTIAL BILL GAITHER TRIO DISCOGRAPHY: *Because He Lives* (1972), *Alleluia!* (1973), *Jesus, We Just Want To Thank You* (1975), *Fully Alive In His Spirit* (1983), *Hymn Classics* (1990)

The Bishops

From humble beginnings in the hills of central Kentucky in 1984, the Bishops became a household name in Southern Gospel. Starting on the front porch of their parents' house, brothers Mark and Kenny Bishop along with their dad, Kenneth, began a successful career.

With encouragement and financial support from the brothers' grandmother, the Bishops recorded *He Gave His Life*. Nashville producer Eddie Crook subsequently signed them to a recording contract. Under Crook's guidance, the group had a string of radio hits with songs like "Lazarus Come Forth" and "He's in the Midst," which was number one on the *Singing News* chart from February through April in 1991. After leaving the Eddie Crook Company in the mid-1990s, they signed with Homeland Records. The Bishops achieved success with songs like "When Jesus is All That I Have", "You Can't Ask too Much of My God", "What I Have" and "Reach the World". After leaving Homeland, the group signed with the newly formed Cathedral Records and released two more recordings.

Just before the National Quartet Convention in September 2001, the Bishops abruptly disbanded without public explanation. Kenneth retired from the road, Kenny became involved in politics, and Mark continued to sing as a soloist. Since then, the Bishops have reunited only for brief select performances. One reunion took place at the National Quartet Convention in 2002, and another was held during the Mark Bishop Homecoming in July 2003.

---James Hales contributed to this entry

Bishop, Mark

When the Bishops disbanded in 2001, Mark Bishop launched a solo ministry. Writing many of the Bishops best known songs, Mark had already established himself as an astute songwriter. In October of 2004, he had a number one single on the Singing News charts titled "Can I Pray For You," a rarity for a soloist. He reached number one again in April of 2005 with "I Got Here As Fast As I Could."

---James Hales contributed to this entry

Blackwood, James Webre
(1919 - 2002)

James Blackwood formed the Blackwood Brothers Quartet in the 1930s along with his two older brothers (Roy and Doyle) and a nephew (Roy's son, R. W.). The group turned heads over the next twenty years, but their career really began to skyrocket in 1954 when they won a competition on Arthur Godfrey's television program and were signed to record with RCA Victor. Tragedy also struck the group in 1954 when two members (R. W.

Blackwood and bass singer Bill Lyles) were killed in a plane crash in Clanton, AL. J. D. Sumner and Cecil Blackwood joined the group at that time and Wally Varner soon became their pianist.

James Blackwood and J. D. Sumner are noted for jointly designing the first bus for group touring purposes. They also started the National Quartet Convention, which grew to become the largest annual event in Southern Gospel music. Later Sumner and Blackwood purchased the Stamps Quartet and in time Sumner left the Blackwood Brothers to manage that group.

Following the formation of the Gospel Music Association in 1964, Blackwood served on the GMA board of directors. In 1971, Blackwood found himself at the center of an ethical scandal over methods the Blackwood Brothers used when selling GMA memberships at concerts. Ultimately, the Dove Awards were nullified for that year and Blackwood issued an apology to the industry. After the GMA expanded to cover all forms of Christian music in the 1980s, Blackwood frequently criticized the organization for promoting what he deemed to be worldly influences.

In the 1980s, Blackwood joined Hovie Lister, Jake Hess, J. D. Sumner, and Rosie Rozell to form the Masters V. The group was very popular on the concert circuit. Blackwood frequently performed "His Eye Is On The Sparrow" and "More And More Like Jesus Everyday," going out into the audience and delighting them by ending the song in tenor territory. Blackwood was in his mid-60s at the time.

After that group disbanded, he started the James Blackwood Quartet. This group included several former Blackwood Brothers members. Blackwood was also a frequent guest on the Gaither Homecoming videos in the 1990s until his death in 2002. He was inducted into the SGMA Hall Of Fame in 1997.

Blackwood, R. W.
(1921 - 1954)
R. W. Blackwood was a founding member of the Blackwood Brothers Quartet at the age of 13. For 20 years, he sang baritone alongside his uncle James as the group began its rise to national fame. R. W. was killed in a tragic plane crash along with the group's bass singer Bill Lyles in 1954. The SGMA recognized Blackwood's contributions to Gospel music in 2002, when he was inducted into the Hall Of Fame.

Blackwood Brothers
(1934-present)
Background
The Blackwood Brothers came from a large and musically gifted family. At least one photo of the family exists from 1899 that shows the Blackwood String Band. In that group were Emmitt Blackwood (father to Roy, Doyle, and James), and seven other aunts and uncles.

The Blackwood Brothers formed in 1934 in the midst of the Great Depression when preacher Roy Blackwood moved his family back home to Mississippi. His brothers Doyle and James (only 15 at the time) already had some experience singing with Vardaman Ray and Gene Catledge. Adding Roy's 13-year-old son R. W. to sing tenor, the brothers began to travel and sing locally. By 1940, they were affiliated with Stamp-Baxter to sell songbooks and were appearing on 50,000-watt radio station KMA in Shenandoah, Iowa.

The Roaring 50s
The quartet relocated to Memphis, TN in 1950. The move proved to be profitable for the group as they began to appear on television station WMCT in coming years. On June 14, 1954, the Blackwood Brothers won the *Arthur Godfrey's Talent Scouts* competition on national television with their rendition of "Have You Talked To The Man Upstairs?" The excitement was short lived however, when a fatal plane crashed claimed the lives of R. W. Blackwood and bass singer Bill Lyles just 16 days later in Clanton, AL. The popularity of the group was so strong at this point that 5000 people attended the joint funeral.

J. D. Sumner replaced Lyles at the bass position. In the following years, he and James Blackwood put a number of innovative ideas into play. They were the first to customize a bus for group travel and are the founders of the National Quartet Convention. Sumner also contributed to the group as a songwriter, sometimes writing all the songs for an album. The Blackwood Brothers were also setting new standards in the studio. Their RCA Victor recordings from this time period are now prized collectors' items.

The Blackwood Brothers formed a partnership with the Statesmen to tour as a team in the 1950s. By the end of the decade, the team was making up to $1500 per performance, an amount unheard of at the time. Due to their popularity, the team had a great deal of clout with concert promoters. The two groups were able to dictate who sang where and when. This dominance lasted for about a decade until the rise of gospel television shows in the late 1960s began to give competing groups wider exposure. The Blackwood Brothers were still a major force in the industry at the end of the 1960s. In 1969, they collected nearly 200,000 signatures on a "God And Country" petition in retaliation to the banning of prayer in school.

GMA Issues And The Longest Number One In History

In 1971, the Blackwood Brothers were at the center of a scandal that led to the Dove Awards being nullified for that year. An extraordinary number of Gospel Music Association memberships had been sold by the Blackwood Brothers the previous year, which skewed the final results of the Dove Awards in their favor (and in favor of groups they recommended to their fans). James Blackwood, who was on the GMA board of directors at the time, issued an apology to the industry on behalf of the Blackwood Brothers.

In 1970, the Blackwood Brothers shared a number one song on the *Singing News* chart with the Stamps called "The Night Before Easter," but their biggest success on the chart would come six years later. From August of 1976 to October of 1977, the Blackwood Brothers had the number one song on the *Singing News* chart for an unprecedented 15 months in a row. The song was "Learning To Lean." These were the only two songs that ever reached number one for the group, but it's safe to say they would have dominated in a similar fashion if a national gospel chart had been published during the 1950s and 1960s.

After the departure of James Blackwood, the Blackwood Brothers continued to sing together with various lineups for the rest of the 20th century. When the group disbanded after the death of Cecil Blackwood, James announced the group name was also to be retired. However, his son Jimmy put the name back to use following James' death. Various members of the Blackwood family have also formed groups that employed the banner of the family name...the Blackwood Singers, the Blackwood Gospel Quartet, and The Blackwoods being three variations from recent years. James Blackwood had a group in the 1990s billed as the James Blackwood Quartet.

A PARTIAL BLACKWOOD BROTHERS DISCOGRAPHY: *Hymn Sing* (1956), *Paradise Island* (1959), *Blackwood Family Album* (1964), *How Big Is God* (1966), *Just A Closer Walk With Thee* (1969), *L-O-V-E* (1972), *What A Beautiful Day For The Lord To Come Again* (1975), *On The Jericho Road* (1980), *The Answer* (1986), *Beulah Land* (2000)

Blue Ridge Quartet

The Blue Ridge Quartet formed in Dallas, Texas in 1946 as a part of the Stamps organization. The group soon moved to Raleigh, NC and then to Burlington, NC before settling for good in Spartanburg, SC in the late 1940s. They appeared on radio station WPSA. In their first few years, the group lineup changed often until the team of Elmo Fagg (lead & manager), Ed Sprouse (tenor), and Kenny Gates (baritone and pianist) got together in the early 1950s.

Burl Strevel was the bass singer for a while. George Younce sang bass later, and this core group remained together until Younce left to join the Cathedrals in 1964. The group hired Jim Hamill as baritone and later hired Bill Crowe. Crowe remained with the group until they disbanded. Burl Strevel returned to the group after the departure of Younce and remained with the group until his death. When Elmo Fagg retired in 1969, Laverne Tripp replaced him at the lead position. Tripp's songwriting skills and intense delivery brought a new appeal to the group. They experienced some of their finest moments with the personnel of Fred Daniel, Laverne Tripp, Bill Crowe, Burl Strevel, and Kenny Gates, adapting a country sound.

The Blue Ridge Quartet shared the number one song on the *Singing News* chart with the Oak Ridge Boys from February through November of 1971. The song was "I Know." Other number one songs for the group include "That Day Is Almost Here" (December 1971-February 1972) and "After Calvary" (October-November 1972). A number of personnel changes occurred in the 1970s. The quartet added a band, and began to sing country music in addition to gospel songs. Burl Strevel died after a massive heart attack in the late 1970s, and the group disbanded shortly thereafter.

The Blue Ridge Quartet was the first gospel group to record for Decca records. They were also the first professional gospel group to perform in a Catholic church. They recorded for Sing and Skylite in the 1960's and for Canaan in the 1970s, releasing over 100 albums in total. The group was also instrumental in forming the *Gospel Singing Caravan* with the Lefevres, Prophets, and Johnson Sisters. Other former members of the Blue Ridge Quartet include Otis Forrest, Don Seabolt, Norman Allman, Gary Timbs, David Reece, and "Tiny" Jack Taylor.

Kenny Gates, Bill Crowe, Fred Daniel are fixtures at the Grand Ole Gospel Reunion each year. Ed Sprouse, George Younce, Norman Allman, and Donnie Seabolt have joined them on the GOGR stage in the past.
---John Crenshaw contributed to this entry.

Bo Hinson and Purpose
See: **Hinsons**

Bob Poole's Gospel Favorites
Originally broadcast on WFBC in Greenville, SC, *Bob Poole's Gospel Favorites* was a syndicated music program on television in the late 1950s.

Booth Brothers

The original Booth Brothers of the late 1950s included Ron, Charles, James, and Wallace Booth. They were based in Detriot, MI and functioned as a regional group until 1963 when Ron left to sing with the Toney Brothers. Ron would go on to sing with the Rebels Quartet, the Thrasher Brothers, and the Stamps.

The second incarnation of the Booth Brothers formed in 1990, when Michael and Ronnie joined their father Ron. Over the next decade the group would come to be known for their infectious energy on stage. Ron Sr. retired and was replaced in 1995 by former Perfect Heart member Joseph Smith. Winning over fans at the Grand Ole Gospel Reunion and keeping a strong connection to traditional fans by involving legend Mosie Lister in their recordings, the group had a major hit with "Still Feeling Fine," a sequel to Lister's classic "I'm Feeling Mighty Fine."

Singer/songwriter Jim Brady took Smith's place after Smith joined the newly formed Mark Trammell Trio in 2002. The Booth Brothers subsequently signed with Spring Hill, releasing a self-titled project for the label in 2003 and a follow-up project in 2005 titled *The Blind Man Saw It All*. They also provided vocals for a worship song called "Adoration" that featured a significant stylistic turn from their typical Southern Gospel sound. The song can be found on a 2005 various artists release titled *Songs From The Bennett House.*

Bowling, Mike

With a voice often compared to the late Kenny Hinson, Mike Bowling carved out a successful career as a soloist in Southern Gospel. Many fans got their initial exposure to Bowling when he was singing with a group, though. He sang first with the LeFevres as a teenager during the 1970s and later formed a group with his brother Jeff called Family Tradition that performed on a regional basis for about ten years. In 1995, Bowling joined the New Hinsons, participating in the recording of their number one song, "Oasis." Later that same year, he moved to the Perrys where he stayed for the next four years and was instrumental in their success.

Bowling married Kelly Crabb in 1998. Their daughter Loryn Hope was born in 1999. After the birth of his child, Bowling joined the Crabb Family band so he could be closer to his family. It was then that he began releasing solo recordings on a regular basis.

Bowling had a great deal of success from the outset of his professional solo career. With the Crabb Family's band backing him during live appearances and the family's successful approach to radio promotion, Bowling's first single, "Forgiven, Forgotten, Forever, Amen" peaked at number four on the

Singing News chart. "Thank God For The Preacher" and "The Call" (from his project titled *The Call*) were back-to-back number ones, a first for a soloist. "I Take Him Back" was also a number one song in August of 2003.

Bowling has achieved recognition for his songwriting and his role as a producer for groups like the McCraes, the Hoskins Family, and the Crabb Family. In 2005, Bowling launched a mixed quartet called the Mike Bowling Group. Two former members of Family Tradition (his brother Jeff and their cousin Karen) joined Bowling along with Jeff's wife Kim.

Brian Free and Assurance
See **Free, Brian**

Brock, Dwight Moody
(1907 - 1988)
Dwight Brock was playing piano in a drugstore when a member of the Frank Stamps Quartet named Otis Echols discovered him. With the endorsement of Echols, Brock became a member of the group. This was the beginning of what became the traditional male quartet format: four singers plus a piano player. In the past, one of the singers had typically pulled double duty as the accompaniment either on piano or guitar.

Brock's talent and showmanship elevated the pianist to a more prominent role. He is credited as being the first pianist to add "turnarounds" between verses. He played for various Stamps quartets in the 1920s and 1930s and ultimately became president of the Stamps-Baxter Music Company.

Brock was with the Stamps when they first recorded "Give The World A Smile," a song J. D. Sumner would revive years later when he began to manage the Stamps Quartet. Brock also performed with the Vaughan Radio Quartet. His sister Lena became the matriarch of the legendary Speer family.

Brock was inducted into the Southern Gospel Piano Roll of Honor in 1996, and into the SGMA Hall Of Fame in 2003.

Brown's Ferry Four
Formed in 1946, the Brown's Ferry Four gospel quartet consisted of four Country music singers. Alton and Rabon Delmore were already established as a Country act called The Delmore Brothers when the group formed. Merle Travis and Louis Marshall Jones ("Grandpa" Jones of *Hee Haw* fame) would be more widely recognized in years to come. One of the first songs

recorded by the group was Cleavant Derrick's classic "Just A Little Talk With Jesus."

Brumley, Albert Edward
(1905 - 1977)
Albert E. Brumley wrote approximately 700 gospel songs. Many are now classics that even non-gospel fans will immediately recognize. Songs like "I'll Fly Away," "Turn Your Radio On," "If We Never Meet Again" and "I'll Meet You in the Morning" are still sung often in churches and concert halls across the country.

Brumley first began writing songs when he was a student at E. M. Bartlett's Hartford Music Institute. Brumley later worked there as an instructor. By 1943, he had established his own music publishing company.

Brumley's induction as a charter member of the Nashville Songwriter's Hall of Fame demonstrates his impact on the secular music industry. The SGMA Hall Of Fame inducted him in 1997. Each year, a four night concert series in Fayetteville, Arkansas commemorates the life of Albert E. Brumley. The event has been held annually since 1969.

Bruno, Nick
Nick Bruno was a key contributing member of several groups during in the 1960s and 1970s. As a teen, he was a member of the Keystone Quartet with Richard Sterban. He and Sterban moved to the Eastman Quartet in the mid-1960s, but later returned to the Keystone Quartet. Future Oak Ridge Boys member Joe Bonsall and future Imperials member David Will would get their first full time singing jobs with the Keystone Quartet. Bruno began producing, arranging and working as a session piano player at Baldwin Sound Productions when the Keystone Quartet was based in Harrisburg, PA in the late 1960s.

He traveled with the Stamps for a year or so during their early Elvis years before joining the Kingsmen in 1972. Later, Bruno produced the novelty song "Excuses" for the Kingsmen. The song held the number one position on the *Singing News* chart for ten months in 1981-82. Bruno would produce another mega-hit for a former Kingsmen Quartet member not long after the success of "Excuses." The song was "Beulah Land" and the singer was Squire Parsons.

Bruno worked in Branson, MO for five years producing live shows for some of the top secular acts there. He later returned to Nashville, TN where he produced recordings that helped elevate artists like Quinton Mills and the Booth Brothers.

In recent years, Bruno has become a mentor of sorts to young artists. He writes a regular article for Sogospelnews.com that typically focuses on the business side of the industry. He has also written a book about the industry called *The Gospel Music Truth*. Meanwhile, Bruno has continued to record and produce. His most recent venture is a record label called Song Garden that is designed for up-and-coming Southern Gospel artists.

Burger, Anthony
(1961-)
After suffering third degree burns on his hands at eight months of age, Anthony Burger's doctor told his parents he wouldn't likely be able to move his hands in the future. Despite the odds, Burger was healed. At the age of five, he was accepted at the Cadek Conservatory in Chattanooga, TN. A child prodigy, Burger was playing classical piano repertoire within a few years.

Burger's first recording, *Anthony Burger At The Lowry Organ* was released in 1975 when he was 14 years old. He joined the Kingsmen while still a teen and remained with that group until 1992. During that time, Burger recorded nineteen projects with the group and was voted the Favorite Pianist in the *Singing News* Fan Awards for an unprecedented ten years. The award was renamed the Anthony Burger Award for several years after that. During this period, Burger presented the award to the winner each year, but was ineligible to receive it.

In 1992, Burger left the Kingsmen Quartet to pursue a career as a solo pianist. He joined the Gaither Homecoming tour the following year and has since been featured on more than 65 Homecoming videos. Burger has continued to release piano solo recordings and headline concerts, but his solo schedule is now balanced by about 80 Gaither Homecoming dates per year. Adding more variety to his schedule, Burger formed an impromptu group with Ivan Parker and Kirk Talley in 1998 called The Trio. The group performs at several events each year. (Shane Dunlap has since replaced Parker.) Burger's piano folios are popular among keyboard players. The Hazelton Brothers piano company also honored Burger when they began offering an "Anthony Burger Signature" model.

Burke, Charles
Charles Burke is an entrepreneur with business interests ranging from Southern Gospel to funeral homes. He was an original member of the Pine Ridge Boys. Burke also owned and managed one of the more popular quartets in the 1980s, the Singing Americans. He owns Tape Corporation of

America, a factory based in Maiden, NC that services many Southern Gospel artists with cassette and CD replication as well as graphic design.

Butler, Don

Don Butler sang baritone with the Sons Of Song trio in the late 1950s. He later moved to working behind the scenes in the gospel music industry. In the 1980s, Butler served as the Executive President for the Gospel Music Association.

Canaan Records

Formed in 1963 as a division of Word, Inc., the Canaan label was managed for years by Marvin Norcross. The Canaan roster included the Florida Boys, the Cathedrals, the Happy Goodmans, the Inspirations, the Speer Family, and many other top groups in the industry.

Carter, Anna (Anna Carter Gordon Davis)
(Feb. 15, 1917-Mar. 5, 2004)

Effie Carter's bout with pneumonia at the age of 18 prompted her father David Carter to audition with son Ernest and daughter Lola for a job singing on radio station KFYO in Lubbock, TX. When the job was secured, he requested an advance to pay for Effie's medical expenses. Effie recovered and joined the group to sing alto. The group was initially known as the Carter Quartet.

The following year, Effie was given the radio name "Anna" by talent agent Cy Leland. Although Effie had a 12-year old sister named Anna, she assumed it would only be a temporary change. The group name was soon changed to the Chuck Wagon Gang Of the Air, which was later shortened to the Chuck Wagon Gang. They were known for singing simple arrangements of western songs and using just an acoustic guitar for accompaniment. After a few years, they began limiting their song selection to gospel numbers.

Anna later married Howard Gordon, who served as the Chuck Wagon Gang's guitar player. After her husband died in 1967 and with her brother Roy off the road, Anna, Jim Black and Anna's children Greg and Vicki made up the Chuck Wagon Gang for several months. In 1968, Anna re-married to songwriter Jimmie Davis, a former governor of Louisiana and composer of the Country music classic "You Are My Sunshine." She soon began singing regularly with Davis in a trio. Her son Greg went on to sing with the Imperials in the early 1970s.

In the early 1970s, the Chuck Wagon Gang did not tour. They did continue to record for Columbia Records, and Anna made herself available for the recording sessions. After the group began to tour part time in the late 1970s, she sang with them sporadically, but eventually withdrew from the road permanently.

Carter, David Parker "Dad"
(1889 - 1962)
Like other groups that rose out of the depression, Dad Carter formed the Carter Quartet in 1935 to escape the low paying, back breaking work of the cotton fields. He was joined by three of his nine children, Effie, Rosa Lola, and Ernest. Under Dad's guidance, they signed to record for Columbia the following year. Dad also secured the group a spot on WBAP in Fort Worth, TX where they came to be known as the Chuck Wagon Gang. The group would sing on the radio and sell recordings for the next fifteen years before they ventured out to tour.

The SGMA Hall Of Fame inducted Dad Carter into membership in 1997.

Carter, Roy
(Mar. 1, 1926-Aug. 4, 1997)
Roy Carter served in the Navy near the end of WWII and was ultimately discharged in February of 1946. In 1947, Roy majored in Bible and education at Abilene Christian College using his G.I. Bill supplement of $90 per month to pay expenses. He completed his double major in three years. After trying his hand at preaching, teaching, and selling insurance, he moved back home to Texas to sing bass with his family's group, the Chuck Wagon Gang, who had just started actively touring after 15 years singing almost exclusively on radio.

After five years on the road, Roy took a break from the Gang in 1957 to sell school supplies for Weber-Costello. The group itself entered a period of semi-retirement at this time, though they continued to record. Roy returned to the group in 1963, but in 1967 he came off the road again, this time to try his hand at teaching once more and focus his attention on earning his Masters degree. As before, the group reduced its touring schedule and ultimately ceased to tour after Anna Carter married former Louisiana governor Jimmie Davis in 1968.

In the mid-1970s, Roy reorganized the Chuck Wagon Gang with his sisters Ruth Ellen and Bettye. Ronnie Page and Pat McKeehan alternated on the fourth part and Anna Carter Davis sometimes sang in place of Ruth Ellen when her schedule permitted. At first, they only sang on a summer schedule to allow Roy to continue teaching. Once the group stabilized with McKeehan and Ruth Ellen around 1977, Roy began making plans to return to full time touring. In 1987, Roy retired from teaching and realized his dream of touring full time once again. He continued to sing with the Chuck Wagon Gang for the next ten years until his death in 1997.

Roy Carter received the Marvin Norcross award in 1989.

The Cathedrals
(1963-1999)
The Cathedral Trio was formed in 1963 as a ministry of Rex Humbard's Cathedral Of Tomorrow in Akron, OH. Original members included Glen Payne, Danny Coker and Bobby Clark, all previous members of the Weatherford Quartet whose owners Earl and Lily Fern Weatherford had decided to return to an active touring schedule. Bass singer George Younce joined the group in 1964, transforming the Cathedrals into a quartet.

Over the next 30 years under the leadership of Payne and Younce, the Cathedrals became a household name among Southern Gospel fans. The group had their first number one song on the *Singing News* chart in October of 1983 with "Step Into The Water," a song written by Kirk Talley who was singing tenor for them at the time. The song remained number one through June of the following year. The Cathedrals had five more number one songs in the years that followed, including "Can He, Could He, Would He" (October-November, 1986), "Boundless Love" (April-May, 1987), "I Can See The Hand" (April-May, 1989), "Wedding Music" (November 1992-January 1993), and "He Made A Change" (May 1999).

Driven by Payne's energetic lead vocals and Younce's comedic appeal as the group emcee and bass singer, the group dominated the *Singing News* Fan Awards in the 1990s and appeared on the GMA sponsored Dove Awards broadcast. A farewell tour and the death of Glen Payne ended the Cathedrals' run in 1999.

Some of the group's most popular concert tunes included "This Old House," "Goin' In Style," "Champion Of Love," and "Oh, What A Savior." The group released more than 100 original and compilation recordings over the course of their 36-year history.

Several former Cathedrals members went on to establish their own successful groups in Southern Gospel. These include Mark Trammell (Greater Vision/Mark Trammell Trio), Gerald Wolfe (Greater Vision), Roger Bennett and Scott Fowler (Legacy V), and Ernie Haase (Signature Sound). They all credit the guidance of Payne and Younce during their time as Cathedrals as a key to their current success.

A PARTIAL CATHEDRALS DISCOGRAPHY: *Introducing the Cathedral Trio* (1963), *The Last Sunday* (1973), *Statue of Liberty* (1974), *Then & Now*

(1977), *Master Builder* (1986), *Symphony Of Praise* (1987), *Radio Days* (1996), *Faithful* (1998), and *A Farewell Celebration* (1999)

Charles Johnson and the Revivers
See: **Johnson, Charles**

Christian Minstrel
Published in 1846 by Jesse Aiken, the *Christian Minstrel* was the first songbook to employ what is now accepted as the de facto system for shape note notation. Subsequent editions were published for the next 30 years.

Chestnut Grove Quartet
(1945-1994)
Chestnut Grove Methodist Church in Washington County, VA had no musical instruments in the years following the second World War, so church members Bill Nunley, Jim Nunley, Archie Reynolds, and Gale Webb learned how to read shape notes and sang a cappella. By the mid-1950s, they were Sunday afternoon regulars on WBBI in Abingdon, VA and traveling to other states like Kentucky and Tennessee.

Ray Roe took over the baritone spot after Reynold's death in 1962. The group's regional fame increased after they began recording at Arthur Smith Studios in Charlotte, NC. At the height of their popularity, the Chestnut Grove Quartet sold more than 50,000 LPs in one 18-month period. This group was a significant influence on popular bluegrass artists who perform a cappella gospel such as Ralph Stanley and Doyle Lawson.

Following Roe's death in 1987, Bill's wife Ann Statzer Nunley joined the quartet. The group traveled and sang on radio broadcasts for another seven years.

Chuck Wagon Gang
(1935-present)
David Carter formed the Carter Quartet in 1935. He was initially joined by three of his nine children, Effie, Rosa Lola, and Ernest. They sang on KFYO radio in Lubbock. A year later, they had secured a recording deal with Columbia that would continue for an unprecedented 40 years. They also were appearing on a daily radio broadcast from WBAP in Fort Worth.

The group was soon hired to fill a radio spot on WBAP sponsored by Bewley's Mill Flour. At this point, the group name was changed to the Chuck

Wagon Gang Of The Air. The flour company also sponsored a touring male quartet called the Chuck Wagon Gang, but when that group disbanded, the Carter family became the only Chuck Wagon Gang. At the encouragement of talent agent Cy Leland, the group members began to use more "radio friendly" names. David became "Dad," Ernest was "Jim," Rosa Lola was shortened to "Rose," and Effie became "Anna" (despite having a 12-year old sister named Anna).

After 15 successful years on WBAP, the Chuck Wagon Gang embarked on their first major tour in 1951. It was a huge success. Brothers Roy and Eddie Carter soon replaced Jim and Dad and Anna's husband Howard Gordon joined to play guitar.

At various points in the Gang's 70-year history, eight of the nine Carter family siblings sang with the group. Mom Carter sang at times as well. Roy took a couple of extended breaks from touring (as did the group), but he became the most constant Carter family representative. Other notable members included Ronnie Page, Pat McKeehan, Debby Trusty, Mae Kutz, and Roy's daughter Shirley. Although guitar was used almost exclusively for accompaniment throughout the 70-year history of the Chuck Wagon Gang, they did have one piano player, Harold Timmons, during the late 1980s.

Following Roy Carter's death in 1997, the group name was retired. Anna Carter's granddaughter, Shaye Truax, re-established the Chuck Wagon Gang in 1999. Rose Carter's son Rick Karnes was also a member of the new Gang in 1999, along with another former member Darrell Morris. Long time member Ronnie Page returned to sing tenor and emcee for the group in 2003.

Combs, Michael
(1957-)
Michael Combs has been singing gospel music since 1991 after giving his heart to Christ in 1989 at the age of 31. An ad campaign for a recording called *Lambitus* introduced him to Southern Gospel fans. Curiosity was sparked at first by advertisements stating that the singer had a rare "disease," which was later revealed to be Lambitus.

With Combs combining his somewhat unorthodox vocal style with a string of popular and at times, controversial songs, he soon had a dedicated group of fans. The Solid Gospel radio network refused to air "Not For Sale" due to what they deemed to be low production quality, but fans requested the song so much that it still landed at number five on the *Singing News* chart. Other popular songs by Combs include "It's Time To Get Up" and "Drinking From My Saucer."

Cook, Martin Alfred
(1936 -)

Martin Cook played piano for the Kingsmen early in his career. He later taught chemistry and physics at Swain High School in Bryson City, NC. It was there in 1964 that he convinced four of his students to form the group that ultimately became the Inspirations. Cook retired from teaching in 1969 to devote his attention to full time gospel music. The move would prove to be successful for Cook as the Inspirations had a number of hit songs during the 1970s, including "When I Wake Up To Sleep No More" and "Touring That City." Cook has developed a recognizable style at the piano. The SGMA Hall Of Fame recognized Cook for his achievements in 2003.

The Couriers
(1955 - present)

The Couriers formed in 1955 at the Assemblies Of God Central Bible Institute in Springfield, MO. They became full time professionals in 1958, with group members Neil Enloe (lead), Duane Nicholson (tenor), Don Baldwin (baritone), Dave Kyllonen (bass), and Eddie Reece (piano). Harrisburg, PA became the group's home after they scouted the country for areas where their competition would be minimal. The group soon secured a spot singing on radio station WCMB.

By the early 1960s, the Couriers were key concert promoters as well as performers. In 1964, they became one of the original groups included on the nationally televised *Gospel Singing Jubilee*. In 1967, the Couriers scaled back to a trio format and released *Here Come The Couriers*. The group also popularized the use of pre-recorded soundtracks. The Vicounts (a group that was started by the Couriers and traveled often with them all across the US) actually initiated the practice.

The Couriers experimented with producing their own television show as early as 1966 on WHP in Harrisburg. They discontinued their initial venture due to finances, but re-established a television presence in the early 1970s on WGAL.

The Couriers commonly stood in contrast to the rest of the entertainment driven industry with their ministry approach during concerts. Although other groups certainly promoted the gospel, the Couriers' program had an altar call as its primary focus. Neil Enloe wrote a hit song for the group in the early 1970s called "Statue Of Liberty" that became their signature tune. Unlike most southern gospel style groups, the Couriers have experienced the bulk of their success in the northeastern United States and Canada.

In 1980, the group went on hiatus for two years following Duane Nicholson's unsuccessful 1978 throat surgery. Kyllonen became involved with his own family's ministry, so former member Phil Enloe rejoined Neil Enloe and Nicholson in 1982 after Duane's voice had healed. The group continued until 2001 when the men retired and the Couriers name was turned over to the New Couriers, who they had been mentoring. In 2004, Dave Kyllonen, Nicholson, and Neil Enloe went back on the road together billed as "Dave, Duane, and Neil."

---Cliff Cerce contributed to this entry.

A PARTIAL COURIERS DISCOGRAPHY: *Nothing But The Gospel Truth* (1963), *Here Come The Couriers* (1967), *Statue of Liberty* (1974), *Ovation* (1976)

The Crabb Family

Gerald and Kathy Crabb organized the Crabb Family in the mid-1990s. Their five children joined them in the venture. Based in Kentucky, the group was quickly accepted by Southern Gospel radio and concert fans. Their live band stood out in a genre where many groups perform with only one instrumentalist or none at all. Siblings Jason and Aaron play guitar, and their brother Adam is a masterful harmonica player. Kathy played keyboard during their early years, as well, and all the group members sing.

Written by Gerald Crabb, the song "Please Forgive Me" was the number one song on the *Singing News* chart from July through October in 1998. Other number one songs for the Crabb Family during the 20th century include "Trail Of Tears" (March-April, 1999), "The Lamb, The Lion, And The King" (October 1999), "I Sure Miss You" (February 2000), and "Through The Fire" (May-July 2000).

The Crabb Family then went 14 months without a number one song, their longest dry spell. In October of 2001, "That's No Mountain" hit number one and the frequency of their visits to the top spot accelerated to an unprecedented pace. They would claim the record for the most number one songs in *Singing News* chart history by June of 2004, surpassing the previous record of 11 set by the McKameys in 2002. Since then, they've had two more number ones, giving them a total of 14.

The group's nine number one songs since 2001 are "That's No Mountain" (October 2001), "The Reason That I'm Standing" (March-April, 2002), "Don't You Wanna Go" (September 2002), "Please Come Down To Me" (January-February, 2003), "The Walk" (July 2003), "The Cross" (November-December, 2003), "Jesus Will Do What You Can't" (June 2004), "He Came Looking For Me" (January 2005), and "The Shepherd's Call" (October-November, 2005).

Gerald and Kathy withdrew from the concert stage to a degree after the turn of the century. Their daughter Terah also stopped touring for a period of time. The cover of the 2004 recording *Driven* displays siblings Jason, Kelly, Adam, and Aaron. With pop influenced songs like "Sacrifice Of Praise," a Southern rock feel with "Chapter 2" and a remake of "Through The Fire" with Donnie McClurkin joining the group on vocals, the new recording opened a number of doors to the Crabb Family and garnered Dove Award nominations for the group in categories where Southern Gospel artists are typically overlooked.

By 2005, Gerald Crabb was established as a soloist, preacher and songwriter. The group had also helped launch the careers of artists like the McCraes and the Hoskins Family through their own record label. Creative marketing techniques combined with events like Crabbfest and the Crabb Jam tour constantly keep the group's name in front of their fans. By mixing compatible names from the contemporary genre (Avalon, Michael English, etc.) with more traditional Southern Gospel acts at their events, the Crabb Family is often viewed as a uniting force in gospel music.

Crabb, Gerald

A former alcoholic, Gerald Crabb's testimony of salvation and God's grace is a driving force behind his songwriting and preaching. In the mid-1900s, his wife and children joined him in forming a traveling music ministry known as the Crabb Family. Ten years later, the group had seen 14 songs (all composed by Crabb) reach the number one position on the *Singing News* airplay chart. Mike Bowling, the Perrys, and the Talley Trio have also had number one recordings using Crabb's material. He has been also been lauded by BMI and the GMA for his songwriting.

Crabb reduced his appearances with the family group in 2002 to focus on preaching in revivals and camp meetings. He has one solo recording called *Roads That I've Traveled.* Although he ceased touring as heavily, he has continued to write songs. The Crabb Family's 2004 release *Driven* includes twelve of Gerald Crabb's songs, including a remake of an early hit called "Through The Fire." Other well known songs written by Crabb include "The Healer," "Please Forgive Me," "Thank God For The Preacher," and "That's No Mountain."

Crosby, Fanny
(1820-1915)

Fanny Crosby wrote more than 8000 gospel song texts in her 95 years. Blind from the age of six, she wrote both secular and sacred poetry as well. In addition to her own name, Crosby used more than 200 pseudonyms when publishing her songs. A few of Crosby's most popular song texts include "Rescue The Perishing," "Blessed Assurance," "To God Be The

Glory," "Tell Me The Story Of Jesus," and "Near The Cross." Most modern collections of hymn recordings include at least one Crosby song.

Cross, Phil

Phil Cross first made a name for himself as a songwriter. A number of high profile groups recorded his songs in the 1980s. His most notable song is arguably "Champion Of Love," which was popularized by the Cathedrals and won a Dove Award. Other songs by Cross from that time period include "When I Get Carried Away," "Saved To The Uttermost," "Miracle In Me," and "Wedding Music."

Cross formed Poet Voices in 1991. Their song "Jesus Built A Bridge" was number one on the *Singing News* chart from December 1991 to February 1992. The group returned to the top position with "I Am Redeemed" in 1998 and again in 2002 with "The Key." Around this time, the group disbanded for a couple of years, but formed again as a trio in 2004 with Cross, Mark Lanier, and Greg Crowe. In addition to his work with Poet Voices, Cross is president of a choral music publishing company called Cross Music Group. He has continued to write songs for other artists as well.

The Crusaders

Formed by former Statesmen tenor Bobby Strickland in the early 1950s, the Crusaders were based in Birmingham, AL and recorded for the Bullet and Bibletone labels. Strickland was one of many gospel music singers that came from the Sand Mountain, AL area. The Crusaders were an immediate hit due in part to their daily program on radio station WVOK in Birmingham.

The quartet went through a few personnel changes at first, but began to gel when Strickland had Buddy Parker singing lead, Hershell Wooten on bass, and Dickie Matthews playing the piano. These three young gentlemen were relatively new to professional gospel music, but all went on to have long careers in the industry. In addition to Strickland's work with the Crusaders Quartet, he also taught voice to various students in the Birmingham area. The Thrasher Brothers were among his young students.

Unfortunately, the Crusaders were short lived. Strickland was killed in an automobile accident in September of 1953 at the age of 33. Initially, the remaining member of the group asked another Sand Mountain tenor named Bill Hefner to replace Strickland, but the arrangement didn't work out. The Crusaders soon disbanded.

Buddy Parker, Herschel Wooten, and Bill Hefner later sang with the Harvesters Quartet, a popular act on radio station WBT in Charlotte, NC. The Crusaders Quartet left behind about twenty songs recorded on 78rpm

vinyl. Although their career was short and recording output limited, they were on the cusp of greatness prior to the death of Bobby Strickland.
---John Crenshaw contributed to this entry.

Crumpler, Denver Dale
(1914 - 1957)
Denver Crumpler was a native of Magnolia, Arkansas. He first sang with the Stamps Melody Boys in the 1930s. He joined the Rangers Quartet in 1938 just before they began a five-year stint at radio station WBT in Charlotte, NC, and stayed with them for more than 10 years. Crumpler subsequently joined Hovie Lister and the Statesmen in 1953. Noted for his Irish tenor style on tunes like "Climbing Higher and Higher," Crumpler was only 43 when he passed away in 1957. 40 years later, Crumpler was inducted into the SGMA Hall Of Fame.

Daniel, John Tyra
(1906 - 1961)
John Daniel formed the Daniel Family Quartet with his brothers and sisters in Alabama during the early 1920s. They became a full time male quartet headed by Daniel and his brother Troy in the 1930s. Partnering with hymnal publishers like Showalter, Vaughan, and Stamps-Baxter, the group (now billed as the John Daniel Quartet) ultimately ended those affiliations in 1942 to sing on WSM in Nashville, TN. This in turn led to them joining the cast of the Grand Ole Opry. With the popularity of the Opry broadcasts over WSM's powerful AM clear channel, the John Daniel Quartet became one of the most heard groups in the 1940s and 1950s. The SGMA recognized Daniel for his leadership in gospel music in 1997 when they inducted him into their Hall Of Fame.

Davis, James Houston "Jimmie"
(1899 - 2000)
Jimmie Davis got his start in the music business writing country songs in the 1920s and 1930s. His most popular tune is "You Are My Sunshine," written in 1940. He also played roles in several westerns filmed by Columbia Pictures in the 1940s. It was also during the early 1940s that Davis pursued a political career, ultimately becoming governor of Louisiana in 1944. In his later campaigns for political office, Davis would sing gospel music while the Plainsmen Quartet backed him up. This endeared him to voters, and he served a second term as governor in the early 1960s.

Davis recorded on the RCA Victor label and also on Decca, and was best remembered for his vocal performances of the songs "Suppertime" and "Mansion Over A Hilltop." He also wrote a number of gospel songs including

"Someone To Care" and "Sheltered In The Arm Of God" (co-written with Dottie Rambo). Davis served a term as President of the GMA in 1967, and married Chuck Wagon Gang member Anna Carter Gordon the following year. The Nashville Songwriters, Country Music, and SGMA have inducted Davis into their respective Halls Of Fame.

Daywind Records

With the demise of the Canaan (Word) and Heartwarming/Riversong (Benson) labels in the late 1980s and early 1990s, Daywind Records emerged as a primary record label for Southern Gospel artists. Initially developing new artists like the Steeles and the Freemans, Daywind became the home to more established artists like Greater Vision, Gold City, and Legacy V as the 20th century drew to a close. Much of Daywind's success can also be credited to their large line of accompaniment soundtracks and the success of their sister company, New Day Distribution.

Deep South Quartet

Jimmy Jones had a storied career in gospel music prior to forming the Deep South Quartet. He had been the bass singer and stand-up bass guitarist for the Melody Ranch Boys, a group that performed western swing music in addition to their gospel fare. Jones had also sung bass with the Rangers Quartet for several years, filling in for Arnold Hyles who was in an automobile accident in 1951. Once Hyles returned, Jones sang baritone for the Rangers for a short time before departing the group to form the Deep South Quartet.

Jones moved to the Atlanta area and hired several seasoned quartet veterans to sing with him. Jone's brother, Brownie Jones, sang baritone. Cat Freeman was their tenor, and Bob Crews was the group's first lead singer. The group hired another quartet veteran, Wally Varner, to play piano. Wally is best known for his stint with the Blackwood Brothers, which would come later, but he was already famous in gospel music circles when he joined the Deep South Quartet, having played previously with the Melody Masters and the Homeland Harmony Quartet.

The original Deep South Quartet became popular on the quartet circuit, but as with so many groups of this era, changes in personnel came fast and frequently. Crews left to sing with other Atlanta-based groups before rejoining the Harmoneers. Varner and Freeman both joined the Revelaires. Jones subsequently hired two men to replace the three that had departed. Future Kingsmen Quartet member Kermit Jamerson joined the group as tenor and former Rangers Quartet member David Reece came on board to fill a dual role as pianist and lead vocalist. Jones and Reece were both comfortable with the four-man group, as they had quite a bit of experience with this aggregation in the Rangers Quartet.

After David Reece left the group, he returned to his home state of North Carolina where he joined the newly formed Harvesters Quartet. The Harvesters were made up of several members of the now defunct Crusaders Quartet. The former pianist of the Crusaders Quartet, Dickie Matthews, moved to Atlanta and became a member of the Deep South Quartet, essentially swapping places with Reece. Lewis McKinney sang lead for a short time after Reece's departure, but was soon replaced by Tommy Rainer. Several of the Deep South Quartet's most popular songs featured Rainer's unique vocals.

Bob Robinson followed Dickie Matthews as pianist. Before joining the Deep South Quartet, Robinson had been a pianist and vocalist with the LeFevres. When Kermit Jamerson left the group, Jimmy Jones offered Bobby Clark his first professional job in gospel music. Clark would later sing with a number of successful gospel quartets including the Oak Ridge Quartet, Weatherford Quartet, and Dixie Echoes. Clark is best known for his stint as the original first tenor for the Cathedral Quartet. Unfortunately, the group made up of Clark, Rainer, the Jones brothers and Robinson never made any recordings. The Deep South Quartet was offered an opportunity to move to the Washington, D.C. area that they accepted. After working there for a few months, the group disbanded.
---John Crenshaw contributed to this entry.

Derricks, Lister Cleavant
(May 13, 1910 - 1977)
Baptist minister Cleavant Derricks was a writer of gospel songs whose works are counted as standards among Southern Gospel quartets today. "Just a Little Talk With Jesus", "When He Blessed My Soul", "We'll Soon Be Done With Troubles and Trials", and "When God Dipped His Love in My Heart" are just a few of the more than 300 songs he contributed to gospel music. Many of his songs were published by Stamps-Baxter in the Depression era. In addition to songwriting, Derricks served as pastor and choir director in Tennessee, Wisconsin, and Washington, DC.

Derrick's son (also named Cleavant) began a career in entertainment by following in his father's footsteps initially. The two co-wrote a Grammy nominated project called *Satisfaction Guaranteed* in 1976, which was released on the Canaan label a year before the elder Derricks' death. It was a follow-up to the 1975 release *Just A Little Talk With Jesus*. The son is better known for his acting career that followed. He was an original cast member on the sci-fi television series *Sliders,* portraying the character Rembrandt "Crying Man" Brown. He also won a Tony Award for his work in the Broadway production *Dreamgirls*.

27

The elder Derricks' efforts were recognized by the GMA in 1984 when he was posthumously inducted into their Hall Of Fame. The SGMA Hall of Fame inducted Derricks as well in 2001.

Dixie Echoes

J. G. Whitfield formed the Dixie Echoes in the early 1960s with his brother Joe Whitfield, Joe's wife Sue, Jack Toney, and George Forbus. When Toney left to replace Jake Hess with the Statesmen, Dale Shelnut was hired to sing lead for the Dixie Echoes. Shelnut was noted for his renditions of Negro spirituals and his quick wit.

The Dixie Echoes were part of the regular cast on the *Gospel Singing Jubilee*. After Whitfield left the group, Shelnut assumed the owner/manager responsibilities. This continued until Shelnut's death in 1983 at the age of 47. The ownership of the group then fell to his son Randy who had been playing guitar with the group for several years.

Randy still sings lead for the group. A third generation of the Shelnut family joined the Dixie Echoes later in the form of Randy's son "Scoot," who plays bass and sings baritone. Former Florida Boys bass singer Billy Todd was with the group for several years, and Stewart Varnado has been a consistent presence at the piano.

Dixie Melody Boys

The Dixie Melody Boys formed as a part time group in the 1960s and became full time by the 1980s. The group had a number one song on the *Singing News* chart in 1982 called "Antioch Church Choir." They changed the group name to the DMB Band in the mid-1980s and performed in a Christian Country style, but returned to the original group name and traditional quartet style after that proved to be unsuccessful.

Under the leadership of bass singer Ed O'Neal, the Dixie Melody Boys became a seed group for many of the top groups in the industry. A number of recognizable names got their musical training at the "School of Ed O'Neal." McCray Dove, Derrick Selph, Harold Reed, and Devin McGlamery are just a few of the singers who got their first national exposure with the Dixie Melody Boys

Dollywood

The Dollywood theme park in Pigeon Forge, TN is the site of the Southern Gospel Hall Of Fame and Museum, which was first opened to the public in 1999. The park has long promoted Southern Gospel with special concert events each fall. The Kingdom Heirs have been a daily-featured group there since 1986.

Don Light Agency

Formed in 1965, the Don Light Agency was one of the first booking agencies to represent Southern Gospel artists on a wide scale. In 1968, former Oak Ridge Boys member Herman Harper joined Light in his venture. Harper eventually split from the Don Light Agency to form his own booking agency, Harper and Associates, which remains in the present day as one of the largest agencies in Southern Gospel.

Dorsey, Thomas A.

Although he is most recognized as the father of black gospel music, Southern Gospel artists have frequently performed and recorded Thomas Dorsey's compositions. "Precious Lord, Take My Hand" (1932) and "Peace In The Valley" (1939) in particular are standards for many groups. The most popular rendition of the latter song is probably Red Foley's 1951 version where he is backed up by the Sunshine Boys.

Dove Awards

The Gospel Music Association (GMA) presents the Dove Awards annually. The awards were first presented in 1969, five years after the GMA was formed. The Dove Awards were established to recognize achievement in the gospel music industry and were patterned after the voting procedures used for the Grammys, which recognize all forms of music. For the first decade or so, Dove Award winners were typically traditional Southern Gospel artists. As Christian music styles began to broaden in the late 1970s and 1980s, the Dove Award categories also expanded to reflect the new musical trends. The album award was split into Southern Gospel, Inspirational, and Pop/Contemporary categories in 1976 and three more album categories for Black Gospel had been added by 1981.

A number of prominent Southern Gospel artists have expressed their growing disgust over the years regarding the expansion of the Dove Awards, particularly since 1980. However, the GMA has continued to recognize Southern Gospel music with categories for Song and Album. A top Southern Gospel group is typically invited to perform on the Dove Awards program each year as well. In 1988, a Country category was added to distinguish Country artists from Southern Gospel, and a new category for Bluegrass was established in 1998.

Dove Brothers Quartet

The Dove Brothers formed in 1998 and quickly made a splash in the Southern Gospel music industry. Veteran lead singer McCray Dove (formerly with the Dixie Melody Boys) recruited his brother Eric to sing baritone. John Rulapaugh (tenor), Burman Porter (bass), and Richard Simmons (pianist) completed the initial lineup. The group recreated the classic style of the Statesmen and Blackwood Brothers by bringing back tunes like "Get Away Jordan" and "He's Already Done What He Said He Would Do." Audiences delighted in the group's "rain dance" on the song "Didn't It Rain" as well. Within a few years, the group had been chosen to provide live music for the Quartet Legacy Tour, an event produced by Grand Ole Gospel Reunion promoter and SGMA director Charlie Waller featuring video clips of artists from days gone by.

After a few years, the Dove Brothers (now with Jerry Martin on tenor and David Hester on bass) realized the market was being flooded with nostalgia acts. Even though they had been the group that started the trend in the late 1990s, they felt it was time to modernize their sound. *Anything But Ordinary, Everything But Typical* was the title of their CD released in 2005. The new sound of the Dove Brothers blends a Country music production style with traditional quartet vocals.

The Downings

Virginia Ann Sanders was fresh out of high school when she joined the Speer Family in the early 1960s, a position she would keep for five years. Ann later married bass singer Paul Downing who had been a student of Lee Roy Abernathy and a former member of the Rangers and the Dixie Echoes. Ann and Paul formed The Downings soon after their marriage in the late 1960s. They hired Sue Chenault (soprano), Greg Gordon (lead), and Dickie Matthews (pianist).

The Downings were quickly recognized by the industry. The first Dove Awards were issued in 1969 and Ann received the award for Female Vocalist that year. Joy Dyson replaced Chenault at soprano in 1970 and Dony McGuire began filling a dual role as pianist and lead singer. This lineup remained consistent until 1977. 18 of the Downings songs reached the Top 20 of the *Singing News* monthly charts during that same time period, with their greatest success coming on the very first chart the magazine published in January of 1970. Three songs by the Downings were listed in the Top 20 that month, including the number one song, "Jesus Is Coming Soon." "Sheltered In The Arms Of God" reached number one in October of 1970 as well. Readers of the *Singing News* recognized Paul and Ann as Favorite Bass and Queen Of Gospel Music in the 1973 Fan Awards. The group would later be known for the song "Operator," featuring Paul's distinctive bass voice.

Dyson and McGuire (who were married by this point) left the Downings in 1977, and the group itself disbanded the following year. After spending more than a decade off the road, Ann and Paul were in the process of making a return to the concert stage in the early 1990s. Before their plans could fully take shape, Paul died after suffering a heart attack on February 23, 1992. Ann has since continued to record and make concert appearances as a solo artist. She has also been a regular on the Gaither Homecoming video series. Fellow Downings alumnus Joy Dyson (now remarried and known as Joy Gardner) is also a frequent guest on the video series.

Ann Downing was inducted into the Gospel Music Hall of Fame in 1998 and recognized by the Grand Ole Gospel Reunion as a Living Legend in 1997.

A PARTIAL DOWNINGS DISCOGRAPHY: *Sheltered In The Arms Of God* (1969), *This Is How It Is...Live* (1971), *Greater* (1973), *Praise Him...Live!* (1975)

Easter, Jeff and Sheri

Jeff and Sheri Easter grew up with musical families in the bluegrass tradition. Jeff's father is a member of the Easter Brothers, while Sheri's mother is Polly Lewis Copsey of the Lewis Family. The two met in 1984 at the annual Albert E. Brumley gospel singing and were married ten months later.

Jeff and Sheri traveled with the Lewis Family until 1988. At that point, they took their own family act on the road. Jeff's brother Steve "Rabbit" Easter joined them for several years, singing backup and playing an array of instruments (including steel guitar). Greg Ritchie joined the group to play drums in the mid-1990s. Rabbit introduced Greg to his future wife Charlotte Ritchie at a Gaither taping in 1995, and Charlotte joined the group to sing soprano soon after that. Although the group is still marketed and billed as a vocal duo, they have actually been a trio for a number of years with Jeff, Sheri, and Charlotte providing vocals both on recordings and in concerts.

In 1998, the group won the Dove Award for Country Album with a recording called *A Work In Progress*. They received another Dove in 2002 for Country Recorded Song with "Goin' Away Party." Sheri has won numerous Favorite Alto recognitions in the *Singing News* sponsored Fan Awards. The group signed to record on the Spring Hill label in the late 1990s and have been regularly featured on the Gaither Homecoming videos and tours.

Ellis, Vesphew Benton "Vep"
(1917 - 1988)
Vep Ellis served as a minister in the Church of God denomination for 49 years. During this time, he also published more than 500 songs and released five recordings. He was the music director for Oral Roberts Ministries and the Tennessee Music and Printing Company. Some of Ellis' more popular compositions include "Do You Know My Jesus," "My God Can Do Anything," and "The Love of God".

The SGMA Hall Of Fame inducted Ellis in 2001.

Enloe, Neil
See **The Couriers**

Ernie Haase and Signature Sound
See **Haase, Ernie**

Fagg, Elmo
See **Blue Ridge Quartet**

Florida Boys
(circa 1948-present)
J. G. Whitfield formed the Gospel Melody Quartet following WWII with Roy Howard, Guy Dodd, Edward Singletary, and "Tiny" Merrell. Howard passed away in 1951 following a radio performance. By 1952, Glen Allred had replaced Dodd in the group to sing baritone and play guitar. Les Beasley came on board to sing lead the following year.

Inspired by Wally Fowler's introduction of the group as "those boys from Florida," Whitfield changed the group name to the Florida Boys in 1954. Derrell Stewart joined the group in 1956 to play piano. Whitfield left the road in 1958 after the death of his first wife and a subsequent re-marriage. At that time, Beasley assumed the management responsibilities for the group.

Under Beasley's leadership and with the continued support of their founder, Mr. Whitfield, the Florida Boys embraced modern technology to enhance their fame. In 1961, Whitfield began producing a black and white television program with the Florida Boys called *The Gospel Song Shop*. A few years later, the Florida Boys were called on by Showbiz, Inc. to anchor the *Gospel Singing Jubilee*, with Les Beasley co-producing and Whitfield selling ads. In addition to the Florida Boys, the *Jubilee* featured a cast of groups including the Lefevres, Couriers, Happy Goodmans, and the Dixie Echoes. The show was ultimately syndicated into 90 markets and ran for more than a decade.

The success of the Florida Boys on television secured them a spot on the Canaan record label, a division of publishing giant, Word, Inc. After recording on Canaan for 20 years, they moved to Homeland and when that label went out of business, to Cathedral Records. In January of 1970 when the *Singing News* published their first monthly chart, the Florida Boys had the number one song with "Jesus Is Coming Soon." (This honor was shared with three other groups that had recorded different versions of the same song.) Other number one songs include "Standing On The Solid Rock" (1979), "When He Was On The Cross" (five months at the top in 1985), and "I Lean On You, Lord" (1988).

In 2000, Les Beasley "fired himself" from singing lead, though he continued to travel with the group as the emcee and bass player. He hired Josh Garner to sing lead in his place. Celebrating 50 years together in 2006, Allred, Beasley and Stewart have toured together longer than any other full-time gospel music threesome.

A PARTIAL FLORIDA BOYS DISCOGRAPHY: *Up Tempo* (1966), *Here They Come!* (1975), *Vintage Gospel* (1977), *Keep Rolling On* (1983), *I'm Forgiven* (2000), *I'm Gonna Rise* (2002)

Foust, Ira T.

Ira Foust was an original member of the first professional Vaughan quartet in 1910. A singing school instructor by trade, he sang the written alto line an octave lower. In 1912, a higher singer replaced him so the Vaughan groups could introduce the new method of having a tenor sing the alto line at the actual pitch.

Fowler, John Wallace "Wally"
(1917 - 1994)

A native of Rome, GA, Wally Fowler got his start in gospel music singing baritone with the John Daniel Quartet in 1940. At the time he was already an established country and gospel music songwriter, having appeared on the cover of *Billboard*. After singing with the Daniel Quartet, Fowler formed the Georgia Clodhoppers, a group that originally sang mostly Country music. In the mid-1940s, he told an audience in Oak Ridge, TN that he was going to rename his group after them, and so they became the Oak Ridge Quartet (now known as the Oak Ridge Boys).

Fowler would actually form four groups called the Oak Ridge Quartet over the next 20 years. The initial group left Fowler and regrouped under another name. The second bought the name from Fowler, but then failed to succeed. The third group also bought the name, and modified it slightly to the Oak Ridge Boys. When Fowler formed a fourth group called the Oak Ridge Quartet, the Boys from the third group filed a lawsuit that ultimately forced him to stop using the name.

While organizing and reorganizing his groups, Fowler was also responsible for popularizing the "All Night" gospel sings. His idea was first put into motion in 1948 at the legendary Ryman Auditorium in Nashville, TN, and later it spread across the South. When Fowler billed the Gospel Melody Quartet as "those boys from Florida who have sand in their shoes and a song in their heart," it prompted the group's owner J. G. Whitfield to change their name to the Florida Boys.

Also noted for his songwriting abilities, Fowler's song "Wasted Years" is his most recognized tune. He was inducted into the SGMA Hall Of Fame in 1997.

Fox, Eldridge Locke "Foxy"
(July 10, 1936 - 2002)
Eldridge Fox was a noted innovator in Southern Gospel Music. A native of Mars Hill, NC, Fox first performed with the Silvertones in 1952. In 1957, he joined the Kingsmen Quartet of Asheville, NC and became the group's manager by the early 1960s. Joined by lead singer Jim Hamill in 1971, Fox subsequently molded the Kingsmen into one of the industry's top male quartets. At one point, they were billed as the "Ton Of Fun," due to several hefty sized members including Fox.

Under Fox's tutelage, the group offered a unique and spontaneous brand of male quartet music that set them apart. In his later years, Fox was credited with assisting many young artists as they learned the ropes of the gospel music industry. He wrote the song "Gone" which was popularized by Teddy Huffam and the Gems. The SGMA inducted Fox into their Hall Of Fame in 1998.

Frank Stamps Quartet
See: **Stamps Quartet** and **Stamps, Frank**

Free, Brian
Brian Free got his start singing tenor for Gold City in the 1980s. Some of his early hits with them included "The Greatest Of All Miracles" and "No Other Word For Grace But Amazing." Along with Tim Riley, Ivan Parker and

pianist Garry Jones, Free and Gold City were a dominant force in the industry during the 1980s and early 1990s.

After leaving Gold City in 1993, Free formed his own quartet billed as Brian Free and Assurance. Mike Lefevre (another former Gold City member) joined him in the venture. This group had a number one song on the *Singing News* chart in December of 1997 titled "For God So Loved."

Free put aside Assurance in the late 1990s and toured as a soloist with moderate success. He returned to the quartet format before the turn of the century. Free's son Ricky joined him to play drums around 1999. The group had a number one hit with their live version of the James Cleveland spiritual "Long As I've Got King Jesus" in 2005. The performance was recorded at Christ Tabernacle in New York City. Other vocalists singing with the 2005 version of Assurance included Keith Plott (bass), Derrick Selph (baritone), and Bill Shivers (lead).

The Freemans

When Chris Hawkins married Darrell Freeman in 1980, she left the Hinsons to join Darrell's family group, the Pathways. With the addition of Chris' sister, Diane singing alto and Darrell's cousin, Joe playing keyboards, the group name was changed to The Freemans in the mid 1980s.

Releasing three albums in the 1980's on the Calvary label and experiencing moderate success with such songs as "Little David" and "Always," the Freemans briefly recorded at Sonlite label before striking out on their own with Goldenvine Productions. In September of 1991, the group landed their first number one song with "Going Back" from the album of the same name.

The group eventually came out of independency to sign with Daywind in the mid-1990s. They released three recordings under that label and had several charting songs...most notably "He'd Still Been God" and "Children of the Dust." Also, "Hello In Heaven" was the number one song for January 1997.

After four fruitful years with Daywind, the group once again struck out on their own, returning to their in-house record company, Goldenvine Productions. They had continued success with the release of songs like "He'd Have to Walk Through the Blood" and "Put Your New White Robe On."

The Freemans have experienced few changes, remaining solely a family group. Diane married Joe Freeman and came off the road to work in the group's office in Nashville, TN. Joe took over the vocal position that Diane held while continuing to play keyboards. Darrell and Chris' children Misty and Caylon have joined the group as vocalist/guitarist and drummer respectively. Misty also released a solo album entitled *It's All True*. She

enjoyed reasonable success with her first two singles, "What Judas Didn't Know" and "There Is A Cross In Your Way."
---James Hales contributed to this article.

Freeman, Claris G. "Cat"

Cat Freeman, already a noted tenor singer at the time, introduced his younger sister Vestal to Howard Goodman, her future husband. Freeman sang tenor for the Melody Masters and the Statesmen in the late 1940s. He also pulled a brief stint with the Oak Ridge Quartet in the 1950s.

Gaither Gospel Series
See: **Homecoming**

Gaither Trio
See: **Bill Gaither Trio**

Gaither Vocal Band
(January, 1981-present)

Formed in 1981 on the spur of the moment before a concert, the Gaither Vocal Band quickly gained recognition in contemporary Christian music with songs like "Alpha And Omega" and "Passin' The Faith Along." The addition of lead vocalist Michael English and comedian/baritone Mark Lowry gave the group a unique blend of powerful vocals and entertainment value. With their gospel roots project *Homecoming* in 1991, most Southern Gospel fans welcomed the Vocal Band with open arms. A follow-up recording called *Southern Classics* cemented their relationship with fans.

Strengthened by the popularity of the Homecoming video series, the Vocal Band added Guy Penrod at lead and David Phelps at tenor in the 1990s. After Lowry's departure, Imperials alumnus Russ Taff sang baritone for a couple of years. When Taff returned to solo work, Marshall Hall was his replacement. Wes Hampton succeeded Phelps in 2005.

During the 1990s and into the first few years of the 21st century, the Gaither Vocal Band mastered the art of mixing classic Southern Gospel with Country and Inspirational styles. This gave the group a broad fan base that reached beyond the typical domain of Southern Gospel. Despite the immense popularity of the Gaither Vocal Band, they've only had one number one song on the *Singing News* chart. "Yes, I Know" held the top position from July to October of 1997. Other popular tunes by the Gaither Vocal Band include "Let Freedom Ring," "Count On Me," "The Baptism Of

Jesse Taylor," and "When Jesus Says It's Enough. "The group routinely performs classic Southern Gospel songs including many written by Bill and/or Gloria Gaither like "He Touched Me," "I Believe In A Hill Called Mount Calvary," and "Sinner Saved By Grace."

A PARTIAL GAITHER VOCAL BAND DISCOGRAPHY: *The New Gaither Vocal Band* (1981), *Passin' The Faith Along* (1983), *A Few Good Men* (1990), *Homecoming* (1991), *Southern Classics* (1993), *Lovin' God & Lovin' Each Other* (1997), *God is Good* (1999), *Everything Good* (2002), *a cappella* (2003)

Gaither, William James "Bill"
(1936 -)
Bill Gaither married his wife Gloria when they were teaching high school English in the 1960s. The two soon became a songwriting team. "He Touched Me," "Because He Lives" and "The King Is Coming" are some of their earliest contributions. These songs were recorded by popular groups of the day like the Speer Family and the Cathedrals as well as by the Gaither Trio, which consisted of Bill, Gloria, and Bills' brother Danny.

As the 1980s rolled around, the Gaither Trio had begun to tour with an entourage of established and upcoming singers. Sandi Patty, Carman, and the Cathedrals are just a few of the regular guests who appeared with the Gaither Trio around this time. These appearances were billed as PraiseGathering events in the 1980s, which later morphed into the Gaither Homecoming Tour when the focus became more about Southern Gospel groups. Along the way, Gaither formed a quartet called the Gaither Vocal Band, which excelled in contemporary music in the 1980s and rose to a highly regarded position in Southern Gospel in the 1990s with hits like "Yes I Know." Gaither developed a knack for making his public appearances be viewed as major events in the eyes of fans, and the fans responded in droves. Since the late 1990s, the Gaither Homecoming Tour has annually been listed as one of the top drawing musical tours in the world, often outdrawing major secular tours.

In addition to his concerts, Gaither has spearheaded the Homecoming video series. Titles in this series have consistently generated gold and platinum level sales. Gaither is also the publisher of *Homecoming Magazine* and is involved at the ownership level with several record labels. Throughout their lives, Bill and Gloria have continued to write gospel songs. Some of their later contributions include "I'm Gonna Sing," "These Are They," and "I Heard It First On The Radio."

Gatlin, Earl Smith "Smitty"
(1935 – March 20, 1972)
Smitty Gatlin joined Wally Fowler's Oak Ridge Quartet in 1956. Gatlin bought the group from Fowler in 1958 and turned them into a household name. During this time, the group came to be more commonly known as the Oak Ridge Boys. Wally Fowler attempted to capitalize on the name change by starting another group called the Oak Ridge Quartet, but a lawsuit filed by Gatlin soon forced him give up all rights to the name.

Gatlin continued to managed the Oak Ridge Boys until 1966 when he sold his interest in the group to the remaining members: Herman Harper, Willie Wynn, and William Lee Golden. Gatlin then served as a minister of music at the First Baptist Church in Dallas, TX. After a few years, he returned to the concert circuit with the Smitty Gatlin Trio and continued to travel and sing until his death in 1972. He was only 37 when he passed away with cancer.

Gatlin was inducted into the SGMA Hall Of Fame in 1999.

Goff, Jerry
(May 1, 1935 -)
Jerry Goff got his start in gospel music with the LeFevre family, producing their *Gospel Singing Caravan* for two years as well as the *LeFevre Family Show*. He gained further popularity producing and performing on *America Sings* from 1967 to 1971 in partnership with the Thrasher Brothers. Goff performed with his own group called The Singing Goffs during the 1970s and 1980s where he continued to develop his appeal with fans both as a singer and a gospel trumpet player. The group had a number one song on the *Singing News* chart in June and July of 1976 with "Please Search The Book Again."

In recent years, Goff often serves as an emcee and host for events such as the National Quartet Convention. The SGMA Hall Of Fame added Goff's name to their roll in 2002. He married "Little Jan" Buckner (formerly of the Sunliters) in 2005.

Gold City
(1980-present)
The Mississippi based Christianairs were renamed Gold City at the stroke of midnight on New Year's Eve to begin the year 1980 with Dallas Gilliland singing bass, tenor Bob Oliver, lead singer Jerry Ritchie, and baritone Ken Trussell making up the group. Floyd Beck owned the group initially. Bass singer Tim Riley would replace Gilliland as the permanent bass singer in July of 1980 after the group relocated to Georgia.

Gold City was an instant success in the industry, appearing on the main stage of the National Quartet Convention in October 1981. By 1982, tenor Brian Free, lead Ivan Parker, and pianist Garry Jones had joined Riley, forming a nucleus that would remain together until 1993. Their recordings of upbeat tunes like "I Think I'll Read It Again" and inspirational songs like "No Other Word For Grace But Amazing" and "Midnight Cry" catapulted the group to the upper ranks of Southern Gospel. The last recording by this popular lineup was the critically acclaimed *Acapella Gold* (1993).

After the departure of Free, Jones and Parker, the next consistent lineup for the group included Jonathan Wilburn singing lead, baritone Mark Trammell, and tenor Jay Parrack. Over the years, the group developed a trademark style that relied on brass heavy arrangements for their more driving songs and moving lyrics for their inspirational anthems. Riley's sons Doug and Danny now manage Gold City on the road, but Tim is still active with the group behind the scenes and appears at selected events. Bill Lawrance replaced Riley at the bass position. The group had traveled with a band for the bulk of their history, but scaled back to using a piano player and accompaniment tracks in 2005.

Gold City has had nine number one songs on the *Singing News* chart. These include "I Think I'll Read It Again" (April-June, 1984), "John Saw" (April-July, 1985), "When I Get Carried Away" (June-September, 1987), "Midnight Cry" (January-June, 1988), "Gettin' Ready To Leave This World" (February 1990), "One Scarred Hand" (November 1991), "I'm Not Giving Up" (February 1996), "In Time, On Time, Every Time" (February 1999), "He Said" (March-April, 2000),

A PARTIAL GOLD CITY DISCOGRAPHY: *Live!* (1982), *Double Take...Live* (1986), *Movin' Up* (1987), *Windows Of Home* (1992), *Acapella Gold* (1993), *Walk The Talk* (2003)

Golden, William Lee
William Lee Golden joined the Oak Ridge Boys in 1964 to sing baritone and was joined in the group by Duane Allen in 1966. The group continued to sing gospel music until 1975. At that point, with former Stamps Quartet member Richard Sterban singing bass and Joe Bonsall singing tenor, the group turned to Country music and became major figures with songs ranging from novelty numbers like "Elvira" and "Bobby Sue" to tear jerkers like "Thank God For Kids." By 1987, Allen, Bonsall, and Sterban were becoming increasingly unhappy with Golden's "mountain man" image among other issues, so they voted to fire him from the Oak Ridge Boys. Golden sued and they settled out of court.

After his dismissal from the group, Golden recorded a solo project and made appearances with other artists. When ten years had passed, the Oaks welcomed him back to the group. By then, their Country music career was in decline, so in 2001, the Oaks returned to their gospel roots with a project called *From The Heart*. It was their most popular recording in recent years and garnered them a radio hit with "Working On A Building." Golden continues to sing baritone. They released another gospel project in 2004 titled *Common Thread*.

Golden Gate Quartet

The Golden Gate Quartet was a popular black group that performed on programs regularly with white quartets like the Statesmen and Blackwood Brothers in the 1940s. The original group members were Eddie Griffin, Henry Owens, Bill Johnson, and Robert "Peg" Ford." The group was known for their spirituals as well as their novelty imitations of train whistles, auto engines, and other sounds. They recorded for the Bluebird and Victor labels and sang on radio station WBT in Charlotte, NC. A 1952 promotional photo album shows the group scheduled to appear on a *Battle Of Songs* event along with 18 white groups. Unfortunately, tensions in the South after the Supreme Court's "Brown vs. Board Of Education" decision in 1954 made audiences less receptive to the group. The group relocated to Europe after conducting a successful tour there in 1955.

Golden Keys Quartet

The Golden Keys Quartet was a long-standing "weekend" group. Based in Portsmouth, OH, they formed in 1945 as a trio called the Campmeeting Boys. Original members included Jim Hill, Harold Patrick, and John Conley. The group changed their name to the Golden Keys Quartet in 1947 when a bass singer was added.

The group stabilized when baritone Pat Duncan and bass Clarence Claxon joined. Except for a short time that Jim Hill spent with the Ambassadors Quartet, the Hill/Patrick/Duncan/Claxon lineup remained intact for many years. The group was one of few part-time groups invited to perform at the National Quartet Convention. Their vocal arrangements were not extremely challenging, but the emotion with which they presented their songs made them exciting. Their programs often showcased the tenor vocals of Jim Hill on sacred classics such as "The Ninety and Nine," "I Walked Today Where Jesus Walked," "God Bless America" and "The Stranger of Galilee."

Hill wrote the classic "What a Day That Will Be" in the early 1950s. It was first presented by the Golden Keys Quartet and initially recorded by the Homeland Harmony Quartet. It became one of the most requested songs by the Golden Keys Quartet. The Speer Family had a popular arrangement of the song and Ben Speer eventually published it.

The Golden Keys Quartet not only furthered the writing career of Jim Hill, they were also were responsible for bringing the songs of then fledgling songwriter Bill Gaither to the gospel music community. They recognized the vocal talents of Gaither's younger brother, Danny, as well. After Danny Gaither graduated from college, he moved to the Portsmouth area to begin his teaching career. Soon after that, Harold Patrick relinquished his role as lead singer for the Golden Keys Quartet and Danny Gaither moved into that position. With Patrick able to concentrate on the piano and Gaither's vocals, the Golden Keys Quartet continued to polish their sound.

The popularity of the Golden Keys Quartet may have eventually led to their dissolving. All of the members had full time jobs, but the requests for bookings continued to come in. Although they were in great demand, it still wasn't enough for the group to become a full-time quartet. However, Jim Hill felt the calling to full time gospel music, and accepted the call from Doyle Blackwood to join the "New" Stamps Quartet in 1962. Al Harkins replaced Hill in the Golden Keys Quartet. Dean Hickman later replaced Harkins. Danny Gaither left the group in 1966 and Harold Patrick again resumed double duty as pianist and lead vocalist with the quartet until the Golden Keys Quartet name was retired.

Bill Gaither has often given the Golden Keys Quartet credit for introducing his songs such as "I'm in Love with Jesus," "Have You Had a Gethsemane," "I've Been to Calvary," "Old Fashioned Meeting," and "Lovest Thou Me.". One of the first Gaither songs ever produced as sheet music featured a picture of the Golden Keys Quartet on the cover page.
---John Crenshaw contributed to this entry.

Goodman, Charles F. "Rusty"
(1933 - 1990)
Rusty Goodman began singing when he was 16 years old under the leadership of his older brother Howard. He left the family group to join the US Army and served during the war in Korea. After he returned from service, he sang with Martha Carson and the Plainsmen Quartet. Goodman rejoined the family group in the 1960s, just before their rise to national prominence. Over the next 20 years, the group would record a number of songs written by Rusty that have since become gospel standards. Some of these titles are "Had It Not Been," "Who Am I," and "Look For Me." The Happy Goodmans sang together as a family into the early 1980s and returned to record a final project called *Reunion* with Rusty and Sam Goodman in 1990, just before Rusty's death.

Rusty was inducted into the SGMA Hall Of Fame in 1997.

A PARTIAL RUSTY GOODMAN DISCOGRAPHY: *The Singer* (1975), *You Make it Rain for Me* (1978), *Escape to the Light* (1981), *Family Band* (1984), *To Be Honest With You* (1986)

Goodman, Howard
(1921 - 2002)
In the 1940s, Howard Goodman put together a family group with his brothers and sisters: Sam, Charles (Rusty), Bobby, Ruth, Eloise, Stella and Gussie Mae. Various formations were used at different times. In 1949, Howard married Vestal Freeman, who soon joined the family group. Vestal's brother Cat Freeman was already an established gospel music singer at this time.

After singing together for 20 years or so, the Happy Goodman Family rose to national fame in the 1960s when appearances at the National Quartet Convention brought them to the attention of national concert promoters. Howard continued to lead the group with his distinctive singing style and unique showmanship at the piano.

After leaving the group in the early 1980s, Howard and Vestal served as ministers in their church. In the 1990s, the Happy Goodmans re-formed as a trio consisting of Howard, Vestal, and a former band member named Johnny Minick.

Howard was inducted into the SGMA Hall Of Fame in 2003 after his death in 2002.

Goodman, Vestal
(December 13, 1929 - 2004)
Known for her unique vocal style, her towering hairdos, an ever-present white hanky, and her "curly-cue" endings that hung above the final pitch before resolving with a flourish, Vestal Goodman was one of the most loved characters in Southern Gospel. She was frequently referred to as the "Queen Of Gospel Music."

Vestal married Howard Goodman in 1949, and stood by his side as their fame grew. Traveling with a full band and singing songs written by Howard's brother Rusty, the Happy Goodmans saw their fame hit a peak in the 1970s. Television audiences often saw Vestal and the rest of the Happy Goodmans on the *Gospel Singing Jubilee.* Later Vestal and Howard would be regularly featured on Jim Bakker's PTL television broadcasts.

In the bitterly divided and sometimes hostile gospel music industry of the 1980s and 1990s, Vestal was one Southern Gospel artist who built bridges with her contemporary Christian and Country music counterparts. She recorded songs with many including Kathy Troccolli, the Newsboys, Dolly Parton and George Jones. Vestal was also frequently asked to appear on the Dove Awards broadcasts.

Encouraged by the popularity of the Gaither series of Homecoming videos, Vestal and Howard began recording and touring again as the Happy Goodmans in the late 1990s. They continued to sing together (with Johnny Minick) until Howard's death in 2002. Vestal released several solo projects as well as two collections of duets with various artists.

Gore, Tony

Tony Gore was raised in Clanton, AL. He began to sing in local churches at the age of 14, and in time joined a regional group from Birmingham called the Southmen. While there, he recorded the song "Death Could Not Hold Him." The bulk of Gore's national popularity came after he joined the Wilburns in the mid-1980s. They charted a number of songs during his nine-year tenure, including the popular "Outside The Gate."

Gore formed Tony Gore and Majesty with John Lanier and Calvin Thornton in 1993 and they hit the road the following year. The group was successful on radio as well as the concert circuit. Their first two singles ("Thank God" and "I Know What It's Like") made it to the Top 5, and their third ("Put On A Crown") was in the Top 10. "Meanwhile In The Garden" held the number one slot on the *Singing News* chart for two months in 1996.

Majesty had a number of personnel changes during its nine-year history. Daniel Riley, Jason Runnells, Greg Cook, Lance Driskell, and others passed through Majesty before the group retired in 2002. Gore embarked on a solo ministry at that point. In 2005, Gore brought back the original lineup of Majesty for an "encore tour." Gore, Lanier, and Thornton performed at several key events during the year and planned to continue in 2006.

A PARTIAL TONY GORE/MAJESTY DISCOGRAPHY: *Cool, Clear Water* (1994) *All Access Live* (1996), *Healing* (1997), *The Story Vol. 1* (2000), *Can't Stop* (2003)

The Gospel Greats

Paul Heil's radio broadcast called *The Gospel Greats* began in 1980, based in Lancaster, PA. Presented in a Top 20 countdown format with artist interviews added for color, the two-hour weekly program has been successfully syndicated across the United States for more than 25 years.

Gospel Harmonettes/"Get Away Jordan"

The Gospel Harmonettes were a black female trio from Birmingham, AL who first sang and subsequently taught Hovie Lister the song "Get Away Jordon." Lister learned it in the early 1950s and adapted it for the Statesmen. It quickly became one of the most popular songs in the Statesmen repertoire.

Gospel Music Association

Founded in 1964 to promote Gospel music, the Gospel Music Association (GMA) membership consists of individuals who derive a portion of their income from Christian music. This includes gospel artists, concert promoters, church music leaders, record label employees, retailers, and radio employees. The GMA is best known for the Dove Awards, an annual awards presentation that began in 1969. Southern Gospel groups dominated the awards for the first several years, but the GMA has since broadened the categories to include all popular forms of gospel music. This expansion caused a great deal of distress in the Southern Gospel industry as they saw contemporary music taking over the organization in the late 1970s and early 1980s. A competing organization called the Southern Gospel Music Association (SGMA) arose in the 1980s to award traditional forms of gospel music only. The first SGMA eventually folded, but would emerge again in the 1990s with a different focus.

In addition to presenting the annual Dove Awards, the GMA sponsors a number of workshops and talent competitions throughout the year. The organization also hosts an annual Gospel Music Week in Nashville, TN, with tracks for all facets of the Christian music business.

Gospel Music News

Like most songbook publishers, the Stamps-Baxter Music and Printing Company published a newsletter. It was called the *Stamps-Baxter News* when it was first published in 1927. Later the name was changed to *The Southern Music News*. Once the circulation began to reach into areas outside the South, the name was changed to the more generic *Gospel Music News*. J. I. Ayres served as the newsletter's editor, and the circulation ultimately reached 50,000.

Gospel Singing Caravan

The *Gospel Singing Caravan* was a television program produced by the LeFevres in partnership with the Blue Ridge Quartet beginning in 1961. Other Southern Gospel acts appearing on the show included the Prophets and the Johnson Sisters. Once the television show became popular, the four groups also started touring together. Martha White Flour was the key sponsor for the show, which was ultimately syndicated to more than 40 stations.

Gospel Singing Jubilee

The *Gospel Singing Jubilee* was a color television program produced by Showbiz, Inc. beginning in 1964. Les Beasley co-produced the show along with Showbiz rep Jane Dowden. J. G. Whitfield was a key figure in the program's marketing. The Florida Boys, Dixie Echoes, Couriers, and Happy Goodmans were regularly featured artists. Stanback Headache Powders and the Chattanooga Medicine Company were national sponsors for the program, with each syndicated station also having an allotted time to show local ads. The program ran into the 1970s and was seen in 90 markets.

In 2003, Daywind Records released a 24-song compilation of artists who had been featured on the old *Jubilee* broadcasts. The collection also included the popular *Jubilee* theme song. The recording isn't a historically accurate representation of the television show, however. The songs are mostly taken from studio recordings rather than from the original TV broadcasts, and several songs on the compilation were recorded after the program went off the air.

Gospel Singing World

One of the first publications to employ a modern magazine approach was the *Gospel Singing World*, published from 1954-1958 by E. O. Batson. Unlike the shape-note company newsletters that focused on singing convention schedules, Batson's *Gospel Singing World* kept readers up to date with news and commentary about the artists themselves. A number of quality photos were also included in the publication, along with concert schedules for the artists. Like magazines of today, Batson sold print ads to supplement income from subscriptions, though he ultimately could not sell enough ads to continue publication. Charlie Waller reprinted portions of the *Gospel Singing World* in 1996 to publicize his annual Grand Ole Gospel Reunion event.

The Gospel Song Shop

The Gospel Song Shop was a half-hour black and white television show produced by Showbiz, Inc. that first aired in Greenville, SC. It was a forerunner to the *Gospel Singing Jubilee*. The *Song Shop*'s key sponsor was the Chattanooga Medicine Company, makers of Black Draught powdered laxative. The show launched in 1961 and featured the Florida

Boys. Producer Jane Dowden would oversee the transition of the show to the *Jubilee*'s hour-long color format in 1964.

The Gospel Voice
The Gospel Voice began publication in 1988 as an outgrowth of another magazine, *The Music City News*. It was sold to Gottem Entertainment, Inc. in the mid-1990s. A relatively low circulation eventually caught up with the *Voice*, and it ceased publication in 2001.

Grand Ole Gospel Reunion
Charlie Waller started the Grand Ole Gospel Reunion in 1988. This multi-day event is held each August in Greenville, SC. Typically reuniting a number of classic groups to perform for the evening audiences, the GOGR also features classic video footage, a talent competition, and an exhibit hall where recordings and other memorabilia can be purchased. A video is recorded each year of the event and offered for sale. Waller also offers a number of special showcases with current groups and organizes a roast for an unsuspecting artist each year. Talented keyboard players are inducted into the GOGR's Piano Roll of Honor.

Grand Ole Opry
The Grand Ole Opry has long been known for its live broadcasts of Country music on radio station WSM in Nashville, TN, but the Opry has also promoted gospel music throughout its existence. The Vaughan Recording Quartet, led by Kieffer Vaughan, was one of the earliest gospel quartets to appear on an Opry broadcast in 1927. In the 1940s, the John Daniel Quartet became a regular member of the weekly Saturday night show. As the 20th century drew to a close and the 21st century began, numerous gospel acts appeared as special guests on the program, including the Stamps and the Crabb Family.

Greater Vision
(1990-present)
Greater Vision formed in 1990 with Gerald Wolfe, Mark Trammell and Chris Allman as founding members. The trio has had very little turnover. Wolfe continues to sing lead, emcee, and play the piano. Trammell left to join Gold City in 1994 and was replaced by baritone/songwriter Rodney Griffin. The following year, tenor Jason Waldroup took Allman's place.

In 1998, Greater Vision released a unique project that utilized the Budapest Philharmonic Orchestra and the Hungarian Radio Symphony. Titled *Far*

46

Beyond This Place, the CD gave Greater Vision a unique sound that was recreated on future projects. The recording marked a major turning point for Greater Vision. Since its release, they have accumulated numerous Fan Awards for Favorite Trio, Favorite Male Vocalist, and Favorite Songwriter.

Baritone Rodney Griffin is a prolific songwriter whose songs are recorded by numerous artists in addition to Greater Vision. "My Name Is Lazarus," "Just One More Soul," and "He's Still Waiting By The Well" were number one songs on the *Singing News* airplay charts between 1999 and 2001 for Greater Vision. Griffin wrote all three.

Greater Vision has appeared on the Dove Awards television broadcast, the Gaither Homecoming videos, and on *In Touch* with pastor Charles Stanley. Their *Live At First Baptist Atlanta* project was recorded at Stanley's church in 2002. A unique recording called *Quartets* followed in 2003. For *Quartets*, Greater Vision recorded 15 songs using a different bass singer on each song. Using old masters, they were able to record several songs with singers who were already deceased including Rex Nelon, Brock Speer, and J. D. Sumner. The remainder of the recording includes performances of newer songs (several written by Griffin) employing the top bass singers of today such as Tim Duncan, Gene McDonald, and Tim Riley.

A PARTIAL GREATER VISION DISCOGRAPHY: *On A Journey* (1991), *20 Inspirational Favorites* (1993), *The Church Hymnal Series Vol. 1* (1996), *Far Beyond This Place* (1999), *Quartets* (2003)

The Greenes

The Greenes trio formed in 1978. Based in Boone, NC, Everette Greene played piano in the original group made up of his children, Kim, Tim, and Tony. Their recording of the song "Gloryland" was a Top 40 hit in 1983. The group started hosting an annual gospel singing in 1983 as well. The weeklong event held each August has since been renamed the Everette Greene Memorial Gospel Singing Jubilee.

Kim left to join the Hoppers in 1989 after marrying Dean Hopper. This was around the time the Greene's song "When I Knelt, The Blood Fell" was enjoying a three-month run at number one on the *Singing News* chart. Amy Lambert replaced Kim and traveled with the Greenes for approximately five years. The group had two other songs reach number one during this time; "In The Twinkling Of An Eye" was number one for three months in 1994, followed by "Jesus Rocking Chair" in 1995. Milena Parks succeeded Lambert, recording hits like "The Blood Covered It All."

The next female vocalist for the Greenes ultimately became part of the family. Taranda Kiser joined the group in 1997 and married Tony Greene in February 2001. Tony proposed in front of the crowd at the National Quartet

Convention in September 2000. Taranda Greene is best known for singing "Glorious City Of God." Meanwhile, Tony Greene has made a recording of standup comedy titled *Life's Too Short Not To Laugh.*

A number of songs recorded by the Greenes have been written by Tim, who also manages the group's studio, The Loft. Tim has recorded several solo releases in addition to his recordings with the Greenes. He has served as a pastor, and has also been a host for the radio program *America's Gospel Countdown.* Tim's version of the wedding song "Butterfly Kisses" won the Dove Award for Southern Gospel Song of the Year in 1998. Health issues became a major issue for Tim in the next few years when he contracted a rare brain disease. Tim left the road in 2005 and relocated his studio to Ocean Isle, NC. Brad Hudson was named as Tim's successor.

An authorized biography of the Greenes was released in 2004. Written by Mike Collins, the book is titled *Hold On* and published by Woodland Press.

Griffin, Rodney
See: **Greater Vision**

Haase, Ernie
(Dec. 12, 1964-)
Ernie Haase began his career singing tenor with Squire Parsons' and Redeemed in 1986. In 1990, he followed Kurt Young's brief tenure with the Cathedrals and sang with them until they retired in 1999. While with the group, Haase was regularly featured on the classic "Oh, What A Savior" and recorded the versions of "Wedding Music" and "He Made A Change" that reached number one on the *Singing News* chart. Haase also married Lisa Younce, daughter of legendary Cathedrals bass singer George Younce.

After the Cathedrals retired, Haase embarked on a solo career, releasing projects titled *Songs Of The Savior, What A Difference A Day Makes* and *Never Alone.* During this same period, he reunited with his father-in-law to form a part-time group called Old Friends Quartet. Other group members included Jake Hess and Wesley Pritchard. Garry Jones was the group's piano player. They released two projects, *Encore* and *Feelin' Fine,* and appeared at select events like the National Quartet Convention and Gaither Homecomings.

In 2003, Haase gave up his solo career to form a new quartet called Signature Sound along with Garry Jones. The group immediately began to turn heads with their exciting vocal blend, choreographed steps on stage, "bed head" hairstyles, and short ties. Group members initially included Shane Dunlap (lead), Tim Duncan (bass), and Doug Anderson (baritone).

48

Jones and Dunlap left after a year and were replaced by Roy Webb and Ryan Seaton respectively. The group's initial success was with the song "Stand By Me," featuring Duncan.

Hall, Connor Brandon
(1916 - 1992)
Connor Hall is best known for his stint as tenor singer with the Homeland Harmony Quartet, which began in 1943. Prior to that, Hall was a minister of music in Greenville, SC. Connor Hall had a natural clear tenor voice. The Homeland Harmony Quartet was based in Atlanta, GA, singing on radio station WAGA and appearing on television station WSB in the mid-1950s. They also sent their transcription recordings to stations across the nation.

In 1961, Hall became the Music Editor for the Tennessee Music and Printing Company, publishers of the famous "red back" *Church Hymnal.* Under Hall's leadership, the company bought the Vaughan Music Company. Hall was also the president of Sing Music Company. He was the first choice for the tenor position in the Masters V, though he was quite a bit older than the other members. Proper singing kept Hall's voice strong and clear into his 70s.

In 1997, the SGMA inducted Hall into their Hall Of Fame.
---John Crenshaw contributed to this entry.

Hamblen, Stuart
Stuart Hamblen was already noted for his work in radio in Los Angeles when he was converted at a Billy Graham Crusade in 1949. Following his conversion, Hamblen wrote a number of gospel songs that are now considered to be classics. Some of Hamblen's songs include "This Old House," "Until Then," "First Day In Heaven" and "It Is No Secret What God Can Do."

Hamill, Jim "Big Jim"
(1934 -)
Jim Hamill's father, Rev. James Hamill, preached at the Blackwood Brothers' home church in Memphis, TN. Jim got his start singing with the Songfellows in 1952. He also pulled short stints with the Weatherfords, the Blue Ridge Quartet, the Rebels, and the Oak Ridge Quartet. Hamill is best remembered for the 25 years (1971-1996) he spent singing lead and doing emcee work for the Kingsmen Quartet of Asheville, NC. His unique brand of comedy and song arranging was key to the unique Kingsmen sound. After retiring from the road, he continued to appear at select dates with the group at events like the National Quartet Convention. Hamill's induction into the

SGMA Hall Of Fame came in 2004 after a petition was circulated among Southern Gospel fans and submitted to the organization.

Happy Goodmans
(mid-1940s-1983, 1990, 1996-2002)
The Happy Goodman Family began in the 1940s under the direction of Howard Goodman and seven of his eight brothers and sisters. Brothers Howard, Sam, and Bobby continued to sing together as their sisters married and left the group while their brother Rusty pulled a stint in service. Howard married, and soon his wife Vestal joined the group as well. Rusty sang with the Plainsmen Quartet for a while after returning from service, but ultimately made his way back the family group.

1960-1970s
The fame of the Happy Goodmans grew considerably in the early 1960s. Appearances at the National Quartet Convention got them in front of promoters who in turn booked them across the country. Their first full-length recording was *I'm Too Near Home*, initially released in 1963 and later re-released on Canaan/Word in 1965. In 1968, they were honored with a Grammy award for their 1967 album *The Happy Gospel of the Happy Goodmans*. Ten years later, they received another Grammy for *Refreshing*.

The Goodmans broke new ground in gospel music during the 1960s and 1970s by implementing a live band and creating their own unique sound. It was during these years that they developed their now classic "grab a note and hang on" endings. Sam's humorous emcee work, Howard's showmanship at the piano, Rusty's songwriting, and Vestal's hairdos and white handkerchiefs all rose to a new level of prominence. Tenor Johnny Cook joined the group in 1974 and Rusty's daughter Tanya was added in 1976.

The Happy Goodmans have had several number one songs on the *Singing News* chart. These include "Thank God I'm Free" (April and September, 1970), "The Lighthouse" (June, August, September, and December, 1972; January-June, 1973 except February), "He Pilots My Ship" (September 1973), "What A Beautiful Day" (March 1975-January, 1976), and "Better Hurry Up" (September and November, 1980).

Seperate Paths
Around 1980, creative differences about musical styles caused a division in the family. Christian music was expanding considerably at this time, and Howard and Vestal wanted to maintain their traditional sound. Rusty, Sam, and Tanya wanted take the group in a more contemporary direction. Ultimately, Howard and Vestal decided to leave the group. Rusty, Sam, and Tanya carried on with Johnny Cook returning at tenor. Michael English joined them a couple of years later.

Reunion

Aside from a one performance at the 1984 National Quartet Convention by Sam, Rusty, Howard and Vestal, the Happy Goodmans did not sing together from 1984 to 1990. In 1990, news that Rusty had contracted cancer prompted the family to record a project together called *The Reunion*. Although they initially planned to tour in support of the project, Rusty's health deteriorated rapidly. He passed away in November of 1990. Sam followed his brother in death the next year.

The Final Stand

In 1996, former Happy Goodman band member Johnny Minick joined Howard and Vestal on vocals. As a trio, they brought back the Happy Goodman sound to the delight of fans. Several projects were released over the next five years and they were regular fixtures at Gaither Homecoming events. Their last project was appropriately titled *The Final Stand* (2001). In 2002, a biographical video titled *More Than The Music...Life Story* chronicled the history of the Happy Goodmans. Vestal wrote her autobiography and released a number of solo projects before her death in 2004, including two *Vestal and Friends* CDs featuring duets with a diverse array of vocalists.

A PARTIAL HAPPY GOODMANS DISCOGRAPHY: *The Happy Gospel...* (1967/Grammy winner), *Good Times With...* (1970), *Wanted Live* (1971), *Happy Goodman Family Hour* (1975), *In Concert...Live* (1977), *Refreshing* (1978/Grammy winner), *The Reunion* (1990), *The Final Stand* (2001)

Happy Two

The Happy Two was a novelty "two man quartet" made up of Lee Roy Abernathy and Shorty Bradford in the 1950s.

The Harmoneers

Baritone singer Fred Maples formed the Harmoneers during World War II. He was a native of Cleveland, TN, a central location for quartet music in those days. Other original group members included Herbert Newman, Paul Stringfellow, Sidney Braden, and Charles Key.

During a war imposed recording ban, the group released several recordings as the "Maple Leaf Quartet" on Lee Roy Abernathy's "Quartet" label. The name change was a result of their exclusive recording contract with RCA Victor. If you come across any recordings by that group, you'll be listening to the Harmoneers.

At the end of the war, Maples revamped the quartet. He hired Bobby Stickland to sing tenor, Ermon Slater to sing baritone, and A. D. Soward to sing bass. They relocated to Knoxville, TN and began an affiliation with the Chattanooga Medicine Company. This company was known for a product called "Scalf's Indian River Medicine", which the Harmoneers sold during their broadcasts on radio station WROL.

The personnel of the Harmoneers changed several times over the next few years. Strickland and Soward left the group and were instrumental in the formation of the Statesmen Quartet. Slater left the group to join the Rangers Quartet. Bob Crews (lead), Wallace "Happy" Edwards (tenor), and Seals "Low Note" Hilton (bass) replaced them and became core members of the Harmoneers for the years that followed.

The group relocated to Decatur, GA in 1949 where they sang live on Atlanta radio station WEAS, now WGUN, and later on NBC and CBS radio. "Happy" Edwards kept the audience on their toes with his humor. Fred C. Maples retired in the mid-1950s, and soon the Harmoneers reorganized with "Happy" Edwards, Bob Crews, Shorty Bradford, Seals Hilton, and Charles Key. Jimi Hall soon joined the group as pianist and lead singer. The four-man group (Edwards, Hall, Crews, and Hilton) continued for several years and released their first long-playing album on the Sing label in 1959 titled *This Little Light of Mine*. Prior to this, eight songs by the Harmoneers were released on a 10" RCA album titled *Church in the Wildwood*.

The group experienced several personnel changes prior to their retirement in the early 1960's. Other notable members include Fred Elrod, Troy Lumpkin, Joe Moscheo, Mack Evans, and Byron Burgess. Harmoneers members were recognized as "Living Legends" at the 1995 Grand Ole Gospel Reunion in Greenville, SC. Crews, Key, Hilton, and Hall have performed at the reunion in recent years. The Harmoneers Quartet has been recognized by the Georgia Music Hall of Fame and are recipients of the coveted Mary Tallent "Pioneer Award."
---John Crenshaw contributed to this entry.

Harper, Herman Clay
(1938 - 1993)
Herman Harper had a multi-faceted career. He was a songwriter, producer, talent agent, and singer. He was also the founder of the Gospel Music Trust Fund. Harper sang bass for the Oak Ridge Quartet for a period of 13 years in the 1950s and 1960s. After working at the Don Light Agency, he launched one of the top Southern Gospel talent agencies, Harper and Associates, in 1985.

The SGMA added Harper to their Hall Of Fame in 1997.

Harper And Associates
See: **Don Light Agency** and **Harper, Herman Clay**

Hartford Music Company

Patterned after successful music companies like Vaughan and Stamps-Baxter, the Hartford Music Company was founded in Hartford, Arkansas by E. M. Bartlett. In 1921, the Hartford Musical Institute was founded. It grew to include more than 400 students annually by the 1930s. The company itself also expanded with new locations in Texas and Oklahoma. Meanwhile, Bartlett began publishing a newsletter called *The Herald Of Song* to promote the company sponsored quartets and his songbooks.

In 1926, the Hartford school acquired its most famous pupil in the young Albert E. Brumley. By 1929, Brumley was representing the company with a quartet known as the Hartford Quartet. Marvin P. Dalton, composer of "Oh What A Savior," sang tenor for the group. Although the group sang mostly gospel music, they'd sometimes perform a novelty song written by Bartlett called "Take An Old Cold Tater And Wait," a move that served to broaden the appeal of gospel music as entertainment. Brumley later played piano for another Hartford sponsored quartet, the Melody Four, from Harrison, AR.

In the early 1930s, it was Hartford singing school instructor Vardaman Ray who first heard the teenage brothers James and Doyle Blackwood at a singing school and convinced them to join him in a quartet.

Harvesters Quartet

The Harvesters Quartet was formed from remnants of the Crusaders Quartet, which had been based in Birmingham, AL. The Crusaders were a highly lauded group until a car accident took the life of the group's owner, Bobby Strickland. Bill Hefner took Strickland's place at tenor for a short while, but the group soon disbanded.

In the mean time, WBT radio of Charlotte, NC was looking for a gospel quartet, so several members of the defunct Crusaders relocated to North Carolina. Original members of the Harvesters Quartet in 1953 included Bill Hefner, Buddy Parker and Hershell Wooten of the Crusaders plus David Reece and Pat Patterson.

Unlike most groups of the 1950s and 1960s, the Harvesters had very few personnel changes. Hefner and Parker set the foundation for the group at the tenor and lead slots, and remained there for their entire professional career. One change occurred at the baritone position in 1958 when Don

Norman replaced Pat Patterson. The bass part changed more often as Fred Rose, Jay Simmons, Bob Thacker, and Noel Fox followed Wooten. Also Jack Clark, Earl Brewer, Phil Ross and Gary Trussler played piano for the group after David Reece's departure.

The Harvesters Quartet was known for tight harmony, great arrangements, and fine entertainment skills. Bill Hefner served as emcee in addition to singing tenor. He constantly kept the audience laughing. Lead singer Buddy Parker had the range of a first tenor. Few groups retire when they are at the top of the pack, but it could certainly be argued that the Harvesters did.

Like so many groups that retire, though, it wasn't too long before the Harvesters name was brought back. Hefner promoted concerts throughout North Carolina, and often had a part-time group that performed on the events using the Harvesters moniker. This arrangement lasted for several years until politics came to call on Hefner. He was elected to serve as a North Carolina congressman in the 8th district. Jack Bryson, Richard Coletrain, Richard Lee, Joe Ferguson, Gene Player, Danny Parker, CR McClain Jr., and Phil Barker were all among these part-time Harvesters. The Harvesters continued to perform after Hefner's departure. The current group is quite active and maintains the quartet sound popularized in the 1950s. Danny Parker (brother of Ivan Parker) has been the manager of the current group for several years.

The Harvesters had a reunion concert featuring four of the former members of the older group a few years ago. Appearing were Bill Hefner, Don Norman, Hershell Wooten, and Jack Clark. Danny Parker filled the vocal part of Buddy Parker as the "Old Harvesters" thrilled the audience singing songs they had popularized in the past.
---John Crenshaw contributed to this entry.

Heartwarming Records
For more than 20 years, the Heartwarming record label was considered to be one of the best in Southern Gospel. From the Oak Ridge Boys in the 1960s to Gold City in the 1980s, the label was home to many of the top groups. It was formed in 1962 by the Benson Company and endured until the leadership at Benson began to focus exclusively on contemporary Christian music during the 1980s.

Heil, Paul
See: **The Gospel Greats**

Hemphills

The Hemphills had considerable success as a family group in the 1970s and 1980s. Several of their songs reached the number one position on the *Singing News* chart. Their biggest hit was a song called "He's Still Working On Me." Actually a children's song, it nonetheless found its way to the top of the *Singing News* chart and remained there for eight months (December of 1980 through July 1981). Other number one songs by the group include "Thank God I'm Free" (September 1970), "I'm In This Church" (July 1980), "Good Things" (May 1982), and "It Wasn't Raining When Noah Built The Ark" (October through December, 1984).

A PARTIAL HEMPHILLS DISCOGRAPHY: *Ready to Leave* (1974), *Sing The Glory Down* (1974), *One Live Family* (1975), *In God's Sunshine* (1977), *Workin'* (1980)

Hess, W. Jake
(December 24, 1927 – January 4, 2004)

Jake Hess gave his first performance at five years old with the Hess Brothers, a family group. He was 16 when he joined his first professional group, the John Daniel Quartet. In the midst of the Depression period, Hess later explained that he was in a group so poor they all slept in the same room and sometimes had to steal food in order to keep from starving.

In 1948, Hess sang with the Melody Masters in Omaha, NE, along with bass singer Jim Wetherington and piano wizard Wally Varner. Later that same year, Hess got the call from Hovie Lister to join the Statesmen. It was there for the next 15 years that Hess established his identity as one of the most recognized voices in gospel music. Hess sang his vowels broadly and dipped into his notes, all the while sporting a broad grin that endeared him to his fans.

With a desire to unite the top voices of the day, Hess left the Statemsen in 1963 and formed the Imperials. They recorded numerous LPs in the months that followed, but health problems forced Hess to leave the road just four years later. This caused a chain reaction with the Imperials as concert promoters cancelled 93 previously scheduled dates when they learned Hess was leaving. As these doors were closing, other doors were opening for the Imperials to pursue a more contemporary audience.

As his health returned, Hess formed a group with his son and daughter called the Sound of Youth. They sang primarily on the west coast. In the early 1980s, Hovie Lister and J. D. Sumner approached Hess to sing with the Masters V. This group had substantial success for several years during the 1980s until Hess, James Blackwood, and Steve Warren left the group.

Hess sang briefly with the Statesmen when they re-formed in the early 1990s until his health again forced him to cut back on his touring schedule.

Hess continued to perform as a solo artist on the Gaither Homecoming videos and concert tours in the 1990s and early 2000s. After the Cathedrals retired, Hess and George Younce formed the Old Friends Quartet to perform at Gaither events and a few other special dates like the National Quartet Convention. They released two recordings, *Encore* and *Feelin' Fine*. Hess passed away in January of 2004.

As a child, Hess had been called W. J. Hess, with no names to go with the initials. When he joined the John Daniel Quartet at the age of 16, Daniel gave him the nickname "Jake" to avoid confusion with another singer in the group named J. W. Phillips (who got the nickname Jud). This was in 1944. Hess later registered for the draft. It was then he got his "real name" of William Jesse. Hess had always assumed his original initials were on his birth certificate since that's what he had been called as a child and as an early teen. It wasn't until he needed a passport in the late 1990s that he discovered the name listed on his birth certificate was "Manchild Hess." His son, Jake Hess Jr., thought it was funny and named his record label Manchild Records in honor of his father.

Hill, Ed

Ed Hill got his start in the 1950s with Jerry (Jay) Berry and the Kings Men Quartet out of St. Louis, MO. The two relocated to Knoxville, TN in 1959 where they formed the Prophets Quartet along with tenor "Big Lew" Garrison. Hill would remain with the group as the manager, baritone, and emcee until it folded in 1973. At that point in time, Hill was preparing to go to work for the Sumar Talent Agency, but agreed to fill in temporarily with the Stamps singing baritone. The position eventually became permanent. Other members of the Stamps at the time included Ed Enoch, Bill Baize, and J. D. Sumner.

In time, Hill became a delight to fans as the brunt of J. D. Sumner's jokes. Sumner often introduced Hill at concerts referencing his tenure with the Prophets as a "successful quartet manager," then saying, "In 1973, he successfully managed them out of business." Sumner also liked to hit a low note, wipe his hand across his mouth, and then wipe it off on Hill's head during a concert. The most significant recording by the Stamps in the 1970s was a double length project titled *Live At Murray State*.

After the death of Elvis Presley and the retirement of the Stamps, Ed Hill joined the Singing Americans where he worked with some of the best upcoming talents. Ivan Parker, Danny Funderburk, Michael English, Rick Strickland, and Clayton Inman are just a few of the well known artists who got their start while Hill was with the Singing Americans.

In the late 1980s, Ed Hill returned to sing with J. D. Sumner in the Masters V. He continued with the group when the name was changed to the Stamps and within a couple of years, Ed Enoch had joined the group again. They sang together after Sumner's death as Golden Covenant for a few years until they started to use the Stamps again. In 2005, Hill had some health issues that became a factor in him leaving the group. He planned to continue to make some appearances as a solo artist.

Hill, Jim

Jim Hill grew up in Portsmouth, OH. He studied opera and auditioned with the Cincinnati Conservatory of Music and the Metropolitan Opera Company. However, his background in church music prevailed, and he continued to perform gospel music. From 1945 to 1962, he sang tenor and managed the Golden Keys Quartet. (He did take a hiatus from the group to sing with the Ambassadors Quartet, but this was only for a short time.) After his extended stint with the Golden Keys, Hill accepted the invitation from Doyle Blackwood to join the "New" Stamps Quartet. He remained with the group for some time after J. D. Sumner bought the name and joined the group. In 1968, Hill gave up his tenor position with the Stamps to sing lead with the Statesmen. He remained with them until the early 1970s.

Hill is also notable for his songwriting talent. Songs such as "Each Step I Take," "For God So Loved," "No One Ever Cared So Much," and "I'll Make it to Heaven" are just a few examples from Hill's writing output. His best-known song is the classic "What a Day That Will Be." Hill was nominated for a Dove Award as Songwriter of the Year in 1969. In more recent years, he has been a frequent crowd favorite at the Grand Ole Gospel Reunion and on selected Gaither projects.

Hinsons
(1968-1988, 1990-present)

The Hinsons were one of the few groups from the West Coast to succeed in Southern Gospel Music. Hailing from Salinas, California, the Hinsons began around 1968 as a family group made up of siblings Ronny, Kenny, Larry and Yvonne. The group gained national attention in 1972 singing a song Ronny wrote entitled "The Lighthouse." The group recorded the song on an album of the same name with California based Calvary Records. The song was further popularized when the Happy Goodman Family discovered the song. The song went on to win the *Singing News* Fan Award and the Dove Award for Song of the Year in 1972. With his trademark country stylings, akin to that of Merle Haggard and George Jones, Kenny became a legend in the minds of Hinson fans everywhere. Between Kenny's singing and Ronny's songwriting, the limits of this group seemed endless.

Success

The group eventually moved to Madisonville, KY to work closely with the Happy Goodman Family. Yvonne married and left the group in 1974. Chris Hawkins came on board to sing and became quite popular with the fans, winning the Singing News Fan Award for Queen of Gospel Music in 1976 and 1977. The 1970's were very successful years for the Hinsons. They were regulars on the *Gospel Singing Jubilee* television show, and the group won several fan awards during this time including Favorite Band, Favorite Group and Song of the Year. After spending a few years being mentored by the Goodmans, the group moved their home base to Nashville, TN.

Chris Hawkins left the Hinsons in 1980 when she married Darrell Freeman. Yvonne returned to sing with the Hinsons. During this transitional period, Larry decided to come off the road and pursue an evangelistic ministry. Eric Hinson joined the group for a few years. Ronnie's son, Bo Hinson came along to fill the vacancy after Eric left the group.

The 1980s were successful years for the group. "God's Gonna Do The Same For You And Me" was the number one song on the *Singing News* chart for July-August in 1982. The group performed at Carnegie Hall around this time. Their 1982 release entitled *Hinsongs* featured two number one songs in "Two Winning Hands" (July-September, 1983) and "Call Me Gone" (July-August, 1984). Ronny Hinson was awarded Song of the Year honors in 1986 for co-writing "When He Was on the Cross." The group also had a number one song with "Mercy Built A Bridge" (August-October, 1988).

The Ending Of An Era

The Hinsons disbanded in 1988, but the original group including Larry and Yvonne came back together in 1993 for a reunion tour and an album called *One More Hallelujah*. The tour ended abruptly when it was discovered that Kenny had developed cancer. As time went on, Kenny's health failed and on July 27, 1995, at age of 41, Kenny passed away.

Ronny Hinson has continued to write songs for other groups. He travels and sings on occasion as well. Larry continues to travel as an evangelist. The group gets together from time to time for reunion concerts.

New Hinsons

Bo Hinson and his wife Rhonda formed their own group called Bo Hinson and Purpose in 1990. After releasing one recording under Calvary Records, they signed with Daywind Records. The group eventually changed their name to the New Hinsons and more recently shortened it to the Hinsons. The group released two recordings with Daywind, *Generations II* and *Oasis*, and garnered several hit songs. The song "Oasis" was number one on the *Singing News* chart from April through July in 1996. "Old Ship Of Zion" was number one in December that same year.

The group started their own label called House of Hinsong and released a live recording entitled *Light up the Night*, which featured a reunion of sorts with the remaining original Hinsons. Since the release of *Light up the Night*, the group has released several recordings featuring new versions of classic Hinson material. The group evolved into a 'New Hinson Revival' of sorts, mostly staging original Hinson songs, mixed with a few of their own recent hit songs.

Though not nearly as successful as the original Hinsons, this incarnation of the group has experienced moderate success and continues to travel and sing.

A PARTIAL HINSONS DISCOGRAPHY: *The Lighthouse* (1971), *Live & On Stage* (1976), *High Voltage* (1976), *On the Road...Live* (1978), *Prime* (1979), *Hinsongs* (1982)
 ---James Hales contributed to this entry

Hinson, Kenny
(1954 - 1995)
Kenny Hinson was a regular fan favorite at the National Quartet Convention in the late 1970s. He's best known for his unique rendition of "The Lighthouse," a classic gospel tune. He traveled with his family group, the Hinsons, for over 20 years. Hinson introduced Country style diction to Southern Gospel that would sound right at home alongside George Jones or Randy Travis. When the Hinsons stopped touring in 1988, Kenny became a pastor of a church in Texas. He learned that he had cancer in 1993, and passed away at the age of 41 in 1995.

Hinson was inducted into the SGMA Hall Of Fame in 2004.

Holm, Dallas
Dallas Holm is rightly regarded as one of the founding fathers of modern Christian music, but he also enjoyed his share of crossover success in Southern Gospel. Holm's song "Rise Again" spent six months at the top of the *Singing News* chart from December 1977 to May 1978.

Homecoming (Gaither Gospel Series)
The Homecoming video series began on February 19, 1991 with a group of old friends gathering around the piano at the Masters Touch studio in Nashville, TN to sing after a video recording session. It ultimately became the best selling music video series ever.

In 1991, despite the objections of their record label, Star Song, the Gaither Vocal Band recorded an audio project titled *Homecoming*. Previous Vocal Band projects on the Star Song label had been tailored to compete in the contemporary Christian market, but *Homecoming* had strong Southern Gospel roots with only a touch of soul from lead singer Michael English. The Vocal Band was joined on the recording by a number of their heroes including Vestal Goodman, James Blackwood, Hovie Lister, Jake Hess, the Gatlin Brothers, George Younce. These singers were featured singers on the song "Where Could I Go," so the group decided to record a concept video of the song with all the singers present.

After the formal video taping session was over, the singers gathered around a piano in the studio and began singing just for the fun of it. Gaither kept the cameras rolling, thinking the footage would be great to have for his personal collection. After viewing the footage, he thought it could have commercial value, so he had it edited with some narration added. Star Song supported the project and packaged it to match the audio recording, including the polished concept footage of "Where Could I Go" as well.

The project was a financial success, so Gaither decided to shoot another video in 1992, this time with more advance planning. The resulting project was called *Reunion*. The demand was great again, so next he tried putting out two titles at the same time. These were titled *Turn Your Radio On* and *Old Friends*. By now, the series was up and rolling at full steam. Every three to four months, another pair of videos was released. They weren't exactly cheap at $30 each, but the fans didn't seem to mind.

Using an infomercial approach over cable TV channels like The Nashville Network, Gaither developed a lucrative direct mail business for his videos and associated products like songbooks. This approach annoyed shoppers at Christian retail outlets, because stores weren't allowed to stock new titles until after the direct mail route was employed for several weeks. Artists who appeared on the series also had copies to sell at concerts well in advance of stores. Once products did release to retail, Gaither's company typically failed to manufacture and send the distributor enough copies. The demand that fans placed for the series was simply wider than anticipated. The wrinkles of distribution were finally ironed out after a few years. The delay between direct sales and retail availability was shortened significantly and a "street date" was displayed in print ads to inform fans of the exact date when new titles would be available in stores. Stores began receiving an ample supply of stock once Gaither's company realized each title would probably sell as well as the previous title and manufactured enough units to meet the potential demand.

Gaither has released several dozen Homecoming video titles since 1991. Most titles are ultimately certified Gold (50,000 units for video titles) and several have reached the Platinum sales mark (100,000). *Old Friends*, *Turn*

Your Radio On, and *Ryman Gospel Reunion* are double Platinum (200,000). (RIAA certification figures reflect domestic sales only.)

While many Homecoming projects were released a few months after the original taping, others (*Red Rocks Homecoming, Hymns, Church In The Wildwood*) were held for a few years before being release. This delayed release schedule proved to be effective after several of the older generation of singers passed away (Howard and Vestal Goodman, Jake Hess, James Blackwood, Hovie Lister, etc.). Fans were eager to see the previously un-released footage of their heroes.

Gaither already had a popular traveling tour established with various artists from different musical backgrounds before the Homecoming craze set in. It soon became known as the Homecoming Tour to coincide with the video title and concept. Appearing in 50-70 major cities each year, the tour now ranks as one of the top draws of all time, including both secular and gospel. In addition to Southern Gospel artists, the Homecoming Tour includes traditional black gospel artists and inspirational acts. This mix of styles has come to be reflected in the video series as well.

In addition to bringing many of the older gospel artists back to the attention of fans, the Homecoming phenomenon helped launch the careers of several major artists. The Martins, Signature Sound Quartet, and the Talley Trio gained much of their initial publicity through Homecoming appearances and video tapings. Other previously unknown artists like Lynda Randle, Stephen Hill, Mike Allen, and Reggie Smith became regular Homecoming fixtures.

Homeland Harmony Quartet

The Homeland Harmony Quartet name was first used in connection with a singing group in 1935. Members included Otis McCoy, Doyle Blackwood, Fred C. Maples, and B.C. Robinson. The group originated as an outreach of the Church Of God Bible Training School. The group got its name from the title of a songbook published in 1936 by the Church Of God owned Tennessee Music and Printing Company. Early group member Otis McCoy credited Alphus LeFevre, who named the songbook *Homeland Harmony*, as also being the source for the group name.

The group went through a re-organization in 1943. For a few months the personnel consisted of Eva Mae LeFevre, Otis McCoy, James McCoy, and B.C. Robinson. When Urias LeFevre returned from the military service, Eva Mae rejoined him in the LeFevre Trio and Connor Hall became the tenor for the Homeland Harmony Quartet, a title he would retain until his death in 1992. The group was based in Atlanta, GA, where Hall and baritone James McCoy were joined by a string of lead and bass singers, among them Paul Stringfellow, Bob Shaw, Jim Waits, Aycel Soward, George Younce and Rex

Nelon. Piano players like Hovie Lister, Wally Varner, Lee Roy Abernathy and Jack Clark also pulled stints with Homeland Harmony.

The Homeland Harmony Quartet developed a style all its own. On stage, they had a unique sound built around high harmonies and unusual arrangements. Before this time, most quartets sang songs from the latest songbooks, more or less note for note as written. The Homeland Harmony Quartet became famous for using more difficult arrangements.

In 1948, the group introduced Abernathy's "Wonderful Time Up There." The song proved to be both popular (selling 200,000 copies) and controversial (due to the "boogie woogie" bass part). The quartet released the song on White Church Records. It soon became known as "The Gospel Boogie", much to the dismay of conservative religious leaders who often booked the quartet for singing conventions and worship services. Nearly ten years later, Pat Boone recorded a version of the song that charted quite well on the Billboard charts.

The Homeland Harmony Quartet was based at radio station WAGA in Atlanta during the 1950s. They also had a television show carried on more than 50 stations including Atlanta's WSB. They recorded music on the Bibletone label. The group performed until the late 1950s. Uncle Sam claimed several of the younger members for military service and James McCoy was experiencing some health concerns, so Connor Hall disbanded the group and went to work behind the scenes in the gospel music field.

The group reformed in the early 1960s as a part time group. Hall had been asked to record a solo album for Sing Records, but he wanted the Homeland Harmony in the studio with him. He called on several quartet veterans to join him including two former Harmoneers in Jimi Hall and Fred Elrod; Dickie Mathews, formerly with several groups including the Deep South Quartet and Crusaders, played the piano; and newcomer Bill Curtis sang bass. This group didn't join the full-time quartet circuit, but recorded two albums and made a few select live appearances. In 1968, Jack Clark and J. L. Steele joined Bill Curtis, Fred Elrod, and Connor Hall and formed a part-time Homeland Harmony Quartet that lasted for many years, though they made few live concert appearances.

Connor Hall had a natural clear tenor voice. His ear for music was superb. In 1961, Hall entered a long, productive career as Music Editor of the Tennessee Music and Printing Company. Hall was also the president of Sing Music Company. He was the first choice for the tenor position in the Masters V, though he was quite a bit older than the other members. Proper singing kept Hall's voice strong and clear into his 70s.

The Homeland Harmony Quartet was responsible for several "firsts" in gospel music. They were the first gospel quartet to be featured on a radio network of fifty-five stations. They were also the first quartet to appear on television as they were on the South's first telecast on WAGA-TV in Atlanta, GA. The quartet in conjunction with Lee Roy Abernathy was the first group to produce sheet music. They were also cosponsors, with the Rangers Quartet of the world's first all-night gospel concert held in Atlanta, GA.

Eight former members of the Homeland Harmony Quartet are in the SGMA Hall of Fame. Eight former members are recipients of the Living Legend Award at the Grand Ole Gospel Reunion. Seven former members have been inducted into the Gospel Music Piano Roll of Honor.
---John Crenshaw contributed to this entry.

The Hoppers
(1964-present)
The Hopper Brothers and Connie began as a local church group in Madison, NC. Their career as nationally known artists commenced when they won the talent competition at the National Quartet Convention in 1964. Claude Hopper and his wife Connie shortened the group name to "The Hoppers" once Claude's brothers retired from the road. Their sons Dean and Mike now travel with the group along with Dean's wife Kim Greene Hopper.

The group's first number one song on the *Singing News* chart was "Here I Am" in 1990. Three more number one songs followed in the 1990s: "Milk And Honey" (October 1992), "Mention My Name" (May-June, 1993), and "Anchor To The Power Of The Cross" (August 1996). Although "Shoutin' Time" became their signature song in the 1990s, it never reached the number one position. Number one songs in the next decade included "Yes, I Am" (February-March, 2001) and "Jerusalem" (September 2004).

Over the years, Claude Hopper has positioned himself as a key individual in the gospel music industry. He is a board member of the National Quartet Convention and owns Hopper Brothers & Connie Publishing. Hopper is also a founding member of the North Carolina Gospel Music Hall Of Fame. Connie Hopper has written at least two books. One is *The Peace That Passes Understanding* on the topic of dealing with cancer. The other is a daily devotional titled *Heart Of The Matter*.

Dean Hopper began performing with the group initially as their drummer. He moved to the lead vocal slot in 1981. He has released a solo recording titled *Solo But Not Alone*. He and his brother Mike own a recording studio called The Farm. The two released a comic "rap" recording billing themselves as the Hip Hoppers in the early 1990s. Mike Hopper began playing drums for the group at the age of 13. In addition to his work with the family group, he is the regular drummer for the Gaither Homecoming videos. Mike has appeared on the television show *Touched By An Angel* along with the

Gaither Vocal Band. Kim Greene Hopper joined the Hoppers in 1989 after marrying Dean in November 1988. She formerly sang with her brothers Tim and Tony Greene, billed as The Greenes. Kim has recorded a solo CD titled *Imagine*.

The Hoppers won Favorite Mixed Group at the *Singing News* sponsored Fan Awards from 1997-2003. Kim Hopper won Favorite Soprano during the same period. They have been featured on the Singing At Sea event every year since it first began in 1974.

Hovie Lister And The Statesmen Quartet (TV Show)
See: **Lister, Hovie Franklin** and **The Statesmen Quartet**

Huffam, Teddy
Teddy Huffam and the Gems were the first all black gospel group since the 1950s era Golden Gate Quartet to have significant success in Southern Gospel. The group first came to the attention of Southern Gospel audiences when they won a talent competition in 1973. Their recording of "Gone," a song written by Eldridge Fox, became a hit in 1979, appearing in the top 20 of the *Singing News* annual airplay charts for 1979 (No. 14), 1980 (No. 4), and 1981 (No. 19).

Hyles, Arnold
(1917 – March 15, 1979)
Arnold Hyles was one of the original members of the Rangers Quartet, which formed around 1936. Billed from the outset as "America's lowest bass," Hyles had a unique, gruff bass voice, and the Rangers made the most of it by featuring him often. Hyles was crippled in 1951 as the result of a vehicle accident that claimed the life of fellow Rangers Quartet member Erman Slater, but he returned to travel and sing with the Rangers until they disbanded in 1956.

Hyles joined the ranks of the SGMA Hall Of Fame in 2004.

The Imperials
(circa 1945-1953, 1964-present)
Marion Snider first used the name "Imperial Quartet" in the 1940s. Snider's group quickly attracted the attention of a radio sponsor, the Imperial Sugar Co. The new quartet became the Imperial Sugar Quartet, and began a long association with the Texas Quality Radio Network.

The Imperial Sugar Quartet was popular for nearly a decade as they performed both on the airwaves and the concert stage throughout Texas and surrounding areas. The name "Marion Snider and the Imperial Sugar Quartet" was retired in the early 1950s. Snider was later inducted into the Southern Gospel Music Association's Hall of Fame.

Jake Hess Begins A Legacy
In the 1960s, Jake Hess wanted a quartet that would enter the field of gospel music at the very top of the game. Hess retired from the Statesmen Quartet on December 7, 1963 to put all of his efforts into this all-star quartet. He contacted Marion Snider and requested permission to use the name "Imperials". After receiving Snider's blessings, "Jake Hess and the Imperials" was born.

Hess and former Weatherford Quartet pianist Henry Slaughter chose Sherrill Nielsen (tenor), Gary McSpadden (baritone), and Armond Morales (bass) to complete the new group. At the time, all of the members were active in other major gospel quartets.

Struggles and Successes
The Imperials released five recordings simultaneously to coincide with their debut. They launched a newspaper called *The Imperial Times* to herald their arrival on the gospel music scene. Some groups didn't want to appear on programs with the Imperials initially, because they didn't appreciate the way the group was formed by "stealing" singers from other top groups. In his book *Nothin' But Fine*, Hess details the group's initial struggles on the gospel music circuit.

Influential promoters accepted the Imperials, though, and they began to break down musical barriers. In keeping with their trend-setting ways, the Imperials were soon hired to sing backup for Elvis Presley. The classic Presley recording *His Hand in Mine* prominently features the Imperials.

New Singers
By 1967, Nielsen, Slaughter, Hess, and McSpadden had departed for various reasons. Jim Murray had replaced Nielsen at tenor in 1966, Joe Moscheo took over keyboard duties, and Terry Blackwood and Roger Wiles moved into the lead and baritone positions. Recordings such as *New Dimensions*, *The Imperials NOW*, and *Love is the Thing* put the Imperials back on top in the gospel music industry.

Roger Wiles left the group in 1970 and was replaced by Greg Gordon, a son of Anna and Howard Gordon of Chuck Wagon Gang fame. During this time, the Imperials began to record music that was outside the gospel music realm. Popular songs such as "Bridge Over Troubled Waters", "Let it Be", "My Sweet Lord", and "A Thing Called Love" became part of their repertoire.

In 1972, the Imperials began to stage a pop medley from their album *Time To Get It Together*. At this time, they became one of the first groups to perform in concert with pre-recorded music tracks complimented by Moscheo's piano.

Trendsetting Moves
Gordon's tenure with the group was short-lived. In February 1972, the Imperials became the first interracial quartet in gospel music. Sherman Andrus, a former member of Andrae Crouch and the Disciples was brought in to replace Greg Gordon. They hired a band they called Solid Rock to accompany them in their live appearances.

In the mid-1970s, Terry Blackwood and Sherman Andrus left the Imperials to form the contemporary Christian group Andrus, Blackwood and Company. David Will and Russ Taff replaced them, and the Imperials music took on a definite contemporary edge, with one notable exception. Their novelty song "Oh Buddha" hit the top of the *Singing News* chart in September of 1979 and remained there until May of 1980. There was one break in March of 1980 when a decidedly more pop sounding Imperials song called "Praise The Lord" was number one on the *Singing News* chart.

The 1980s saw the Imperials set the standards for vocal music in the growing Christian pop market. Several former Imperials members such as David Robertson, Russ Taff, and Jonathan Pierce went on to enjoy considerable success as solo artists. Interestingly, four former Imperials later pulled stints with the Gaither Vocal Band. These include Gary McSpadden, Jim Murray, Jonathan Pierce, and Russ Taff,.

After 39 years traveling with the Imperials, Armond Morales retired in 2003. At that time, he passed the torch to his son Jason Morales, who continued the Imperials legacy with tenor Jeremie Hudson, bass Ian Owens, and Shannon Smith singing lead. In 2004, the 1972 version of the group (Sherman Andrus, Armond Morales, Jim Murray and Terry Blackwood) reunited to record a tribute CD along with the Stamps Quartet called *The Gospel Side Of Elvis*. The group has made several appearances billed as the Classic Imperials.

A PARTIAL IMPERIALS DISCOGRAPHY: *Introducing The Illustrious Imperials* (1964), *Talent Times Five* (1965), *New Dimensions* (1968), *Follow The Man With The Music* (1974), *Sail On* (1977), *Sing The Classics* (1984), *This Year's Model* (1987), *Til He Comes* (1995), *I Was Made for This* (2002) ---John Crenshaw contributed to this entry.

The Inspirations
Martin Cook, a former piano player for the Kingsmen and a chemistry teacher at Swain High School in Bryson City, NC, formed the Inspirations in

1964 with several of his teenage students. Cook and fellow original group member Archie Watkins have been with the group since it formed. Original member Jack Laws left the group after a few years, but later returned to sing and play guitar. The Inspirations became full time in 1969, a year after hosting their first "Singing In The Smokies" event. Bass singer Mike Holcomb joined them in 1972.

The 1970s saw the Inspirations rise to national attention with a number of hit songs. Their sound was defined by the piercing tenor vocals of Archie Watkins. The group was also invited to be part of the regular cast on the *Gospel Singing Jubilee* television program. They had the very first number one song on the *Singing News* chart in January of 1970 with "Jesus Is Coming Soon." (This honor was shared with three other groups who had different versions of the same song.) Beginning in November 1973, the group was number one for 12 months in a row. "Touring That City" held the position through February 1974 and "When I Wake Up To Sleep No More" was the most popular song for the next seven months. "Jesus Is Mine" was also a number one song for the group in 1976.

In more recent years, the Inspirations have continued to present concerts with a traditional style and a conservative image. Their songs such as "Cry For The Children" and "We Need To Thank God" have resounded strongly with Christian conservatives and fans of traditional gospel music. 26 years after their last number one song, the group returned to the top position on the *Singing News* chart in 2002 with "I'll Not Turn My Back On Him Now."

A PARTIAL INSPIRATIONS DISCOGRAPHY: Touring That City (1973), When I Wake Up To Sleep No More (1973), A Night Of Inspiration (1976), The Wonder Of Wonders (1983)

The Isaacs

Lily Fishman Isaacs has a Jewish background. Her parents married at the end of World War II. Her father had been forced to serve in a German labor camp and her mother had been confined to a concentration camp during the war. After Lily was born in Germany, the Fishmans immigrated to New York. When Lily grew up, she began singing as half of a folk duo called Lily and Maria. They released an album for Columbia in 1968. She also performed on the off-Broadway theatre circuit.

Joe Isaacs was playing with a group called the Greenbriar Boys when he met Lily Fishman at Gerdes Folk City, a New York City hotspot. The two were married in 1970. One journalist commented that the unlikely match was analogous to "Ralph Stanley joining Joan Baez." Lily and Joe became Christians in 1971 after attending the funeral of Joe's brother and hearing the gospel message that was presented. She now describes herself as a "completed Jew."

After the couple's conversion, they quit performing in nightclubs and began singing exclusively in church settings. Their children Ben, Sonya, and Becky were born between 1972 and 1975. During those years, Joe had a group called the Calvary Mountain Boys. He later headed a group billed as Joe Isaacs and the Sacred Bluegrass. This group was together until 1986.

Early on, the three Isaacs children recorded a project billing them as the Isaacs Trio. They were laughingly referred to as the Chipmunks at the time, due to their high harmonies. As they matured, the three Isaacs children began singing from time to time with their father's group and appearing on a local cable access network.

They re-billed themselves The Isaacs in 1986 with the three children now full-fledged group members. Their music was bluegrass, but their vocals were more akin to Southern Gospel, so they began to have moderate success in both genres. In the early 1990s, the group's popularity grew considerably. They were invited to appear on the Gaither Homecoming videos and were an instant hit. Although Joe and Lily ultimately divorced, Lily continued to perform with the family group.

The song "I Have A Father" came very close to being a number one for the Isaacs on the *Singing News* chart. Their next single was "From The Depths Of My Heart." It did reach number one and it held the position for three months in the summer of 1993. Rebecca married John Bowman in 1994, and John joined the group to play guitar and banjo. Tim Surrett married Sonya and left the Kingsmen to join the Isaacs playing dobro and other instruments. He and Sonya later divorced, after which he returned to sing with the Carolina Boys/Kingsmen.

Sonya Isaacs released a self-titled project on the Lyric Street label in 2000 that was aimed at the mainstream Country market. Vince Gill produced several tracks and it was critically acclaimed. Isaacs also toured some with Gill as a backup singer and featured vocalist around this time. A follow up project with Lyric Street was planned in 2004, but the label first floated a single to radio to test the waters. "No Regrets Yet" peaked at #36 on the Billboard charts in February 2004, but the label and Isaacs parted ways a couple months later with the second recording left unfinished.

Meanwhile in 2003, the Isaacs joined the Homecoming Tour full time and saw another song hit number one on the Southern Gospel charts, "Stand Still," co-written by Sonya and Rebecca. The group released a CD titled *Heroes* in the summer of 2004.

A PARTIAL ISAACS DISCOGRAPHY: *Family Chain* (1989), *Our Style* (1992), *Mountain Praise* (1996), *Increase My Faith* (1998), *Stand Still* (2000), *Eye Of The Storm* (2002), and *Heroes* (2004)

James D. Vaughan Music Publishing Company
See: **Vaughan, James D.**

JD Sumner And The Stamps
See: **The Stamps Quartet** and **Sumner, John Daniel "J. D."**

Jeff and Sheri Easter
See **Easter, Jeff and Sheri**

The Jenkins Family
Andrew Jenkins and the Jenkins Family were early radio pioneers who combined gospel music with evangelistic preaching on the air. They were heard on radio station WSB in Atlanta, GA beginning in 1922. Jenkins, a partially blind songwriter, married a widow with three children in 1919. The family developed the program to include Jenkins' preaching, gospel songs, and instrumental music.

Jensen, Gordon
See: **The Orrells**

Jerry And The Singing Goffs
See: **Goff, Jerry**

John Daniel Quartet
See: **Daniel, John Tyra**

Johnson, Charles
The Nightingales are a top black gospel group with a history spanning more than half a century. Charles Johnson sang with them for more than 20 years, before entering Southern Gospel music in 1984 with his own group, Charles Johnson And The Revivers. Propelled by a hit single called "I Can't Even Walk (Without You Holding My Hand)," Charles Johnson And The Revivers blended Southern and Black gospel styles. The success of this vocal trio paved the way for other black artists to gain acceptance with predominantly white Southern Gospel audiences during and after the 1990s.

The Johnson Sisters

Originating in Birmingham, AL, the Johnson Sisters formed as an all female trio in the early 1950s with siblings Margaret, Judy and Anna Johnson on vocals and their older sister Mary at the piano. Mary was seven years older than Margaret. Judy and Anna are twins born about a year after Margaret. Mary began to teach her younger sisters to harmonize at a very young age. In order to get them all together, Mary came up with an unusual technique. She would grab her sisters one by one and assemble them on top of their old upright piano. They were too small to climb down, so the practice sessions would be held with six little feet in Mary's face!

The Johnson Sisters began appearing on Wally Fowler's All-Nite Sings around 1954 and subsequently on Fowler's Birmingham based television show *Gospel Sing* (on WBRC) a few years later. Fowler also brought the group into the recording studio where they cut a record with guitar whiz Chet Atkins. The sisters recorded their first album on the Sing label when the twins were only nine.

Their association with the Sing record company led to an invitation to join the *Gospel Singing Caravan*. Shortly before the Johnson Sisters joined the Caravan, Margaret fell in love with Larry Willis and left the group, never to return to full time singing. At this point, Mary left the piano bench and began singing the third vocal part. Through television exposure, the Johnson Sisters became known as the "Sweethearts Of Gospel Music." Kenny Gates of the Blue Ridge Quartet played the piano for them and various members of the LeFevres played other instruments during their stage appearances.

The love bug continued to wreck havoc with the group as Anna secretly married Ray Reece in 1963 when she was 17. Following her marriage, Anna left the road for a short time. Sandy Kennedy was hired to sing in her place. Jan Houk would sing with the group as well. Judy Johnson soon found the love of her life and married Johnny Johnson in 1964. All of these girls were excellent singers, had similar appearances, and were quite versatile in their abilities. Being newlyweds, the twins often swapped out with Houk or Kennedy on their tours. Many times, the audiences were none the wiser.

During this time, the sisters' tales of joy and woe were documented in their monthly column in *SING Magazine*. They were some of the first teenagers singing full time gospel music, so fans delighted in their lamentations about curlers, bobby pins, hair spray, broken zippers, and lost shoes each time a new issue of *SING Magazine* came off the presses.

Both twins ultimately returned to the road full time. As a rule, one of the husbands would typically travel with the girls during their tours. A near tragedy occurred on one trip. Neither Ray Reece nor Johnny Johnson was available to make the trip, and their van had a terrible accident on a rain-slicked road in Alabama. None of the girls were seriously injured, but the fear of traveling ultimately brought an end to the Johnson Sisters.

After the group retired from the road, the sisters assumed their own private lives. Mary married Bob Wise in 1967. In 1978, Judy and Anna recorded an album of secular tunes billed as the "Johnson Twins." The trio appeared on television with many great country artists. They also worked in the recording studio as backup singers for various artists including Willie Nelson.

The Johnson Sisters reunited in 1996 at the Grand Ole Gospel Reunion joined by pianist Harold Timmons. They continued to appear at Grand Ole Gospel Reunion events for several years, and recorded a new project in 1997 on the BRG label. The group also joined the cast of *America's Gospel Favorites*, a television program produced by Charlie Waller. A few years after their reunion, Anna again decided to retire from the trio. Jan Houk again joined Mary and Judy. The group no longer performs, but the memory of their lush harmony remains.

---John Crenshaw contributed to this entry.

Karen Peck and New River
See **Peck, Karen**

Kieffer, Aldine Silliman
See: **Shape Note Method (Solfege)** and *Musical Million and Singer's Advocate*

The Kingdom Heirs
Formed in the early 1980s by brothers Steve and Kreis French, the Kingdom Heirs began to enjoy a boost in popularity after 1986 when they began regularly performing at the Dollywood theme park in Pigeon Forge, TN. With the commitment to sing at Dollywood daily, the touring schedule for the group is generally limited to three or four months in the winter. Thanks to this situation, the Kingdom Heirs are able to offer attractive benefits to future group members: a secured singing schedule and more time to be at home with family.

Former Singing Americans tenor Rick Strickland and lead singer Clayton Inman sang with the Kingdom Heirs for several years. During the late 1990s, the group had David Sutton, Eric Bennett, and Arthur Rice joining Steve French on vocals with Jeff Stice on piano. This lineup had the group's first number one song on the *Singing* News chart in September of 2001 with "That's Why I Love To Call His Name."

In February of 2005 with Jeff Chapman now singing bass and Jodi Hosterman singing tenor, "I Know I'm Going There" hit number one on the *Singing News* chart. The group had another number one from the same recording in August with "Forever Changed." The Kingdom Heirs have maintained a long-term relationship with the Sonlite record label. Former Florida Boys and Dixie Echoes member Billy Hodges replaced Hosterman at the tenor slot in mid-2005.

Kingsmen Quartet
(1950s-present)
Several groups have used the Kingsmen name over the years, both in sacred and secular music. The most popular secular artists to use the name were the pop group who had a hit with the song "Louie, Louie" and the Statler Brothers, who changed their name once "Louie, "Louie" became a hit. Other groups have used altered spellings of the name, such at the "King's Men."

In Southern Gospel circles, the male quartet based in Asheville, NC is the best-known group calling themselves the Kingsmen. Brothers Raymond, Reece, and Lewis McKinney formed the group in the 1950s. Eldridge Fox joined in 1957 and began to manage them by the early 1960s. Bass singer Ray Reese joined in the 1960s, followed by popular lead singer Jim Hamill in 1971. Never missing an opportunity for creative marketing, the group was billing themselves as the "Ton Of Fun" by the late 1970s, and indeed, when the entire group at the time (eight individuals including band members) stood on a set of vehicle scales, they surpassed 2000 pounds.

The Kingsmen of the 1980s combined high energy, up-tempo music with an exciting brand of showmanship. They recorded more live projects than the average Southern Gospel group. The concert setting was where they really excelled. Ernie Phillips, Ed Crawford, Wayne Maynard, Squire Parsons, Anthony Burger, Arthur Rice and other individuals passed through the group over the next few years. Burger was very popular with fans during his extended stint with the group, winning the *Singing News* Fan Award for Best Musician ten years in a row. For several years after that, the award was named after him. Popular songs for the group during this time included "Old Ship Of Zion" and the novelty song "Excuses," which stayed at the number one position on the *Singing News* chart for ten months. Other number one songs for the Kingsmen in the 1980s include "Saints Will Rise" (February-March, 1984) and "Stand Up" (December 1986-March 1987).

By the early 1990s, the Kingsmen had joined forces with Gold City to record a series of live recordings called KingsGold. Parker Jonathan was singing baritone for the group by this time. Tim Surrett took on a dual role singing lead at times in Hamill's place, and playing with the band. Andrew Ishee became the group's piano player in the late 1990s. The multi-talented Randy Miller played guitar, harmonica, and was featured on selected songs as a vocalist.

A hit with the sentimental song "Wish You Were Here" featuring Surrett's bluegrass tinged vocals marked a turning point for the group. The song proved the group could have success with a polished studio ballad in addition to their success in emotion driven concert settings. It reached number one on the *Singing News* chart for the Kingsmen in May of 1992 and remained number one through August of that same year. Other number ones for the Kingsmen during the 1990s included "Go And Tell Somebody" (December 1991-January 1992), "He's All I Need" (November 1993), and "I Will Rise Up From My Grave" (June 1995).

In time, Fox and Hamill withdrew from traveling, though they continued to appear at selected events. Greg Fox, son of Eldridge and longtime drummer for the group, assumed road manager duties for a few years. The modern version of the Kingsmen had a song reach the number one position on the *Singing News* chart in May of 2001. That song was titled "The Next Cloud." After the elder Fox's death in 2002, the Kingsmen Quartet name was retired. The legal ownership of the name was turned over to Charles Burke, a businessman from Maiden, NC with ties to the Southern Gospel industry.

The remaining Kingsmen members toured for two years billed as the Carolina Boys Quartet. In April and May of 2003 their song titled "God Sits On High" was number one. Nick Succi had replaced the departing Andrew Ishee at piano when the name change occurred and Tim Surrett returned to sing with the group the following year.

In 2004, the Kingsmen Quartet name was transferred from Charles Burke back to the group, now managed by bass singer Ray Reese. The group subsequently released a project titled *Born Again* that included several previous Kingsmen hits like "Love Will Roll The Clouds Away" and "When I Wake Up To Sleep No More." Their next major release contained mostly new material and was titled *The Past Is Past*.

Citing continuing vocal difficulties, Tim Surrett resigned from the Kingsmen in 2005 and Tony Peace replaced him to sing baritone. Other vocalists for the 2005 version of the group included Phillip Hughes (lead), Jeremy Peace (tenor), and veteran bass singer Ray Reese.

A PARTIAL KINGSMEN DISCOGRAPHY: *Big & Live* (1973), *Chattanooga Live* (1977), *Live...Naturally* (1981), *Stand Up At Opryland USA* (1986), *The Judgment* (1989), *Wish You Were Here* (1991), *Kings Gold* (1992), *Born Again* (2004)

Klaudt Indian Family

One of the most diverse groups to travel the gospel music circuits was the famous Klaudt Indian Family. Reverend Reinhold Klaudt was a German cattleman who married Lillian White Corn Little Soldier of the Arickara-Mandan tribe of Indians. She was a direct descendent of one of General Custer's scouts at the Battle of Little Big Horn and also a descendant of Chief Sitting Bull. Their story began on the Fort Berthold Indian Reservation, ND. Together, they raised a family dedicated to spreading the gospel.

Originally from the badlands of North Dakota, the Klaudts were members of the Church of God. The couple wanted their children to be educated in that faith at the Bible Training School in Cleveland, TN, so they relocated there. All of the children received their formal education at the school, where they also expanded their musical abilities. The family included Vernon, Melvin, Raymond, Ken and their sister Ramona.

The Klaudt Indian Family began performing with Mom, Dad, Vernon, Ramona, and Melvin. The other siblings soon joined the group as well. Dad Klaudt left the performing group after several years to concentrate on being the business manager for the group. They settled in the Atlanta, GA area and soon began traveling across the country holding revival services and singing in gospel concerts. The Klaudt Indian Family featured various instruments in their program including the upright bass, trumpet, tenor saxophone, baritone saxophone, trombone, and piano. Their music had a jazz flavor that helped open new doors to the group. They were one of the first gospel groups to use a custom designed motor coach in their travels. They also used semi-trucks to haul tent equipment that would expand to a seating capacity of 3,000.

Most groups in gospel music were using only a piano for accompaniment, but the Klaudts showcased strings and horns. They were also set apart because they performed in elaborate native Indian costumes. The Klaudts quickly became a fixture on the Wally Fowler All Night Singing programs. In addition to gospel concerts and church venues, they played engagements in Las Vegas, state fairs, professional sports games, and theme parks.

The Klaudt Indian Family also owned a record label. Several other gospel groups recorded on their Family Tone label, and they published sheet music and song folios to distribute to the gospel music community. Except for their pianists, they remained a family group. Vernon, Ramona, Melvin, Raymond, and Ken sang together until Ramona was married. Vernon's wife, Betty, added her talents to the group. Ramona's husband Dr. Charles Carpenter also performed with the family for about a year. Some of the pianists that have taken the stage with the group include Mildred Hunter (former pianist for Mahalia Jackson), Jimmy Doan (uncle of the famous Gatlin Brothers), Mack Evans (noted gospel music vocalist), and Tony Brown (former Stamps pianist and now a noted music executive in Nashville). Solos by Mom Klaudt backed by her boys highlighted each Klaudt Indian Family performance.

Television was a vital part in the growing popularity of the Klaudt Indian Family. They were fixtures on the syndicated program, *Bob Poole's Gospel Favorites*. The group traveled for more than four decades before retiring in the early 1980s. One of their final performances featured Mom Klaudt at age of 90 on the stage of the Grand Ole Gospel Reunion in 1996. Mom Klaudt passed away in March of 2001 and Dad passed away about four months later. Mrs. Klaudt was inducted into the Southern Gospel Music Association Hall of Fame in 2004. Most of her family was there to share in this honor.

The siblings are all still living and involved in various business ventures. They continue to keep the ministry of the Klaudt Indian Family alive. They have established a Klaudt Memorial Foundation to fund scholarships through Lee University in Cleveland, TN where the Klaudt family received their higher education. The purpose of the scholarship is to honor the heritage and legacy of Mom and Dad Klaudt and to promote the teaching of gospel music to a new generation.
---John Crenshaw contributed to this entry.

Klaudt, Lillian Little Soldier "Mom"
(June 29, 1906 – March 3, 2001)
Mom Klaudt often appeared in concert with her family wearing traditional Indian outfits. Along with her husband Rev. Reinhold Klaudt and their five children, the group came to be billed collectively as the Klaudt Indian Family. Fans were naturally curious to hear the group due to their name and heritage. The group was known for playing a wide variety of instruments during their programs. These ranged from brass instruments to guitar, piano and accordion.

As her children grew older, Mom Klaudt relocated her family from the Dakotas to Cleveland, TN so they could attend to the Church Of God Bible Training School. In later years, the Klaudts became one of the more popular groups on Wally Fowler's All Night Singings, ultimately settling to live in the Atlanta, GA area. Mom Klaudt was always a crowd favorite with her heartfelt rendition of "Blessed Assurance."

The SGMA inducted Mom Klaudt into their Hall Of Fame in 2004.

Kyllonen, Dave
See: **The Couriers**

LeFevre, Alphus "Uncle Alf"
(March 2, 1912 - 1988)
Alphus LeFevre first sang in a trio with older siblings Urias and Maude when he was nine. He and his brother Urias sang with a number of quartets over the next few years. Ultimately, they formed a new version of the Lefevre Trio in the 1930s along with Urias' wife Eva Mae. Alphus arranged music for the trio and was a talented performer, playing a variety of instruments ranging from the guitar to the accordian. They became one of the most recognized family groups in the industry. Alphus continued to perform until the 1970s, retiring a few years before the group name was changed to the Rex Nelon Singers in 1977.

The SGMA Inducted Alphus into the Hall Of Fame in 2002.

LeFevre, Eva Mae Whittington
(1917 -)
Eva Mae Whittington was married to Urias LeFevre in 1934. They formed the Lefevre Trio along with Urias' brother Alphus and frequently performed at revivals where Eva Mae's father, Rev. H. L. Whittington was preaching. The LeFevres were the first full time gospel group to be based in Atlanta, GA. Eva Mae was forced to manage the group a few years while Alphus and Urias left to fight in World War II. After the war, Eva Mae and Urias had five children.

As Eva Mae's children grew older, they began to join the group on the road. Pierce played trumpet and sang. Meurice and Andrea played saxophone and trombone. Mylon sang and is the credited writer of the song "Without Him." With Eva Mae's popularity as a pianist and emcee, the LeFevres became part of a television show called the *Gospel Singing Caravan*. The Caravan also toured together. Later Jerry Goff, who was married to Andrea Lefevre at the time, produced *The LeFevre Family Show* for television.

Eva Mae was the last LeFevre to sing with the group. She left the road in 1977. By that point, Rex Nelon was managing the group and his daughter Kelly was a group member as well, so Nelon decided to change the name to the Rex Nelon Singers. Eva Mae has continued to appear at various reunion functions such as the Grand Ole Gospel Reunion and the Gaither Video Series. She was inducted into the SGMA Hall Of Fame in 1997.

LeFevre, Urias
(1910 - 1979)
Urias LeFevre was a member of the original LeFevre Trio with his brother Alphus and sister Maude as a child in 1921. In 1934, Urias married Eva Mae Whittington, who joined the trio to sing alto and play piano. Urias handled the business end of the group and emceed until he and his brother Alphus were called into military service. Upon their return, the emcee duties fell to his wife.

The group was successful on radio and television as well as the concert circuit. They were regulars on the *Gospel Singing Caravan*. Urias was inducted into the SGMA Hall Of Fame in 1997

The LeFevres
(1921-1977)
Group Origins
The original LeFevre Trio consisted of two brothers and their sister: Urias, Alphus, and Maude LeFevre. They were from Smithville, Tennessee. The group first sang country music, but soon switched exclusively to gospel music. When Maude married in the mid-1920s, their sister Peggy took her place briefly. The brothers continued to perform in various configurations.

In 1934, Urias married Eva Mae Whittington, a daughter of a Church of God minister named H. L. Whittington. They promptly re-formed the LeFevre Trio along with Alphus LeFevre. Eva Mae's father helped the group get their start by scheduling them to sing at revival meetings where he was preaching.

The LeFevres secured sponsorships from NuGrape and Orange Crush. Through these sponsorships, they recorded and shipped transcription discs across the United States. They were sometimes billed as the Suncrest Trio.

Substitutions
The three original members remained together for the next 40 years, except during World War II when Eva Mae was left to manage the group while her husband and brother-in-law were overseas. During this time, a variety of vocalists filled in, including Jim Waits, Jimmy Kirby, and Connor Hall. Alphus sang with the Stamps Quartet for a short time after returning from the war, but he ultimately came back to join Eva Mae and Urias.

Then it was Eva Mae's turn to be off the road for a bit. After the war, Eva Mae and Urias had five children. In Eva Mae's absence while raising her children, the group also had a variety of individuals filling in. Some of these included Hovie Lister, Jim Waits, and Troy Lumpkin. With the changes in the musical styles of the day, the LeFevres added a full band to give the music a broader appeal.

In the 1950s, the LeFevres moved to Philadelphia, PA to assist evangelist Thea Jones with his ministry. Eva Mae again became a full time mother for a short time as Urias and Alphus continued to perform. Bill Huie and Bob Robinson sang with them during this time period. In 1957, the group returned to their original base in Atlanta. Rex Nelon joined the group to sing bass and play guitar that year. With Jimmy Jones in the group, he and Nelon performed dual bass vocals on songs like "Hide Me, Rock Of Ages."

LeFevre Children Join The Group
By 1959, the LeFevre children were old enough to start joining the group. Pierce was the first to join as a singer and trumpet player. Instrumental numbers began to be a prominent feature in the LeFevres' music. At various times, they incorporated a wide variety of instruments including accordion, trumpet, fiddle, trombone, and sax. Meurice, Andrea, and Mylon performed with the group as well.

In the mid-1960s, Pierce LeFevre handled the editorial duties of the group's newsletter *Sing*. Often noted for his creative prose, Pierce used his position as editor to criticize promoters like Wally Fowler and the failed Southern Gospel movie *Sing A Song For Heaven's Sake*. He also used the newsletter to endorse Barry Goldwater's campaign for the presidency.

Television Successes
For a number of years, the core members of the LeFevres included Eva Mae, Urias, Alphus, Pierce, Jimmy Jones, and Rex Nelon. Recordings were promoted through their in house record label, Sing. During the 1960s, they formed the *Gospel Singing Caravan* television show along with the Johnson Sisters, the Prophets, and the Blue Ridge Quartet.

After the Caravan left the air, Jerry Goff produced a television program called *The LeFevre Family Show*. Goff was married to Andrea LeFevre at the time and often performed on the program as well.

By 1971, Pierce had left the group. Alphus and Urias retired a few years later and management duties were transferred to Rex Nelon. Ultimately, Eva Mae was the only LeFevre still traveling with the group. In 1977, the LeFevres consisted of Eva Mae, Rex Nelon, Janet Paschal, Kelly Nelon, and Rodney Swain. When Eva Mae retired that year, the LeFevre name was retired with her and the group became known as the Rex Nelon Singers. Alphus LeFevre put together a group billed as "Alphus LeFevre and the LeFevres" that included future Nelons member Karen Peck in 1980 and 1981, but it never gained the popularity enjoyed by the former group.

Eva Mae's son Mylon recorded *Mylon/We Believe* in 1969, which was released on the Cotillion label. Many historians consider it to be the second Christian rock recording ever made, the first being Larry Norman's *Upon This Rock*. The members of Mylon's band in 1969 became key members of the Atlanta Rhythm Section in 1970. During the 1970s, Mylon chased the dream of a secular rock music career, recording for Warner Brothers. He ultimately hit bottom in 1979 and found redemption in Christ. After being delivered from drug addiction, he returned to perform Christian contemporary music in the 1980s and early 1990s with his group Broken Heart. Mylon has focused on preaching and teaching more than singing in recent years. Mylon's daughter, Summer, is married to Peter Furler, the lead singer and drummer for the Newsboys.

Eva Mae has continued to appear at various reunion functions such as the Grand Ole Gospel Reunion and the Gaither Video Series. She was inducted into the SGMA Hall Of Fame in 1997.
---John Crenshaw contributed to this entry.

Legacy Five
(1999-present)
Roger Bennett and Scott Fowler were members of the Cathedrals together from the time Fowler joined the group in 1990. The two men formed a friendship and became business partners, producing recordings for up and coming groups when they weren't touring. When the Cathedrals completed the *Farewell Tour* in 1999, Fowler and Bennett formed a new group, hiring Glen Dustin (bass), Josh Cobb (tenor), and Scott Howard (baritone). In light of their heritage with the Cathedrals, they adopted the name Legacy Five.

Highly acclaimed in 2000 with songs like "I Stand Redeemed" and "Stepping Out On The Water" from their *Strong In The Strength* recording, the readers of the *Singing News* responded by nominating all three of Legacy Five's new faces as Horizon Individuals. Josh Cobb won the award, but he and the group parted ways two days later. Tony Jarman was ultimately chosen to replace Cobb. The group had their first number one song on the *Singing News* chart in September of 2003 with the song "I Found Grace."

Frank Seamans replaced Jarman at the tenor slot in 2004. Roger Bennett's son Jordan came on board to play bass for the group in 2005

A PARTIAL LEGACY FIVE DISCOGRAPHY: *Strong In The Strength* (1999), *Heroes Of The Faith* (2001), *London* (2003), *Monuments* (2004)

Lester, Harvey Bryant
(1902 - 1982)
Harvey Lester was well known for his work as a promoter in St. Louis, MO during the 1950s. His family group had a television show *The Lester Family Sing* for 27 years. The group formed in 1925 and originally sang as a trio consisting of Lester, his wife Opal, and his son Herschel. Herschel's wife Mary Alene joined the group later, and their children Brian and Donna subsequently joined as well when they were old enough to participate. By the late 1950s, the group was hosting an annual concert event at a unique location, the Meramec Caverns in Missouri. The Lesters also operated a music store in St. Louis, MO where they sold instruments and gave music lessons. Lester was inducted into the SGMA Hall Of Fame in 2004.
---John Crenshaw contributed to this entry.

Lewis, James Roy "Pop"
(1905 – March 23, 2004)
Pop Lewis was 20 when he used a ladder to elope with 15-year-old Pauline Holloway in 1925. Their marriage lasted 77 years until Pauline's death in 2003. They had eight children: Miggie, Wallace, Esley, Mosley, Talmadge, Polly, Janis and Roy (Little Roy) Lewis.

Pop oversaw the rise of his children as they were first billed as the Lewis Brothers and later as the Lewis Family. The group ultimately came be known as "The First Family Of Bluegrass Gospel Music." Combining gospel lyrics with comedy and up-tempo picking and grinning, the group has been traveling and singing since the 1950s. Pop was also instrumental in the 38-year run of the *Lewis Family Show*, a television program based in Augusta, Georgia on WJBF. The show was syndicated in 25 markets.

Lewis was added to the SGMA Hall Of Fame in 2000.

The Lewis Family
(1940s-present)
The Lewis Brothers initially consisted of Esley, Talmadge, and Wallace Lewis, with Little Roy Lewis sometimes joining his older siblings. Little Roy has played banjo since he was six, and won a competition playing and singing the song "Juicy Watermelon" at the age of eight. The group initially played secular music, sometimes in a concert setting and sometimes as a backdrop for square dances.

When Esley Lewis entered military service, his father ("Pop") and three of his sisters, Miggie, Polly and Janis, joined the group. At that point, the group name was changed to the Lewis Family for obvious reasons, but the more significant change that came at the same time was the shift in lyrical content to gospel music. The group gave their first performance billed as the Lewis Family in 1951 in Thomson, GA. The first recordings by the group were made in the 1950s on the Hollywood label.

The Lewis Family was pioneers of television. The *Lewis Family Show* was based in Augusta, GA on station WJBF beginning in 1954 and continued for the next 38 years, the longest running show of its kind. Inspired by their success on television and growing popularity on the concert circuit, the group bought a bus and quit their day jobs to become a full time musical act in the early 1960s. By the end of the decade, they were regular fixtures on the bluegrass festival circuit.

Talmadge Lewis left the group in 1972 to concentrate on his automobile business. Wallace Lewis' son Travis joined the group in 1974 to play bass fiddle and remained in that position until 2004. Janis' multi-talented son, Lewis Phillips also became a third generation member of the family group. Phillips sings and plays a variety of instruments. Wallace developed Parkinson's disease and had to come off the road in the 1990s. Pop Lewis passed away in 2004, leaving the group in the hands of his three daughters and Little Roy.

The Lewis Family has been inducted into the Georgia Music Hall Of Fame and won a Dove Award in 1999 for the song "He Still Looks Over Me." They won two more Doves in 2003 for the recording *50th Anniversary* and the song "Walkin' and Talkin'." The following year, they won another Dove for the song "So Many Years, So Many Blessings." Other best remembered songs by the Lewis Family include "Slippers With Wings," "Just One Rose Will Do" (Pop's signature song), "Hallelujah Turnpike" and "Good Time Get Together." Little Roy popularized a comedy routine to go along with the song "Honey In The Rock" that is often requested at concerts.

The group was inducted into the GMA Hall Of Fame in 2005. After recording for the Hollywood label in their early years, they went on to release music on the Sullivan, Starday (15 years), Canaan (16 years), Riversong, and Daywind record labels.

Lister, Hovie Franklin
(September 17, 1926 – December 28, 2001)
Hovie Lister toured with evangelist Mordecai Ham in his younger years. Later he attended the Stamps-Baxter School Of Music, then pulled stints playing piano for the Homeland Harmony Quartet, LeFevres, and the Rangers. With a desire to implement his own ideas in gospel music, he formed the Sensational Statesmen in 1948. This group quickly rose to national prominence. Often billed with the Blackwood Brothers, they also appeared on television and in the movies.

In the 1980s, Lister set aside the Statesmen and joined J. D. Sumner, Jake Hess, Rosie Rozell, and James Blackwood to form the Masters V. The group traveled for several years. After the Masters V retired, Lister traveled for a while with the Palmettos State Quartet before returning with Jake Hess and a new version of the Statesmen. Their first recording was titled *Revival*. Biney English (lead/baritone), Bob Caldwell (bass), and Johnny Cook (tenor) fleshed out the new group. Lister developed throat cancer in 1993, but returned to the road with the group after his recovery. The Statesmen continued to sing together until Lister's death in 2001. Lister and the Statesmen were also regular featured artists on the Gaither Homecoming videos.

The GMA made Lister a member of their Hall Of Fame in 1984. He was added to the SGMA Hall Of Fame in 1997. Despite the immense popularity of the Statesmen and the Masters V, neither group had a song reach number one on the *Singing News* chart.

Lister, Thomas Mosie
(September 8, 1921 -)
In 1939, Mosie Lister studied music at the Vaughan School Of Music in Tennessee. He began his musical career as a singer, performing as an original member of the Sunny South Quartet before World War II. After a four-year stint with the Navy, he worked a few months again with the Sunny South Quartet before forming the Melody Masters in 1946 along with Jim Wetherington, Alvin Tootle, Lee Kitchens, and Wally Varner. Lister remained in Atlanta when the Melody Masters moved to Nebraska. In 1948, Lister was tapped by Hovie Lister to be the original baritone for the Statesmen. (Despite their common last name, similar first names and involvement with the Statesmen, Mosie is no relation to Hovie).

Lister soon gave up his professional singing career to devote his attention to songwriting, but he continued to work as an arranger for the Statesmen. In 1953, he formed the Mosie Lister Publishing Company. Some of Lister's better known tunes include "Then I Met The Master," "I'm Feelin' Fine," "His Hand In Mine," and "'Til The Storm Passes By."

Lister is also a popular arranger of choral music for Lillenas Publishing. He has continued to write songs and produce recordings for popular Southern Gospel groups. The Dove Brothers, Booth Brothers, and Palmetto State Quartet are just a few of the modern groups to recorded songs written by Lister. The Dove Brothers released a project titled *A Tribute To Mosie Lister* in 2004, which Lister also produced.

Lister was inducted into the Gospel Music Hall Of Fame in 1976 and into the SGMA Hall Of Fame in 1997.

Lowry, Mark
(June 24, 1958-)

Mark Lowry was born in Houston, TX, the middle child of Charles and Beverly Lowry. Lowry's mother is a noted songwriter whose songs include classics like "I Thirst" and "The Ground Is Level" as well as more recent songs like "Monuments" (Wilburns). After graduating from Liberty University in 1980, Mark began his career as a solo singer, but he soon began telling jokes to fill in the gaps between songs. The comedy routines he developed ultimately came to be as much a part of his act as the singing.

In 1988, Lowry's popularity took a quantum leap when he joined the Gaither Vocal Band to sing baritone and provide comic relief during concerts. Within a year, he had released a solo comedy recording on the Word label called *For The First Time On Planet Earth*. Following in his mother's footsteps, he began to receive recognition for his songwriting ability in 1990 after Buddy Greene set music to a lyric Lowry had composed in 1984. Since Michael English's initial recording of "Mary, Did You Know?" in 1991, more than 30 major recording artists have released their own versions of the song, including Kenny Rogers, Kathy Mattea, Natalie Cole, and Donnie Osmond.

When the Gaither Homecoming video series exploded in popularity in the 1990s, Lowry had a prominent platform for his creative output. Bill Gaither became the straight man for his comedy. Lowry was regularly featured on solos with the Vocal Band, and developed close friendships with a number of the legends that appeared on the series including J. D. Sumner, Howard and Vestal Goodman, Jake Hess, and others.

During the 1990s, Lowry was quick to take advantage of the then emerging Internet. He launched his own website where he developed a personal connection with fans (which he came to call "reMarkables") and also published an email newsletter he titled "reMarks." During the same time period, Lowry wrote a series of children's books featuring a hyperactive mouse named Piper and hosted a television talk show with Kathy Troccolli. In addition to touring with the Gaither Vocal Band, Lowry did a number of concert tours to support his comedy releases on the Word label. He ultimately moved to the Spring House label in 1998 to release *But Seriously*, a recording that had no spoken comedy and very little musical comedy.

In 2001, Lowry left the Gaither Vocal Band, but continued to maintain close ties with the Homecoming video series. A two-volume set of videos called *The Best Of Mark and Bill* was released in 2004. He has four videos that are certified Gold (50,000 units) and two that have reached the Platinum level (100,000 units). Lowry's tours in recent years are typically booked through one concert promoter and featured a select cast of performers such as Stan Whitmire, Lordsong, and the McCraes.

Lyles, Bill

Bill Lyles sang bass during World War II with the Swanee River Boys, a group that included Lee Roy Abernathy, Billy Carrier and George Hughes at the time. Following the war, Lyles joined the Blackwood Brothers and was instrumental in the growth of their popularity. When the Blackwood Brothers began traveling by airplane, Lyles and baritone R. W. Blackwood became the pilots for the group. On June 30, 1954, both men died in a plane crash before a concert in Clanton, Alabama at the annual Peach Festival. John Ogden, Jr., the son of the concert promoter, also perished in the accident.

Majesty/Tony Gore and Majesty
See: **Gore, Tony**

Maples, Fred Calvin Maples
(1910 - 1987)

Baritone Fred Maples was an early member of the Bible Training School Quartet, a group that later came to be known as the Homeland Harmony Quartet. In 1943, Maples established the Harmoneers Quartet, based in Knoxville, Tennessee and oversaw their rise in popularity for the next 13 years. The group recorded for RCA Victor and performed on radio station WNOX. Maples retired from the concert circuit in 1956 to work as a minister of music.

The SGMA inducted Maples into their Hall Of Fame in 2003.

The Martins

Siblings Joyce, Jonathan, and Judy Martin began singing together when they were still children. Coming from humble beginnings, the group's first big break came in the mid-1990s when they were invited to sing on the Gaither video series. Their tight family harmonies immediately attracted a large base of fans. Southern Gospel fans were particularly drawn to the group due to their tight a cappella arrangements of traditional hymns. With older sister Joyce Martin McCollough as a contributing songwriter, and with the backing of their record label Spring Hill, the Martins proceeded to create a new brand of Southern Gospel that blended Country, Inspirational and Contemporary influences. "Timothy's Burden" was their first hit with a new song, followed by inspirational tunes like "Grace" and "Wherever You Are." By the turn of the century, they were one of the most frequently mimicked trios on the circuit. It seemed that two out of every three mixed trios that came along were attempting to duplicate the sound of the Martins.

Jonathan left the group before their last album (*Above It All*) was recorded. He became actively involved with Mission House Music, a record label designed to launch new acts in Southern Gospel. Paul Lancaster took Jonathan's place in the group. In spite of the popularity of the Martins, only one of their songs ever reached the number one slot on the *Singing News* chart, and it was one of their last singles titled "The Promise" (February-March, 2004).

The trio stopped touring regularly after 2003 as Joyce and Judy focused on raising their respective families and recording solo projects. By 2005, the group (with Jonathan back singing again) had scheduled a few select appearances, but whether or not they were planning a full-fledged return to the touring circuit was still a matter of speculation.

Masters V

JD Sumner and Hovie Lister formed the Masters V in the early 1980s along with Jake Hess, James Blackwood, and Rosie Rozell. The concept of seeing five "living legends" together immediately connected with fans. Shaun Nielsen and Steve Warren would later alternate at the tenor slot.

The Masters V mostly performed songs that were already identified with the individual singers; Rozell's "Oh What A Savior," Sumner's "Old Country Church," Hess' "Faith Unlocks The Door," Blackwood's "I'll Meet You In The Morning," Nielsen's "Gonna Shout Hallelujah," and Lister's "Thanks To Calvary" were all popular concert numbers. The group endured until 1988. At that point, the departure of Hess and Blackwood had diluted the concept of the group name. Lister soon followed them. Sumner continued to sing with replacements Jack Toney and Ed Hill, but he announced a name change during the National Quartet Convention. They became the Stamps at that point.

McClung, John Alexander "J. A."
(1891 - 1942)

John Alexander McClung was known as a teacher, songwriter and singer. He was a popular singing school instructor across the United States. McClung formed the Hartford Music Company in 1918 along with his partners E. M. Bartlett and David Moore. He subsequently sang in several quartets associated with the school. McClung wrote over 300 songs including "Standing Outside" and just before his death, the popular "Just A Rose Will Do."

McClung was inducted into the SGMA Hall Of Fame in 2003.

McCoy, Otis Leon
(1897 - 1995)
Otis McCoy was known as a singer, songwriter, instructor and music publisher. McCoy taught music theory, harmony, voice, brass and composition. He played with the WOAN radio orchestra in the 1920s. By 1927, he was singing lead with the Vaughan Radio Quartet.

McCoy became the manager and music editor of the Tennessee Music and Printing Company when it was formed in 1931 with the support of the Church of God denomination. His most enduring publication while heading the publishing company is the venerated red backed *Church Hymnal*, which is still in print. McCoy's most popular song is "Keep On The Firing Line." He was also a member of the Homeland Harmony Quartet during the 1940s.

McCoy was inducted into the SGMA Hall Of Fame in 2003.

The McCraes
Annie and Kelly McCrae were 16 and 14 respectively when comedian Mark Lowry asked them to be part of his tour. The vocal duo's debut recording on the Family Music Group label garnered them five Top 20 songs on the *Singing News* chart. Those songs were "Mountain Top For Me," "When Nothing But A Miracle Will Do," "I Will Overcome," "Lord Shake These Chains," and "He Bore My Burden For Me." In 2004, the McCraes released their first project on the Daywind Records label. The song "If It Had Not Been The Lord" was number one for the month of December that same year. Acclaimed record producer Bubba Smith produced their second Daywind release titled *Perfect Love*.

The McGruders
The McGruders formed their music ministry in the late 1980s. They hail from Indiana and are made up of husband and wife, Carroll and Priscilla. They typically perform with a third vocalist. Carroll is a noted songwriter. The Hoppers, Gold City, Cathedrals ("I've Just Started Living") and other groups have recorded his songs. The McGruders are best known for songs such as "Saved", "Thanks," "I Lean On You, Lord," "A Great Homecoming" and "Most of All." "I'm Going Home With Jesus" was the group's only number one song on the *Singing News* chart. It hit the top position in December of 1990. Priscilla has also written a book describing her struggles with breast cancer. The book is titled *I've Just Started Living*.

The McKameys
(1954-present)

Dora McKamey established the McKameys as a gospel group in 1954, recruiting her sisters Peg and Carol to complete the trio. Ruben Bean joined the group to play guitar in 1957 and married Peg two years later. Dora and Carol retired from the group in 1971 and were replaced by Peg and Ruben's daughters Connie and Sheryl. Sheryl left the group in the early 1980s and her aunt Carol returned to sing with the group at that time. After leaving the concert circuit, Sheryl continued to contribute to the group with her songwriting. The group has maintained the same lineup of vocalists ever since, joined by musicians Randall Hunley at piano and Roger Fortner (who married Connie) playing bass guitar.

By the 1980s, the McKameys had an increasingly growing group of diehard fans that preferred their brand of heartfelt singing to more polished styles of Southern Gospel. Peg has grown to be recognized as an icon in the industry, winning *Singing News* Fan Awards. She's also noted for her tendency to kick off her shoes during an emotional moment in a song.

The McKameys have had thirteen number one songs on the *Singing News* chart. This impressive run began in September of 1984 with "Who Put The Tears In The Eyes Of The Lamb." They rounded out the 1980s with "Getting Used To The Dark" (October-December, 1987) and "God On The Mountain" (November 1988-March 1989). Their number ones from the 1990s include "God Will Make This Trial A Blessing" (January-February 1991), "Do You Know How It Feels" (February-April, 1993), "A Borrowed Tomb" (October 1993), "Arise" (June-September, 1994), "Right On Time" (November 1997), and "Roll That Burden On Me" (November 1999). The McKameys have had four number one songs since the turn of the century. These include "I've Won" (November 2001), "He Calms Me" (May 2002), "The Good News" (June 2005), and "I Am Home" (December 2005).

A PARTIAL MCKAMEYS DISCOGRAPHY: *Genuine* (1980), *Gone To Meetin'* (1988), *Sing Praises* (1989), *It's Real* (1994), *Always* (1998), *I've Won* (2001), *Fresh Manna* (2004)

The Melody Boys Quartet

The lineage of the Melody Boys Quartet runs deeply into the Stamps Baxter Music Company. In the 1940s, there were quite a few groups that used "Melody Boys" in their name. The version that evolved into the current Melody Boys Quartet was first known as the Stamps-Baxter Melody Boys Quartet. This group featured Hershel Foshee singing bass and Smilin' Joe Roper at the piano as its mainstays. After these men served their time in the armed forces, they reorganized the quartet in Carbondale, IL. The members included Russell Guest (tenor), Horace Comstock (lead), Melvin Red (baritone), Foshee (bass), and Joe Roper (piano).

The group relocated to Little Rock, Arkansas in 1947. They began a long association with KARK radio, and became one of the best-known groups west of the Mississippi River. The quartet always began their programs with "Give the World a Smile". Members of the group were also active in teaching gospel music. It was through this outlet that they made the acquaintance of Gerald Williams. Foshee became a mentor to 14 year-old Gerald Williams, and Williams patterned his rounded tones after Foshee.

Hershel Foshee suffered a heart attack in 1948 at the age of 37, so he attempted to scale back his activities. In the process, he formed the "Hershel Foshee Junior Quartet." Gerald Williams joined James Burleson, Tommy Ashcraft, and Freddy Holmes in this quartet. The Junior Quartet knew many of the songs of the Stamps-Baxter Melody Boys Quartet, and often performed in concert with them. When Foshee passed away in 1949, Gerald Williams became his replacement. He was just 16 years old.

The managerial duties fell into the lap of Joe Roper after Foshee's death. The group was called the "Stamps-Baxter Melody Boys Quartet" prior to World War II, but during their reorganization and relocation, they had become known as "Hershel Foshee and the Stamps-Baxter Quartet". When Foshee passed away, they initially changed their name to "Smilin' Joe Roper and the Stamps-Baxter Melody Boys Quartet." The association of the quartet with the Stamps-Baxter Music Company would prove to be short lived in the coming months. The main function of all group associated with Stamps-Baxter was to sell songbooks. They were expected to use the latest Stamps-Baxter material exclusively, extensively and exactly. Unique arrangements were strictly forbidden. Joe Roper, being a gifted arranger, prided himself on the arrangements he wrote for the quartet, and he didn't like being painted into a corner by the Stamps-Baxter Music Company. Roper ultimately dropped the group's association with Stamps-Baxter Music Company, and billed them as "Smilin' Joe Roper and the Melody Boys Quartet".

The Melody Boys Quartet continued to perform on a regular basis on KARK, and their popularity spread. Roper's arrangements were difficult and demonstrated the fine musicianship of the quartet. The singers stayed well within their ranges. Harmony, blend, timing, phrasing and precision became trademarks of the Melody Boys Quartet. In 1950, the group began to record their radio programs on tape. This allowed them to travel extensively. Many songs the Melody Boys Quartet introduced became gospel standards, including "Peace in the Valley", "Pray", and "I Bowed on My Knees and Cried Holy."

Joe Roper wrote many songs including "Sinner's Plea", "Faith in My Savior", and "What a Happy Day." Roper also had a knack for arranging spirituals, which allowed the quartet to produce sounds similar to the popular black groups of the day.

The Melody Boys Quartet was chosen to sing at the first National Quartet Convention in 1957. By this time, the group was made up of Jerry Venable (tenor), Don Randall (lead), Coolidge Faulkner (baritone), Harold Smith (bass), and Joe Roper (piano). Although the Melody Boys Quartet had very talented musicians, the group was suffering financially. Roper ultimately retired the group, and joined former Melody Boy Jim Boatman in the newly formed Prophets Quartet. With the Melody Boys Quartet officially disbanded, four veterans of the quartet formed the Venable Quartet. T.O. Miller, Gerald Williams, and Fred Smith joined Jerry Venable in a group that became very popular in Arkansas fueled by their daily television program on KARK-TV.

In the ensuing years, Gerald Williams had a desire to return to his Melody Boys Quartet roots. He reorganized the group using several singers with former ties to the quartet. Richard Oliver, Bob Walters, Bill Thompson, and William Garvin joined Gerald Williams in this new version of the Melody Boys Quartet. The group operated part-time with all the members holding down full-time jobs. This aggregation lasted a few years before disbanding.

A few years later, Gerald Williams formed yet another Melody Boys Quartet, this time with former member T.O. Miller, John James, and Gerald's son, Steve Williams. Again operating as a part-time group, the membership changed a bit as Ronnie Smith and Jerry Trammell joined the group. As bookings increased, Doug Boydston and Johnny Minnick became members of the Melody Boys Quartet. However, these increased bookings were not necessarily a blessing, for they infringed on the full-time jobs of the quartet members. The Melody Boys Quartet disbanded again in late 1986.

Williams later heard a young trio called Homeward Bound and was impressed with their sound. They soon joined their talents as the new Melody Boys Quartet. Members included Mike Franklin, Chris Bennett, and Jonathan Sawrie. Bennett ultimately left the group and was replaced by Doug Kramer. This group remained together for nine years. They performed mostly on weekends. As with previous incarnations of the Melody Boys, all the guys held full-time jobs.

When Kramer left the quartet in 1998, the group hired Jeremy Raines from Versailles, MO. as the new baritone. Just before Raines joined the group, the Melody Boys Quartet decided to make the group full time. They were soon featured on the covers of *Gospel Voice*, the *Singing News*, and *Christian Music Perspective Magazine*.

Jonathan Sawrie left the quartet in 2002 and was replaced by Ryan Seaton. Seaton's stay with the quartet was short-lived as he resigned his position in August 2003 to join Ernie Haase and Signature Sound Quartet. Sawrie filled in until Raines moved up to the lead position in 2004 and Ben Blessing joined the group for a short stint as baritone singer and piano player. 17-year-old Joshua Noah joined the group after Blessing, also filling both baritone and pianist positions. Mike Franklin announced his retirement near the end of 2004, ending a long tenure of 18 years. The Melody Boys secured the services of another newcomer Gary Bullock to replace Franklin.

Gerald Williams has written an autobiography called *Mighty Lot of Singin'* about his life experiences. The book was co-written with his daughter, Judy Cox.
---John Crenshaw contributed to this entry.

The Melody Masters

Bass singer Jim Wetherington, baritone Mosie Lister, and lead vocalist Lee Kitchens left the Sunny South Quartet in 1946 to form the Melody Masters. Wally Varner and Alvin Toodle joined them at piano and tenor vocals respectively. Initially located in Atlanta, the group relocated to Lincoln, Nebraska after year or so, now with Jake Hess singing lead and Cat Freeman at tenor. Although the group would only be around for another year or so, their sound was a prototype for groups that would come later, especially the Statesmen whose membership would include former Melody Masters Hess, Wetherington, and Freeman. The only surviving recordings by this group are one 78 single and four 15-minute radio transcriptions.

The Melody Masters name surfaced again around 1960 in Spartanburg, SC as a regional group. At that time, Acton McClellan owned the group and a young Richard Sanders relocated to Spartanburg to become their bass singer.

In the mid-1990s, almost fifty years after the original Melody Masters Quartet was formed, Sanders and Roger Burnett revived the Melody Masters name. They were joined in 1996 by former Singing Americans lead singer Scott Whitener and tenor singer Chris Roberts, who came from a church music background. This group traveled full time for several years with moderate success, appearing on the main stage at the National Quartet Convention and recording for the Journey Record label.

Eric Phillips, Derrick Boyd, and Phillip Hughes passed through the Melody Masters before moving on to other groups. By 2004, the group had returned to the 1996 lineup of Sanders, Burnett, Roberts, and Whitener and reduced their schedule to part time. They have continued to be popularly received by fans, particularly in North Carolina, Kentucky, and Texas. The group released a new CD in 2005 titled *Big Change*.

Mike Speck Trio
See: **Speck, Mike**

Mills, Walt

Walt Mills became a Christian in 1954. By 1959, he was a full-time singer and traveling evangelist. In September of 1990, Mills had his only number one song on the *Singing News* chart with "I've Got A Feeling." The song held the number one position for three months. A number of other songs recorded by Mills have attracted chart attention. Some of these include "Heaven Will Be My Home," "Where The Timbers Cross," and "The Devil's In The Phone Booth." Mills hosts the television program *Revival's In The Land Today* on the Trinity Broadcasting Network.

Morales, Armond

Armond Morales sang with the Weatherfords and Glen Payne in Akron, Ohio as part of the ministry of Rex Humbard's Cathedral of Tomorrow in the late 1950s. Pianist Henry Slaughter was also a Weatherfords member at this time. When the Weatherfords returned to traveling on the road in 1963, Payne formed the Cathedral Trio while Morales and Slaughter joined Jake Hess and the Imperials. Morales became the manager of the Imperials when Hess left the group a few years later.

Noted for his smooth bass voice, Morales oversaw the Imperials as they left Southern Gospel to explore new musical styles in the 1970s, 80s, and 90s. Their success in Christian pop music peaked in the late 1980s.

Morales turned the management of the group over to his son Jason in 2003. He then reunited with former Imperials members Jim Murray, Terry Blackwood, and Sherman Andrus. They made a recording called *The Gospel Side Of Elvis* in 2004. Billed as the Classic Imperials, Morales appears with this group at select dates each year.

Mull, Jacob Bazzel
(1914 -)

J. Bazzel Mull is one of the most popular DJs in Southern Gospel. Blinded from the age of 11 after falling into an open fireplace, Mull began playing banjo with the Valdese Sacred Band. After surrendering to the ministry in 1932, Mull began broadcasting his sermons on the radio in 1939. In 1943, he promoted his first concert. He was instrumental in the early success of the Chuck Wagon Gang. Although the group did not tour very much at first, their success was immediate once they did begin to travel the concert circuit, thanks in no small part to Mull's continuous promotion of their music on the radio.

Mull and his wife Elizabeth's "Mull Singing Convention Of The Air" became a fixture on several stations in western North Carolina and eastern Tennesee. The Mulls have also published songbooks and established several churches. Mull was inducted into the SGMA Hall Of Fame in 2003.

Murray, Jim

Jim Murray sang tenor with the Imperials from 1966 to 1986. During this period, the group transformed from a traditional Southern Gospel quartet to the leading pop vocal group in contemporary Christian music. Their recordings sold in excess of 300,000 units each at the peak of their popularity. After leaving the Imperials in 1986, Murray joined the Gaither Vocal Band where he sang alongside fellow Imperials alumnus Gary McSpadden as well as Michael English and Mark Lowry.

The Gaither Vocal Band was very popular in contemporary Christian pop music during the 1980s as well, but they recorded a complete Southern Gospel project before Murray left in 1992. His last project with the Vocal Band was the original *Homecoming* release. Since 1992, Murray has performed as a soloist and in 2004, reunited with former Imperials Armond Morales, Terry Blackwood, and Sherman Andrus. They recorded a project in 2004 called *The Gospel Side of Elvis* and made an appearance during the National Quartet Convention that same year.

Musical Million and Singer's Advocate

Aldine Kieffer first published the *Musical Million* in 1870. By 1900, the newsletter had more than 10,000 subscribers. It was used to promote shape notes as the next evolutionary step in musical notation. Kieffer firmly believed shape notes should replace round notes in all forms of music, and he used his newsletter to advance his cause. In 1876, Kieffer had adopted Jesse Aiken's seven-shape system of notation. With the money he collected from ads sold in the *Musical Million*, Kieffer was able to form the Virginia Normal, an annual singing school located first in New Market, VA and later relocated to Dayton, VA.

The Music Teacher (Our Musical Visitor)

Patterned after Kieffer's *Musical Million*, *Our Musical Visitor* was published by the A. J. Showalter Company in the late 19th century. After a few issues, it was renamed *The Music Teacher*. When Showalter passed away in 1924, Thomas Benjamin Mosely took over as the newsletter's editor.

National Quartet Convention
(1957-present)

The first National Quartet Convention was held in 1957. Conceived by J. D. Sumner, it featured all the major gospel groups at a three-day event at the Ellis Auditorium in Memphis, TN. After breaking even the first couple of years, the NQC was moved to Birmingham, AL in 1959 and Atlanta, GA in 1960. It returned to Memphis in 1961 and was drawing annual crowds of 20,000 by the mid-1960s. Sumner bought the convention in 1971 and moved it to Nashville, TN, where it remained until 1993. Since then, the convention has made its home in Louisville, KY.

J. G. Whitfield owned the convention from 1980-1982. A group of industry member investors then bought the convention from Whitfield. A board of directors currently operates NQC.

Over the years, the National Quartet Convention grew from three days of concerts to a six-day multi-purpose event. A main attraction at Louisville is the exhibit hall with approximately 500 booths where artists, record labels, CD duplication plants, media entities, booking agents, Christian bookstores, and other industry related organizations display their products and offer their services. Fans also have an ample opportunity to meet and greet their favorite artists in the exhibit area.

A concert is held each evening in Freedom Hall, a 17,000-seat arena that typically approaches sellout numbers for the weekend concerts. These concerts run for six hours or so and feature non-stop music from the major Southern Gospel artists spaced at 10-25 minute intervals. The *Singing News* magazine presents the Fan Awards on Thursday night. Afternoons are devoted to showcases, some for new talent and others for conceptual events. One popular showcase in recent years has been Mike Speck's "Choral Music Extravaganza." Pianorama is another showcase that spotlights the top piano players. There's a talent competition during the week as well.

In addition to the events for the fans, industry members routinely schedule meetings and even recording sessions to coincide with the National Quartet Convention. Groups needing to replace a member make new contacts at NQC and sometimes conduct auditions during the week. Various business deals are made or re-negotiated. Hoping to gain exposure, up and coming artists schedule showcases at nearby hotels. Record labels court radio and media by feeding them meals, taking them on riverboat cruises and facilitating access for interviews with the artists.

In the late 1990s, the convention added three additional events designed to take the Southern Gospel convention experience to regions distant from

Louisville. These new events were the Great Western Convention in Fresno, CA; the Canadian Quartet Convention in Red Deer, Alberta, Canada; and the Central Canada Gospel Quartet Convention in Hamilton, Ontario, Canada. Within a few years, though, they had sold or abandoned those events in favor of focusing on the main event in Louisville.

2006 marks the 50th year in which a National Quartet Convention has been held. NQC is still marketed and described in the words of its founder J. D. Sumner as "the Grand Daddy of them all."

National Singing Convention
(1936-present)

The most prominent publishers of shape note hymnals established the National Singing Convention and held their first event in Birmingham, AL in 1936. These publishers all used Jesse Aikin's seven-note system of shape notes. [See **Shape Note Method (Solfege)**.] Publishers initially included Morris-Henson Company, the Vaughan Quartet, James D. Vaughan Music Publishers, the Hartford Music Company, A. J. Showalter Company, Denson Music Company, Theodore Sisk Music Company, Tennessee Music and Printing Company, George W. Sebren, W. P. Ganus, and the Stamps-Baxter Music and Printing Company. The first convention president was Adger M. Pace.

Initially operated exclusively by the hymnbook publishers, the National Singing Convention's constitution was revised in 1949 to give state singing conventions voting privileges. Stella Baughan wrote a historical article in 1961 for *Vaughan's Family Visitor* titled "History of the Twenty-Five Years of the National Singing Convention."

The organization's annual meeting is typically held in a different small Southern town each year. At the two-day meetings, the president of the convention calls on individuals to lead in the singing. The leader then selects the song and the pianist who will play. Songs are taken from newly published books, which participants have the opportunity to purchase at the end of the convention.

Nelon, Rex Lloyd
(January 19, 1932 - 2000)

Rex Nelon served in the Marine Corps in the early 1950s. After his discharge, he sang with several part-time groups around Asheville, NC. His first full time position was with Homeland Harmony Quartet in 1955.

In 1957, Rex joined the LeFevres in a dual role as singer and guitarist. He continued with the group for the next 20 years and ultimately became the group owner. When Eva Mae LeFevre retired from the group in 1977, Nelon, whose daughter Kelly was already singing with the group, changed the group name to the Rex Nelon Singers and later shortened that to the Nelons.

The Nelons became a trend setting group in the 1980s, often introducing songs that would be classified as "middle of the road" such as "Oh, For A Thousand Tongues To Sing" and "Don't Give Up." After turning the group over to Kelly in the late 1990s, Rex Nelon continued to appear regularly on the Gaither Homecoming videos. He was in London, England at a taping session with the Gaithers when he passed away in 2000. The SGMA Hall Of Fame inducted Rex Nelon in 1999.

The Nelons

The Rex Nelon Singers were formed in 1977 from the remnants of the LeFevres. The name of the group was ultimately shortened to "The Nelons." Original group members included Rex Nelon (bass), Kelly Nelon (alto for the LeFevres since 1972), Rodney Swain (tenor), and Janet Paschal (soprano). The group's first recording for the Canaan label in 1977 was titled *The Sun's Coming Up*. A live recording followed in 1978 which included a song written and performed by Rex Nelon called "I Love To Call His Name." In 1980, a song from the group's 1979 recording *Feelings* became the Nelons' first number one song on the *Singing News* chart. "Come Morning" actually hit the top position three times in non-consecutive months, which is rare.

After Janet Paschal's departure from the group in the early 1980s, Karen Peck became the soprano for the Nelons. Jerry Thompson married Kelly Nelon and began singing with the group as well. The group would enjoy a successful run of popularity with Peck and Thompson. Four songs that are now considered Nelons classics all came from a 1983 project titled *We Shall Behold The King*. Those songs are "We Shall Behold The King," "When I Receive My Robe And Crown," "Oh, For A Thousand Tongues," and "Walk Right Out Of This Valley."

For the rest of the 1980s, the Nelons sang in a style that came to be labeled "middle of the road." They were more progressive than most Southern Gospel groups of the time, but they weren't full blown contemporary in style, certainly not compared to other vocal groups of the day like Second Chapter of Acts or the Imperials. Songs like "God's Way Up," "Don't Give Up" and "Thanks" attracted a younger audience while tunes like "The Sweetest Song" continued to appeal to traditional Southern Gospel fans.

By the early 1990s, Peck had left the group to form New River. The singing members of the Nelons were all relatives for a couple of years with Rex and Kelly and Jerry joined by Todd Nelon. Another Nelons song reached number one on the *Singing News* chart in 1992. The song was "I'm Glad I Know Who Jesus Is."

1992 also began a series changes for the group. At a couple of points, there was a question of whether the group would continue. Jerry and Kelly left the group to pursue a vocal duo career around this time. Rex considered retirement, but discovered a young talent in Charlotte Penhollow and carried on. Jerry and Kelly subsequently returned to the group in 1993.

Amy Roth began singing soprano for the group in 1997. Jerry Thompson and Kelly divorced around this time, and Thompson left the group. The group then went through a number of personnel changes. David Hill was with the group for one CD, as was Paul Lancaster. Ultimately, Kelly married the group's bass player Jason Clark, who began singing with the group. Jason's father Dan Clark joined the group to sing bass and Kelly's daughter Amber Thompson became the group's soprano soon after that, making it a group with all the members related once more (though three of them now had the last name of Clark). Dan came off the road in 2003 and the Nelons subsequently became a trio consisting of Jason, Kelly, and Amber.

The Nelons have won five Dove Awards, including four for best Southern Gospel Album. Kelly Nelon received seven *Singing News* Fan Awards in the categories of Favorite Female Vocalist and Favorite Alto between 1980 and 1990.

A PARTIAL NELONS DISCOGRAPHY: *The Sun's Coming Up* (1977), *Expressions Of Love* (1980), *We Shall Behold The King* (1983), *In One Accord* (1985), *A Promised Reunion* (1994), *Following After* (2000)

New Hinsons
See: **Hinsons**

New River
See: **Peck, Karen**

Newton, Calvin
A boxing champion as a young boy, Calvin Newton sang tenor with the Blackwood Brothers and the Oak Ridge Boys before forming the Sons Of Song in 1957. Newton's trio stood out at the time because of their different sound. The vast majority of male groups in the late 1950s were quartets. The Sons Of Song were best known in later years for their song called "Wasted Years."

The song would prove to be prophetic for Newton, who later became addicted to drugs and spent at least two stints in prison. It was only after Newton was in his 60s that he turned his life around and rededicated himself to the Lord. In his biography *Bad Boy Of Gospel Music*, Newton describes his life as a prodigal daredevil and what brought him back. Now a regular participant in the Gaither Homecoming video series, Newton is again active in the gospel music world.

Nicholson, Duane
See: **The Couriers**

Nielsen, Sherrill "Shaun"
Sherrill Nielsen sang tenor with a number of top groups in Southern Gospel including the Speer Family, the Imperials (original member), the Masters V, and the Stamps. Also a songwriter, Nielsen's best known song is "I'm Gonna Shout Hallelujah."

Norcross, Benjamin Marvin
(1929 - 1980)
Marvin Norcross established Canaan Records in 1964 as a label in the Word Music family. Groups who recorded on the label for the next 30 years included the Happy Goodman Family, the Dixie Echoes and the Florida Boys. In 1974 and 1975, Norcross was President of the Gospel Music Association. Outside Gospel Music, Norcross was known for his work with Little League Baseball in the state of Texas. The *Singing News* magazine remembers Norcross annually when they present the Marvin Norcross Award to an individual who has made an outstanding contribution to the Southern Gospel Industry.

Norcross was added to the SGMA Hall Of Fame in 1997.

Nowlin, Wilmer Berney "W. B."
(1905 - 1994)
W. B. Nowlin was one of the most successful promoters of Southern Gospel from the 1950s through the 1970s. He began by promoting songs to radio in the 1930s and moved on to concert promotion in the 1940s. When his first major concert in 1948 drew 12,000 people, he became a full time concert promoter. His first event was part of the Peach and Melon Festival in DeLeon, TX. The concert included Eddy Arnold with the Frank Stamps All-Star Quartet opening and the Stamps-Ozark Quartet closing.

In 1950, Nowlin began what would later become a regular feature at his events, the "Battle of Songs." In this popular showcase, quartets would engage in friendly singing "duels." For the first 14 years, Nowlin continued to book gospel artists to open or close for established Country acts, but in 1962, Nowlin began limiting his shows to gospel artists. In 1970, Nowlin was the first to promote a Southern Gospel concert in the state of Hawaii.

The SGMA inducted Nowlin into their Hall Of Fame in 1997.

Oak Ridge Boys
(1943-present)
The Oak Ridge Boys grew out of Wally Fowler's group, the Georgia Clodhoppers. The town of Oak Ridge, TN drew national attention after the atomic bomb was dropped on Hiroshima, Japan in August 1945. Fowler, whose group had been popular in the area since 1943, subsequently re-named the group after the town. At first they were known as the Oak Ridge Quartet, but they also referred to themselves using the "Boys" moniker dating back to the early 1950s.

Starts and Restarts
Over the next 20 years, more than 30 members passed through the group including Calvin Newton, Joe Allred, Cat Freeman, and a teen-aged Glen Allred who played guitar and sang baritone whenever Fowler didn't appear with the group. Fowler actually started a group called the Oak Ridge Quartet at least four times. The first group left Fowler to form the Stone Mountain Quartet around 1949. Fowler hired a new group, which he sold to Bob Weber in 1952. It folded a couple of years later. Fowler reclaimed the group name with a third lineup in 1956. Smitty Gatlin was the group manager/lead singer and Ronnie Page sang baritone with the 1956 group. The group members secured the ownership from Fowler in 1958 and with the addition of tenor Willie Wynn, bass Herman Harper, and pianist Tommy Fairchild, they became one of the more popular quartets in the early 1960s.

The 1960s: Success in Gospel Music
During the 1960s, the Oak Ridge Boys had their own television program, which was geared for youth. The program was called *It's Happening*. They also popularized a stage routine called "Go Out To The Program" which featured the Oaks mimicking the popular songs of other artists. (The routine was actually originated in 1953 by the Dixie Hummingbirds, a popular black gospel group.) In one skit, for example, tenor Willie Wynn and the Oaks would sing the song "Higher" in the style of Rose Carter and the Chuck Wagon Gang. This was especially popular on multi-artist events, because the artist they were spoofing would often join them on stage to the delight of the crowd.

By this time, the group was known and marketed as the Oak Ridge Boys, so Fowler started a fourth group and again named it the Oak Ridge Quartet. A lawsuit filed by Gatlin and the other Oak Ridge Boys forced Fowler to stop using that name, though. When Gatlin left the group a few months after the resolution of the lawsuit in 1966, Duane Allen was hired to take his place. William Lee Golden was already singing with the group by this point, succeeding baritone Jim Hamill in 1965 (who succeeded Gary McSpadden in 1964). Noel Fox replaced Herman Harper at the bass position in 1969.

In January of 1970, the *Singing News* magazine began publishing a monthly chart. The Oak Ridge Boys had the first number one song with "Jesus Is Coming Soon." (Three other groups shared the honor with their own versions of the same song.) It held the number one position for three months and returned to the top of the chart for another three months later that same year. The Oaks had another number one in October of 1970 with "Sheltered In The Arms Of God." They continued to dominate the top position in 1971 with the song "I Know" at the top for ten months. "The Flowers Kissed The Shoes Jesus Wore" (April 1972) and "King Jesus" (October 1973) were also number one songs for the Oak Ridge Boys.

The 1970s: Moving from Gospel to Secular
Allen and Golden got to know Joe Bonsall and Richard Sterban over the next few years. When the bass slot came open in 1972, Sterban was hired. He had been singing backup bass for J. D. Sumner in the Stamps and touring with Elvis Presley previously. Bonsall joined in 1973, replacing the 15-year veteran tenor Willie Wynn. The group continued to sing gospel music until 1975, but their increasingly progressive stage presence had begun to worry some promoters. Many fans were bothered as well. 200 people stood and marched out in protest when they performed in Roanoke, VA in 1975, an act the Oaks accused the Kingsmen of putting into motion, but the Kingsmen denied. Jim Hamill was particularly outspoken about the direction the Oak Ridge Boys were going at this time, referring to them as a "night club act." Les Beasley would also speak positively about the image of the Statler Brothers, saying they weren't "Oak Ridge types."

The turning point came when they were booked to open a tour for Roy Clark and were told they were just "three minutes" away from making it big in Country music...that is to say, they had everything they needed to succeed in terms of talent and stage presentation except one hit song. After a couple of lean years attempting to break in the Country industry and failing on the Columbia label, they had success with their 1977 MCA album called *Y'all Come Back Saloon*. Any doubts about whether or not the Oaks were switching to secular were resolved at that point.

Secular Successes
A string of hits in the late 1970s and 1980s established the Oaks alongside the Statler Brothers as Country music's top male vocal groups. With novelty

songs like "Elvira" and "Bobbie Sue" and a Gospel/Christmas/Country genre-crossing classic in "Thank God For Kids," their popularity reached new heights. After Sterban joined the group in 1973, their only change in membership came in 1987 when William Lee Golden was voted out of the group for failing to modify his "mountain man" appearance (among other issues). Band member Steve Sanders took Golden's place, and Golden sued the group for $40 million. The suit was ultimately settled out of court. Golden returned to the group at the beginning of 1996, still a mountain man. Sanders died from a self-inflicted gunshot wound in 1998.

Return to Gospel
For most of their secular career, the Oak Ridge Boys recorded for MCA and RCA. In 2001, the Oak Ridge Boys signed a recording contract with Spring Hill and released *From The Heart*, an all gospel project containing new material. With several Spring Hill recordings now under their belt, the Oaks have won their way into the hearts of gospel fans again, although they still receive criticism from some for continuing to appear at questionable venues such as casinos. The group has been featured on the Gaither Homecoming videos in recent years and has a daily show at the Grand Palace in Branson, MO.

O'Neal, Ed
(1936 -)
Bass singer, Ed O'Neal was born in Raleigh, North Carolina where he grew up singing with his brothers. He joined the Serenaders in 1958 and moved to the Gospel Harmony Quartet in 1960. A year later, he joined the Dixie Melody Boys, where he has remained for over 40 years.

O'Neal took the group in a country direction for a couple of years in the mid-1980s, rebilling them as the DMB Band. He soon returned them to a traditional male quartet format and brought back their original name. As owner and manager of the Dixie Melody Boys, O'Neal has developed a reputation for molding young singers. McCray Dove, Harold Reid, Devin McGlamery, Derrick Selph and others got their formal training singing under O'Neal.

The Dixie Melody Boys are best known for their renditions of "Antioch Church Choir" and an O'Neal composition called "When I Cross To The Other Side Of Jordan." O'Neal became a member of the SGMA Hall Of Fame in 2004.

Old Friends Quartet
See **Younce, George Wilson** and **Hess, Jake**

Old Time Gospel Hour Quartet

Based in Lynchburg, VA and affiliated with Jerry Falwell's *Old Time Gospel Hour* television broadcast, the Old Time Gospel Hour Quartet consisted of Robbie Hiner (tenor), Wyatt Wilson (lead), Jeff Stanley (baritone) and Christian Davis (bass) when they began traveling and singing full time around the year 2000. The group won the Horizon Award in the *Singing News* Fan Awards for 2001 and capitalized quickly with a novelty song and accompanying video called "The Dream." They had another successful song called "There's A Brighter Day" on their first CD.

The group's first two recordings were released on the Daywind Records label. They then began to record for a label called Song Garden that Hiner co-owns with veteran producer Nick Bruno. In 2005, the group underwent a significant change when bass singer Jeff Pearles and tenor singer Robbie Hiner left the group. Jerry Pilgrim and Tony Jarman replaced them respectively.

Orrell, Lloyd
(1907 - 1983)

Lloyd Orrell became a Southern Gospel concert promoter after giving up his day job in Detriot, Michigan. He soon became the most successful promoter in the north and mid-west. Orrell's concerts were held in many of the larger cities for almost 40 years. He was added to the SGMA Hall Of Fame in 1997.

The Orrells

The Orrell Quartet performed during the 1960s with members including Buddy Lyles and Lloyd Orrell's son Larry. The quartet ultimately disbanded, but reformed as a trio with the name shortened to "The Orrells" in 1969. The vocal lineup of the trio remained the same for the next nine years, with the group taking a break from traveling together a couple of times and going through one name change. Members included Larry Orrell, Gordon Jensen, and Wayne Hilton. They recorded on the Heartwarming label in the early 1970s, with Jensen writing most of their songs. A number of Jensen's tunes introduced by the Orrells became well known standards including "Redemption Draweth Nigh," "Tears Are A Language," "I Should Have Been Crucified," and "Jesus Will Outshine Them All."

In 1976, the group name was changed to Gordon Jensen and Sunrise. They disbanded by the end of the decade. Jensen continued to write and record solo projects after the split. Larry Orrell went the vocal solo route as well, while Hilton became a record producer for Heartwarming label groups including the Kingsmen Quartet, the Hemphills, and Heavenbound.

Ott, Doy Willis Ott
(1919 - 1982)
Doy Ott played piano for the Stamps-Baxter Melody Boys, Hartford Quartet, Rangers, and Homeland Harmony in the 1940s. In 1951, he filled in for Hovie Lister with the Statesmen while Lister was in military service. Ott moved to the baritone slot when Lister returned in 1952 and remained with the group for the next 25 years. Because Ott was equally capable as a pianist, he sometimes played so that Lister could move to center stage and sing. He also arranged songs for the group during the height of their popularity.

Ott became a member of the SGMA Hall Of Fame in 2000.

Pace, Adger McDavid
(August 13, 1882 - 1959)
Adger Pace was a native of South Carolina. He performed for 17 years with the Vaughan Radio Quartet. They broadcasted on one of the first radio stations in the South, WOAN. Pace is best known for his contributions as a music teacher, however. He became the music editor for Vaughan publications in 1920, and continued for the next 27 years. In 1937, Pace became the first president of the National Singing Convention.

While at the Vaughan School, Pace influenced many students who later became popular performers in the Southern Gospel industry. He also wrote more than 1000 songs, including "That Glad Reunion Day," "The Happy Jubilee," and "Beautiful Star of Bethlehem."

Pace was inducted into the SGMA Hall Of Fame in 1999.

Palmetto State Quartet
(late 1940s-present)
Early members of the Palmetto State Quartet in the late 1940s included Greenville, SC residents Jamie Dill (pianist), Clarence Owens (tenor), Woodrow Pittman (lead), Malone Thomason (baritone), and Paul Burroughs (bass). The group had a 30-minute program on Greenville radio station WFBC on Sundays at 8:00 AM. Jack Earl Pittman replaced his first cousin Woodrow in 1954. Jack Bagwell replaced Thomason around the same time. The two Jacks would sing together in the group for more than 40 years.

For many years, the group operated as a part-time regional group. Ken Turner sang bass for the group in the 1960s after Burroughs left. Laverne Tripp also filled in for Jack Pittman for a while when Pittman was having health problems. The group actually stopped singing for a while in the late

1960s, but formed again in 1971 with Dill, Bagwell, Pittman, Claude Hunter, and Cliff King. The next change came in 1981 when Joel Duncan replaced King at the bass position. Eddie Broom joined as the group's guitar player in 1984 and became their tenor singer when Hunter left in 1986.

The Palmetto State Quartet began to expand their horizons in 1989. Dill had passed away in 1987 and was replaced by David McCabe at the keys. Jack Pittman took over as the group manager. In 1989, the legendary Hovie Lister replaced McCabe following his stint with the Masters V. The presence and personality of Lister opened up new doors for the group to travel more. Woody Beatty joined them a few months later to augment Lister's keyboard with his synthesizer work. Beatty became the full time pianist when Lister left in 1992 to re-organize the Statesmen.

By 1987, the Palmetto State Quartet was working a full time schedule. Bagwell and Pittman decided to retire in 1997. Bass singer Harold Gilley made his exit from the group at the same time, leaving tenor singer Brion Carter as the only surviving member from the older group. At this point, Kerry Beatty joined to sing lead, Tony Peace became the baritone, and Jeff Pearles was chosen to sing bass.

This lineup was stable for a few years, but the group would undergo a series of changes again. Jerry Kelso replaced pianist Woody Beatty. Andrew Ishee in turn replaced Kelso. John Rulapaugh joined the group to sing tenor in 2002, Aaron McCune became the group's bass singer in 2003, and Rick Fair replaced Tony Peace in 2004. Despite all the changes in personnel, in 2004 the song "Knock, Knock, Knock" became the group's first number one on the *Singing News* chart.

Parker, Ivan

Ivan Parker's first public performance was at the age of two at his church in Sanford, NC. He later sang with a family group known as the Parker Brothers. His first experience singing with a well-known quartet came in 1982 when he joined the Singing Americans. His tenure with that group was brief, however.

He joined Gold City the following year and remained with them until 1994. While with Gold City, Parker quickly became known for his powerful vocals on songs like "I Think I'll Read It Again," "John Saw," "When I Get Carried Away," and "Midnight Cry." All the aforementioned songs reached number one on the *Singing News* charts in the 1980s and "Midnight Cry" became one of Parker's signature songs. From 1988 to 1993, Parker won six consecutive *Singing News* Fan Awards for Favorite Male Vocalist. The group's song, "There Rose A Lamb," which featured Parker, received a Dove Award in 1993 for Southern Gospel Song of the Year.

In 1994, Parker left Gold City to pursue a solo career. Over the next 11 years, he would release 13 solo recordings. He also appeared at a number of Homecoming events with Bill and Gloria Gaither as a member of the Gaither Trio starting in 1996, and later formed a part time group with Anthony Burger and Kirk Talley in 1999 called The Trio. They released two studio recordings and performed at several events each year. Parker left the group in 2004 and was replaced by Shane Dunlap.

From 2001-2004, readers of the Singing News again recognized Parker, now as their Favorite Soloist. In 2002, Parker's song "It's True" reached the number two position on the Singing News chart.

Parris, Conley "London"
(1931 - 1992)
Bass vocalist, Conley Parris was always a crowd favorite. Lee Roy Abernathy nicknamed him "London." Parris spent a short time with the Homeland Harmony Quartet as well as a few months with the Lee Roy Abernathy Quartet prior to joining the Rebels, where he followed popular bass singer Big Jim Waits. He later pulled a stint with the Blackwood Brothers before returning to the Rebels for a brief period of time. In 1970, he formed his own group called London Parris and the Apostles. The group won the Dove Award for Most Promising New Talent in 1972. Parris' most popular tune was "Everybody Ought to Know."

London Parris rose from relative obscurity in gospel music to becoming one of the most beloved singers in a few short years. He consistently sang notes lower than most basses of his day, and had a dynamic stage presence. The fans loved his ever-present handkerchief and his encouragement of the group as his words "Come on boys!" became a part of every big ending by the quartet.

The SGMA Hall Of Fame inducted Parris in 2004.
---John Crenshaw contributed to this entry

Parris, Oren A. "O. A."
(1897 - 1966)
O. A. Parris was a prominent music publisher, beginning his career under James D. Vaughan and Adger M. Pace. Parris founded the Parris Music Company in 1932 and went on to revise the Sacred Harp and Christian Harmony songbooks. Parris was also a noted composer with several hundred songs to his credit. Some of his more popular songs include "When The Home Gates Swing Open," "A Happy Meeting," and "Hallelujah, I'm Going Home." Parris later worked for the Stamps Quartet Music Company for a period of 15 years. The SGMA Hall Of Fame inducted Parris in 1997.

Parsons, Squire

Squire Parsons was raised in West Virginia and attended the West Virginia Institute of Technology where he received a degree in music. In 1975, he joined the Kingsmen Quartet as their baritone singer. He switched to lead when Jim Hamill left the group to sing with the Senators, but moved back to baritone when Hamill returned to the Kingsmen.

Parsons is best known for writing and performing the song "Beulah Land." He won a number of *Singing News* Fan Awards from the mid-1980s to the mid-1990s, most frequently for Favorite Songwriter. Some of his more popular songs include "Master Of The Sea," "He Came To Me," "I Sing Because," and "Hello Mama." The *Singing News* honored Parsons with the Marvin Norcross Award in 1990.

He traveled for a number of years billed as Squire Parsons and Redeemed. Redeemed typically consisted of two backup vocalists. Ernie Haase was in the group before joining the Cathedrals. Fellow Kingsmen alumni "Big Ed" Crawford and "Little Ernie" Phillips were also members of Redeemed. Parsons has traveled in more recent years with his son and Greg Bentley billed as the Squire Parsons Trio. Although the group is typically part-time, they have released a number of recordings. Parsons has continued to release solo projects as well, and supplements his trio schedule with solo dates and Gaither Homecoming video appearances.

Paschal, Janet

Janet Paschal joined the LeFevres in the mid-1970s, first appearing on the 1975 recording titled *Experience...The LeFevres*. She made the name change transition from the LeFevres to the Rex Nelon Singers with the group after Eva Mae LeFevre's departure in 1977. The group released a recording called *Feelings* in 1979 and saw their single "Come Morning" hit the number one position on the *Singing News* chart for the months of June, August, and October in 1980. Another popular tune that featured Paschal with the Nelons was "We Shall Wear A Robe And Crown" from the 1980 *Expressions Of Love* release.

After leaving the Nelons in the early 1980s, Paschal ultimately embarked on a solo career. Her initial solo release was on the Shiloh label in 1986, titled *I Give You Jesus*. By 2004, she had added ten more releases to her solo discography. Paschal's success as a soloist came in the Inspirational market. "God Will Make A Way," "Another Soldier's Coming Home," and "Written In Red" are just of few of the songs for which Paschal is well known. Seven of her singles have reached the Top Ten on the Inspirational chart, including the 1990 number one hit, "Take These Burdens."

Payne, Glen Weldon
(1926 - 1999)

Glen Payne was a native of Royce City, Texas. He studied at the Stamps-Baxter School of Music when he was still a teenager. This led to an office job and a position singing with the Stamps-Baxter Quartet. After Payne served in the Army, he returned to work for the Stamps Quartet Music Company in 1946. While there, he sang with the Frank Stamps Quartet. In 1951, Payne began a six-year stint with the Stamps-Ozark Quartet. In January 1957, he joined the Weatherfords who sang regularly at the Cathedral Of Tomorrow in Akron, OH where Rex Humbard was the pastor.

When the Weatherfords returned to traveling in 1963, Payne, Bobby Clark and Danny Coker stayed at the Cathedral and formed the Cathedral Trio. George Younce joined the group a year later to sing bass, and the group subsequently became the Cathedral Quartet. Over the next 30 years under the leadership of Payne and Younce, the Cathedrals became a household name for Southern Gospel fans. Former Cathedrals members own several of the top groups currently singing Southern Gospel. They all credit the guidance of Payne and Younce as a key to their success.

One of the most memorable moments for fans attending the National Quartet Convention was in 1998 when Payne called in to sing over the phone from his sick bed. He passed away in 1999 after a bout with cancer as the Cathedrals were wrapping up their farewell tour.

Payne was inducted into the SGMA Hall Of Fame in 1997.

The Paynes

The Paynes trace their origins back to 1972 when Mike Payne started singing at the Glorious Church of God in Grafton, Ohio. After Mike's brothers Mark (drums) and Keith (bass guitar/vocals) and wife Loreen joined the group, they became known as the Glorious Gospel Heirs.

Mike began writing songs in the late 1970s. Groups like the Singing Cookes and Cathedrals recorded his music. "If God Before Us," "God Delivers Again" and "That Same Spirit" are examples of songs written by Payne that were recorded by other groups. Before the group signed with Windchime Records around 1981, they changed their name to The Paynes.

The Paynes' first album on Windchime was titled *Ready Or Not*. It released in early 1982 and featured their first chart song by the same title. The group released their second album later that year titled *It's Out of this World*. The title song garnered them their first number one song on the *Singing News* chart. It stayed at the top of the charts for four months in late 1983 and early 1984. *I'm a Jesus Fan* released in 1984. The songs "Jesus Fan" and "The Conversation" charted in the Top Ten. Both songs were also made into concept videos, which was trend setting for Southern Gospel at the time.

In April 1985, the group recorded what was probably their most popular album, *Fire on Stage...Live*, in Dayton, Ohio. It garnered them another four month run at the number one position on the *Singing News* charts with "Angels Step Back." Their next album *Rapture* also produced several popular songs including "Just in Case of Rapture" and "Waiting for the Son to Shine." This album was released on the short-lived record label called Eagle One. The group then signed with Riversong and released two recordings, *This is War* (1988) and *God Wants You* (1989).

The Paynes disbanded in the early 1990s. Mike Payne traveled the next few years as a soloist and had some success with songs like "I'm Still Dancin'," "The Lord Himself," and "Workin' Like the Devil for the Lord." He formed a new version of the Paynes with his wife and daughter during the late 1990s. They released two recordings on the Daywind label, *Storms* and *Made New*. The family got back together for a reunion concert and released a live recording titled *30th Anniversary Reunion* in 2001.

A PARTIAL PAYNES DISCOGRAPHY: *Ready or Not* (1982), *It's Out Of This World* (1982), *I'm a Jesus Fan* (1984), *Fire on Stage-Live* (1985), and *30th Anniversary Reunion* (2001)
---James Hales contributed to this entry

Peck, Karen
Karen Peck first traveled with Alphus LeFevre's group in 1980 and 1981. Her popularity in Southern Gospel was instantaneous from the time she joined the Nelons in 1981. Her contributions to the group's 1983 recording *We Shall Behold The King* yielded an overwhelmingly positive response from fans with songs like the title track, "Oh, For A Thousand Tongues," "Walk Right Out Of This Valley" and "When I Receive My Robe And Crown." She remained with the Nelons until 1990.

In 1991, Peck formed New River along with her sister Susan Peck Jackson. The group initially toured with a live band. Joel Key was a long time member. Peck's husband Ricky Gooch was also a member of the band, but later moved to the position of sound technician for New River. Peck dropped the band and shifted to using sound tracks exclusively after the turn of the century. A string of vocalists have filled the male spot in the trio in recent years including noted songwriter John Darin Rowsey and more recently Devin McGlamery.

A longtime favorite, Karen Peck won the *Singing News* Fan Award for Favorite Soprano for 11 consecutive years. The songs "God Likes To Work" and "Four Days Late" (both featuring Karen) were number one songs on the *Singing News* charts in 1996 and 2000 respectively. "Four Days Late" was also voted the Favorite Song for 2001 in the *Singing News* Fan Awards and also in the SGMA awards for that year.

The Perry Sisters

The Perry Sisters formed in Huntington, WV in 1974. The original group members included sisters Diana, Bonnie and Carol Perry. They traveled for ten years before signing with a major Southern Gospel label in 1984. Bonnie and Carol left the road in 1990 and the group reorganized with Diana and Bonnie's daughter Tammy Underwood now as the key members. Tammy sings soprano and plays guitar. A number of ladies filled the third vocal position over the course of the next several years including Diana's daughter Angela Monehan, Jada Hite and Karen Akemon. The group ultimately changed from a trio to a duet format. Tammy's husband Robbie Underwood plays keyboard and bass guitar for the group while Diana's husband Bob Gillette drives their bus. Diana has written a number of songs for the group over the years including "Wonder How Mary Felt," "There'll Be A Payday," and "Imagine If You Will."

The Pfeifers

The Pfeifers formed in 1979 in Roanoke, VA. After their formation, the group had an ongoing opportunity to perform at evangelist Don Pfeifer's crusades across the country. Mary Jane Carter joined the group in 1982 and John Pfeifer was added to the lineup in 1985. Candy Pfeifer (John's sister) has sung and played horns for the group since it began.

In recent years, the group has come to be known as one of the most versatile acts in Southern Gospel. All the members sing and play horns in a mix of styles that ranges from Country to Big Band. Their performances are augmented by an elaborate light and multimedia show.

Pittman, Jack
See **Palmetto State Quartet**

Plainsmen Quartet

Most of the original members of the Plainsmen initially recorded together for Columbia Records as the Stamps Quartet. In August of 1956, they left the Stamps organization and chose their new name, Plainsmen. The group at the time consisted of Howard Welborn (tenor), Jack Mainord (lead), Bill Randall (baritone), Joe B. Davis (bass), and Easmon Napier (pianist and emcee). This group maintained the "heavy" sound associated with the Stamps organization at first, but their sound was modified after their first personnel change. Rusty Goodman joined the group to sing baritone in December of 1957 replacing Bill Randall.

Goodman shifted to the bass slot when identical twins Ermon and Thurman Bunch joined the Plainsmen. The Bunch twins came from the Jubilaires Quartet and brought many of their unique arrangements to the Plainsmen. That particular group only released one album titled *Songs and Hymns by the Plainsmen Quartet.* It's often referred to as "The Red Album" since most of the copies were pressed on red vinyl.

Ermon Bunch didn't stay with the group for long, and Howard Welborn returned to the baritone slot instead of the tenor slot that he'd earlier vacated. Goodman could sing well into the second tenor range, and Welborn was the former first tenor for the group. High, unusual harmonies prevailed in the group.

Governor Jimmie Davis saw the potential in this quartet, and took them on the campaign trail with him as he sought reelection in 1958. The Plainsmen moved their home base to Baton Rouge, LA. During this time, the Plainsmen also sang secular music. They sang backup for Johnny Horton on his classic song "North to Alaska," and became one of the few gospel music quartets to record secular music on an ongoing basis.

Rusty Goodman left the group in 1963 to join his family group, the Happy Goodmans. Long time Harmoneers Quartet bass singer Seals "Low Note" Hilton joined the group for a short time. After Hilton's departure, Jay Simmons and David Reece joined the Plainsmen. Simmons remained bass singer for the Plainsmen for many years, but Eddie Crook soon replaced Reece. The personnel of Thurman Bunch, Jack Mainord, Howard Welborn, Jay Simmons, and Eddie Crook remained intact for a couple of years, and this group recorded several gospel classics.

Several former members of the Plainsmen moved to Wichita, KS and reunited with former pianist, Easmon Napier to form the Marksmen Quartet. The Marksmen continued the Plainsmen sound, singing both gospel and country music. Howard Welborn, Jack Mainord, and Eddie Crook remained in Baton Rouge, and enlisted the services of Gerald Williams as bass singer. Gerald had sung for many years with the Melody Boys Quartet. Bobby Edwards became the tenor singer for the group.

In the ensuing years, the personnel of the Marksmen and Plainsmen reunited. For several years, the Plainsmen consisted of Thurman Bunch, Jack Mainord, Dwight Hicks, Jay Simmons, and Easmon Napier. This group headlined many country music shows and continued to promote radio stations owned by Mack Sanders much like the Marksmen. After a few years, Gerald Williams once again joined the Plainsmen replacing Jay Simmons. They became headliners at the Landmark Hotel in Las Vegas showcasing a program that consisted of country and pop standards, as well as gospel music.

The Plainsmen then went though a period as a trio, and had numerous changes in personnel. Some former Plainsmen members not previously mentioned include Sherrill Nielsen, Gene McDonald, Jerry Venable, Steve Warren, Jonathan Sawrie, Tank Tackett, and Mike Loprinzi.
---John Crenshaw contributed to this entry.

Poet Voices
See **Cross, Phil**

Polk, Videt Richard
(1919-2002)
Videt Polk was a noted singer, teacher and songwriter who lived in Baton Rouge, LA. There's a street named after him in Baton Rouge. Polk served as president of several singing conventions, including the TriState Singing Convention for a period of 47 years and the Arkansas-Texas Singing Convention for 25 years. He was also president of the National Singing Convention for five years. Polk was in charge of the Jimmie Davis homecoming event for 20 years and was a co-owner of the Stamps-Baxter Music Company. Some of the gospel singing events Polk held at the Governor's Mansion in Louisiana drew as many as 50,000 people.

Polk published and compiled a number of gospel songbooks for Stamps-Baxter and Zondervan/Benson. He also wrote numerous articles on the subject of gospel music. He co-wrote several songs with Bobby Burnett. Their most popular song is the 1958 children's praise chorus "God Is So Good." Polk co-wrote a book with Mrs. J. R. (Clarice) Baxter in 1971 titled *Gospel Song Writers Biography*.

Presley, Elvis
Although Elvis Presley was never known as a Southern Gospel artist, he is credited for using his fame in pop music to advance the genre of Southern Gospel. Presley's recordings and tours featured such artists as the Stamps, the Imperials, the Jordanaires, and the Blackwood Brothers. Shortly before his initial secular success at Sun Records, Presley auditioned for a part-time gospel group called the Songfellows and was turned down. At the time, Presley had difficulty switching from the melody to a harmony part. He was

later offered a position with the group, but by then he was under contract with Sun.

Presley's gospel music performances drew heavily from popular Southern Gospel songwriters. Mosie Lister's song "His Hand In Mine" was chosen as the title cut for one of Presley's critically acclaimed gospel recordings. His recording of "Without Him" helped launched the pop/rock career of the song's credited author, Mylon LeFevre.

Primitive Quartet

The Primitive Quartet formed in 1973. Two pairs of brothers were in the original group: Reagan and Larry Riddle and Norman and Furman Wilson. The group formed after the four went on a camping trip together and ended up picking and singing around the fire at night. After singing together in church, they began to get requests to sing at other churches in western North Carolina. The group was originally known as the Reagan-Wilson Quartet.

Larry and Reagan's brother Mike Riddle replaced Furman Wilson in the late 1970s. The group became full time in 1978. They also had changed the group name by this point to reflect their characteristic style. Two other members have been added to the group since the 1970s. Randy Fox joined in 1986 to sing and play various instruments. Jeff Tolbert joined in 1997 to play banjo, fiddle, and sing. The group is best known for the song "Fallen Leaves."

The Primitive Quartet hosts a singing each summer during July. At this event, the top gospel bluegrass groups in the country come together for several days of singing in Hominy Valley near Candler, NC. They also have a singing in the fall.

Prophets
(1959-1973)
The Prophets can trace their lineage to the Kings Men Quartet from St. Louis, Mo. Ed Hill and Jerry (Jay) Berry were founding members of the Kings Men Quartet. This group was a big hit at the 1958 National Quartet Convention, and shortly after the convention, Hill and Berry decided they wanted to sing on a full time basis. The pair moved to Knoxville, TN where the Prophets were formed in March of 1959. James Lewis Garrison, Rancell D. Taylor, and Gary Trusler made up the rest of the group. They recorded their first album on the predominately pop label, Coral. That first Prophets album is quite sought after by collectors of gospel music.

Soon thereafter, personnel changes began to occur. Fred Rose replaced

Randy Taylor and Jim Boatman became the bass singer. Legendary gospel music teacher, pianist, and songwriter "Smilin'" Joe Roper became their pianist and arranger for a short while. Under Roper's teaching, the group became familiar with unusual arrangements and expanded their abilities.

The Prophets soon became members of the *Gospel Singing Caravan.* Joe Moscheo had replaced Joe Roper as pianist for the group by 1962. "Big Lew" Garrison and Ed Hill had a wonderful stage rapport and always made their programs quite entertaining.

A string of lead singers like Jack Toney and Roy McNeil were members of the Prophets over the next few years. Jay Simmons sang bass briefly followed by Texan Dave Rogers. Future Oak Ridge Boys member Duane Allen sang with the group for a while as well. They released one unusual album that included six piano solos. The quartet took a back seat to its pianist.

In spite of all their personnel changes, the group maintained their characteristic sound and appeal as long as original members "Big Lew" Garrison and Ed Hill were with the group. Once Garrison left the group, the magic was gone. Ed Hill retired the group in 1973. He had planned to go to work for the Sumar Talent Agency next, but agreed to temporarily fill in at baritone for the Stamps. This position soon became his permanent job. In time, Hill also became a delight to fans as the brunt of J. D. Sumner's jokes. Sumner often introduced Hill at concerts referencing his tenure with the Prophets as a "successful quartet manager," followed by, "and in 1973, he successfully managed them out of business."
---John Crenshaw contributed to this entry

Rambo, Dottie Luttrell
(1934 -)
Dottie Rambo got her start in Southern Gospel by writing songs and performing at revivals. She was eight years old when she first became interested in writing songs. By the age of 12, she had left home to sing full time. Governor Jimmie Davis of Louisiana heard her music and signed her to a writing contract when she was still in her teens. She married Buck Rambo when she was 16, and their daughter Reba was born when Dottie was 18. Reba began performing with the group when she was three years old. As she grew older, the Rambos grew to be one of the most popular family trios in gospel music.

In addition to performing, Rambo continued to write. An extremely prolific songwriter, she has written more than 2500 songs. Her tunes have been recorded by dozens of secular artists and hundreds of gospel artists. Whitney Houston's version of "I Go To The Rock" was included on the movie soundtrack for *The Preacher's Wife,* which sold over two million units.

Driven by Houston's performance, the song was recognized with a Dove Award for Song of the Year in 1999.

In spite of her output and the popularity of the Rambos, only two songs by the group reached the number one position on the *Singing News* chart. The first was "Tiny" which was number one in March and May of 1972. The second was "I've Never Been This Homesick Before" which reached the top position in November of 1977. Other popular songs written and performed by Rambo over they years include "Tears Will Never Stain The Streets Of That City," "He Looked Beyond My Faults" (to the tune of "Londonderry Aire" aka "Danny Boy"), "Too Much To Gain To Lose," "If That Isn't Love," and "We Shall Behold Him."

As the years have passed by, Dottie Rambo has endured more than her share of pain and heartache. She suffers with chronic back trouble and has undergone 10 surgeries. At various times, her health problems have left her in comas. On the home front, Rambo's marriage ultimately failed and the subsequent divorce from Buck Rambo was particularly painful. She has experienced a comeback of sorts in later years, though. Barbara Mandrell hosted a televised *Tribute To Dottie Rambo* in 2002. Then in 2003, Rambo released her first project in 18 years, *Stand By The River*, which included a duet with Dolly Parton on the title song.

Like her songs, Rambo's awards are also numerous. She got her first Grammy in 1968 for a solo project called *It's The Soul Of Me*. In 1994, the Christian Country Music Association named her "Songwriter Of The Century". In 2001, ASCAP recognized Rambo with a Lifetime Achievement Award. Rambo is also a dual member of the GMA Hall Of Fame, having been inducted both as an individual and as part of the Rambo Trio.

A PARTIAL RAMBOS TRIO/DOTTIE RAMBO DISCOGRAPHY: *This Is My Valley* (1969), *Soul Classics* (1970), *Alive & Live At Soul's Harbor* (1974), *Naturally* (1977), *Rambo Reunion* (1981), *Stand By The River* (2003)

Ramsey, William Morgan
(August 24, 1872 - 1939)
William Ramsey began teaching the shape note method of singing when he was still a teenager. He eventually became the president and owner of the Central Music Company. In addition to teaching shape note singing, Ramsey wrote several hundred Gospel songs. His most popular tune is "He Whispers Sweet Peace to Me." Ramsey also edited and published over 30 songbooks.

The SGMA Hall Of Fame inducted Ramsey in 2002.

Rangers Quartet

During the Depression Era of the 1930's, Vernon Hyles, Arnold Hyles, George Hughes and Walter Leverette formed a quartet that soon became known as the Texas Rangers. Vernon sang lead and played the guitar. George Hughes was their tenor, and Walter Leverette was at the baritone slot. The showcase of the group was "The World's Lowest Basso Profundo," Arnold Hyles. His voice was loud and rough. The group drew large crowds and was soon commissioned as honorary Texas Rangers. They were also denoted as "Ambassadors of Good Will" for the state of Texas. After a few years of touring, the name was shortened to "The Rangers".

The Rangers were master showmen. As their reputation began to grow, they began traveling outside of Texas. They rode bicycles from Texas to New York City as a publicity stunt before performing on *The Major Bowles Amateur Hour*. George Hughes left the group in 1938 to join the Swanee River Boys. Denver Crumpler was hired to sing the tenor part, and the popularity of the group continued to grow. Crumpler took over the guitar playing and his lyric tenor combined with Arnold Hyles' loud, rough bass voice to give the Rangers a unique sound. The Rangers began to incorporate intricate harmonies and key changes in their music.

In the late 1930s, the Rangers moved from WHAS radio in Louisville, KY to WBT radio in Charlotte, NC. After moving to North Carolina, the Rangers hired their first pianist, Marion Snyder. Around this time, the Rangers were responsible for many innovations in the gospel music industry. They signed a recording contract with Decca records in 1939 and recorded a number of songs for both Decca and Okeh. They were the first quartet to have a commercially sponsored gospel radio network program. The Rangers were also the first gospel quartet to become a full time group with no supplement from side jobs or songbook sales. Other groups soon followed the lead of the Rangers, for the Rangers realized they could be more prosperous by associating themselves with radio stations that would allow them to book their own concerts and advertise their programs on the air. As was typical in that era, their programs featured a mixture of hymns, gospel, pop, and Western tunes.

The Rangers left Charlotte in 1945 and moved to radio station WWVA in Wheeling, WV. When they moved to Wheeling, Denver again pulled out the guitar and the Rangers added more western and cowboy songs to their repertoire. They moved to Richmond, VA for a short time where they procured the services of Lee Roy Abernathy as pianist. Abernathy in turn convinced them to move to Atlanta, GA. Abernathy's commented, "I decided to hunt the world's finest quartet, and play the piano for them just to advertise my piano course by mail. I decided upon the Rangers who were singing on WRVA in Richmond, Virginia. I played with them for fifteen months before they fired me."

While working in Atlanta, the Rangers recorded four songs for RCA Victor. WBT in Charlotte asked the Rangers to rejoin their station in 1947. Although Abernathy said they "fired him," other accounts indicate he really didn't want to leave the Atlanta area, so Hovie Lister left the Homeland Harmony Quartet to join the Rangers in Charlotte. During Lister's short tenure with the Rangers, they recorded four songs for Bullet Records, one being a solo by Lister. Lister soon found he preferred Atlanta to Charlotte as well. He vacated the piano bench to make way for another future Statesman, Doy Ott. When Ottt joined the Rangers, he was known as a pianist and not a vocalist. The Rangers then did a tour of duty at WIBW in Topeka, KS.

When Doy Ott left the Rangers in May of 1949, David Reece, formerly with the Blue Ridge Quartet, became their pianist. On June 1, 1949, baritone Walter Leverette succumbed to a heart attack, and the Rangers were forced to make their first personnel change in vocalists in more than ten years. Former Harmoneers member, Ermon Slater from Sand Mountain, AL became the new baritone. The Rangers soon moved again, this time to sing on WPTF in Raleigh, NC. There they began their own "Record of the Month Club" which they distributed under their own "Rangers" label.

Tragedy again struck the Rangers in early 1951 when Arnold Hyles and Ermon Slater were involved in an automobile accident and were hit by a drunk driver. Slater was killed instantly, and Hyles was severely injured. Vernon considered disbanding the group, but Jimmy Jones joined the group six days after the accident, and the Rangers continued as a four-man group with David Reece playing the piano and singing baritone. The group moved to Dallas, TX to work for the Liberty Broadcasting System.

After a long period of recuperation, Arnold Hyles began making selected appearances with the quartet singing a few songs, but he wasn't up to full time singing. For these performances, he would be in a wheelchair, for his injuries hadn't fully healed. Hyles lived in constant pain for the remainder of his life. David Reece left the group in 1953 and was replaced by Cecil Pollock. Glenn Sessions joined the group as a sixth member, filling in both at lead and baritone. Jimmy Jones moved to baritone when Arnold would return to the group, and switch back to bass when Arnold couldn't make the dates. The last change in 1953 occurred at the same time when Jimmy Jones left to form the Deep South Quartet and Denver Crumpler left to join the Statesmen. Gene Moss replaced Crumpler.

The Rangers decided to pursue a move to Hollywood, but after a short time in California, the Rangers moved to Wichita, KS. The Rangers Quartet disbanded shortly thereafter, closing the career of one of the more popular and innovative quartets in gospel music history.
---John Crenshaw contributed to this entry.

Rangers Trio

The Rangers Quartet was one of the most popular groups in the field of gospel entertainment. In the late 1940s, the Rangers hired a pianist from Lincolnton, N.C. named David Reece. Formerly a member of the Blue Ridge Quartet, Reece's piano technique soon became an integral part of the sound of the Rangers Quartet. He did many of the arrangements for the quartet and sang vocals after a tragic automobile accident took the life of baritone Erman Slater. David remained an active member of the Rangers Quartet for several years before moving to Dallas, TS to play for the Imperial Quartet. The effects of age ultimately took their toll on the remaining members of the Rangers Quartet, so they decided to retire from the road.

David Reece was always a Ranger at heart. He left the Harvesters Quartet in the late 1950s with the desire to form a new Rangers Quartet. After obtaining permission from the Hyles brothers to use the name, Reece was joined by Bobby Clark, Roy McNeil, David Ingles, and Warren Holmes. This quartet wasn't together very long before disbanding.

Although the new quartet didn't last, David had other ideas for his new group. David selected two members (tenor singer Roy McNeil and lead singer David Ingles) from his disbanded Rangers Quartet and formed the Rangers Trio. Although their sound was quite different from the sound of the Rangers Quartet, they were soon affiliated with WBT radio in Charlotte like their quartet predecessor from years before.

In addition to the standard gospel songs of the day, the Rangers Trio also did some novelty songs that became standards for the group. The Four Lads had previously popularized one such song called "The Mockingbird." It became a crowd favorite and remained so for as long as the Rangers performed. David Ingles didn't stay with the group for very long. He left the trio abruptly to join the Rebels Quartet (which he also left just as abruptly). Arthur Smith, the great country musician and gospel songwriter, persuaded Clark Thompson to join the trio. The Rangers were leaving that day for a series of concerts in Florida, so Thompson learned their entire repertoire in the car on the way to their first engagement.

McNeil, Thompson, and Reece became one of the smoothest and most energetic groups in gospel music in the early 1960s. Their programs were full of great music and Reece's classic humor. David Reece was the consummate entertainer. He was one of the funniest people in gospel music. Later in his career, he became a comedy writer for Minnie Pearl. Clark Thompson once said that you never knew what to expect with Reece, so he and McNeil were always on their toes. Thompson also explained that he didn't really have a regular "part" to sing. He had to figure out what Reece was doing and sing something different.

116

The Rangers Trio had a unique sound, and their recordings were state of the art. When many groups were using only piano as accompaniment, the Rangers Trio used other instrumentation including drums. They also employed an echo chamber on several recordings. They recorded "When the Saints Go Marching In" with an introduction that resembled a live performance. *I Believe*, their only project on the Skylite label, is often mentioned as one of the top gospel albums of all time. Many of their songs came from the pen of David Reece. His recording *Musical Meditations* was one of the first instrumental albums by a gospel music artist.

After a few years, Thompson left the trio and was replaced by Mack Evans. McNeil soon left as well to become the lead singer of the Prophets Quartet. Eventually, the Rangers Trio left Charlotte and moved to Nashville where they became active on television and in the studio.

The group reformed with former Oak Ridge Quartet baritone Ron Page and Darrell Johnson. The trio joined the Chuck Wagon Gang on a popular television program called *Gospel Roundup*. This version of the Rangers Trio went back to its musical roots and performed western songs in addition to their gospel standards. This new version of the Rangers Trio was sent overseas by the US Department of Defense as goodwill ambassadors for the United States. They brought gospel music to Spain, North Africa, Germany, France, and Italy. Their efforts were recorded on a live album on the Scripture label.

The Rangers Trio of the 1960s reunited to perform at the first Grand Ole Gospel Reunion in 1988. McNeil, Thompson, and Reece were well received. Other groups derived from the Rangers Trio over the years and embraced the classic Rangers sound. Clark Thompson joined forces with Wallace Nelms and Larry Shipman and performed as the Clark Thompson Trio. They recorded a project of Rangers classics. David Reece also formed the "New Rangers Trio" with Bill Nelson and Greg Harrelson. This group recorded a number of Rangers Trio standards as well.
---John Crenshaw contributed to this entry.

Reader, Naomi Easters Sego
(1931 -)
Naomi Sego began singing with her husband James Sego and his brother from time to time in 1949. She joined the group permanently in 1958, and the group began to be billed as the Sego Brothers and Naomi as she became the dominant voice in the group. Two of their most popular tunes featuring Naomi were "Sorry, I Never Knew You" and "Is My Lord Satisfied With Me?"

After James Sego's death in 1979, Naomi continued to travel and sing with a full band backing the group. She eventually remarried to Vern Reader, who also sang with the group. The group name was modified to Naomi and the Segos. In 2001, the SGMA recognized Reader by inducting her into the Hall Of Fame.

The Rebels

Formed in the 1950s, the Dixie Lily Harmoneers first changed their name to the Dixie Rebels Quartet. Later they shortened that name to "The Rebels." One of the earliest pictures of the group includes Horace Parrish, Lee Kitchens, John Matthews, Norman Allman, and Jimmy Hand. This lineup began singing gospel music as a full time occupation around 1951.

Big Jim Waits, a popular and well-traveled bass singer, joined the group in the early 1950s. Waits laid a solid foundation for the Rebels Quartet that characterized their sound. "Little" Jimmy Taylor, an accomplished pianist, arranged much of the music for the quartet. The Rebels recorded around 20 songs on the Bibletone label with Big Jim Waits. Waits suffered a heart attack in the fall of 1955 that forced him to come off the road. Losing Waits opened the door for Conley "London" Parris.

The nucleus of Horace Parrish, John Matthews, London Parris, and Jimmy Taylor remained intact for over a decade. Jimmy Taylor assumed the dual role of lead singer and pianist during transitional periods between lead vocalists. The Skylite album *When I Stand With God* features the lead voice of David Ingles, although most album covers have Jim Hamill pictured on the cover. Hamill was actually the next lead singer to join the quartet. He added songs like "Hide Thou Me" to the Rebels' repertoire.

Jay Berry left the Prophets Quartet to sing with the Rebels in the early 60's. Berry's vocal stylings were prominent on several of the Rebels' recordings on the Sing and Skylite labels. London Parris took a leave of absence from the Rebels during the 1960s. Bob Thacker and their 1950s bass singer Big Jim Waits filled in during this period. Thacker never recorded with the Rebels, but was featured with them on the *Singing Time in Dixie* television program. Hamill returned for another stint with the Rebels around 1965, having spent a couple of years with the Oak Ridge Quartet. Horace Parrish and London Parris left the group in the late 1960s. A number of singers passed through the Rebels after that, including brothers Charles and Ronnie Booth, John Gresham, Nick Bruno, Buddy Lyles, Dony McGuire, and Rick Fair.

London Parris returned to the Rebels for a short time and revamped the group with Aubrey Bowlus, Curt Lyles and Everette Reece joining the Booth brothers (Charles and Ronnie). However, this was short-lived as Parris quickly pulled several members out of the group and formed London Parris and the Apostles, leaving Ronnie and Charles Booth to regroup the Rebels.

Lee Kitchens and Jimmy Taylor also returned to the group around 1974 and recorded several albums with country music legend Floyd Cramer (Lee Kitchen's brother in law). Several personnel changes occurred around this time before the group retired. Ronnie Booth and John Gresham moved on to join the Thrasher Brothers.
---John Crenshaw contributed to this entry

Reece, David

David Reece was a native of Lincolnton, North Carolina. In the 1940s, he joined the Rangers Quartet as their pianist and arranged a number of their songs. After short stints with the Imperial Quartet in Texas and the Deep South Quartet in Atlanta, he moved back to North Carolina where he helped formed the Harvesters Quartet. They worked for radio station WBT.

In the 1950s, Reece left the Harvesters and secured permission to use the Rangers name for a new quartet. Bobby Clark, Roy McNeil, David Ingles, and Warren Holmes were the vocalists in the new group, but the quartet did not succeed. However, Reece was persistent and soon formed the Rangers Trio with Roy McNeil and David Ingles. When Ingles left the group shortly thereafter, Clark Thompson took his place. This group remained together for several years in the 1960s and experienced great success with Reece's arrangements.

David Reece was an excellent musician and one of the funniest people in gospel music. Later in his career, he became a comedy writer for Minnie Pearl. Clark Thompson once said that you never knew what to expect with Reece, so he and McNeil were always on their toes in anticipation. Thompson also explained he didn't really have a "part" to sing. He just figured out what David was doing and sang something different. Years later, the Rangers Trio reformed to perform at the first Grand Ole Gospel Reunion in 1988. Reece became an annual fixture at the event until his death.
---John Crenshaw contributed to this entry.

Reggie Saddler Family

Reggie Saddler was a well-traveled musical performer long before forming his family group. He has performed with popular secular acts such as Frankie Valli, Jerry Lee Lewis, and the Platters. He also spent 10 years working for the Disney Corporation.

In addition to Saddler, the Reggie Saddler Family includes his wife Bridgette and their two daughters, Ingra and Shivonne. The group has performed across the United States as well as in Mexico, Scotland, Haiti, South Africa and Canada. They have appeared on several Gaither Homecoming videos and have been featured on the main stage at the National Quartet Convention. The group is best known for the song "I've Got Me A Home."

The Revelaires Quartet

Gospel music has had many groups that were on the scene for a short time and have been all but forgotten. The Revelaires Quartet is one of these groups. Dan Huskey, Bobby Shaw, and Big Jim Waits were the founders of the Revelaires Quartet, which was organized in September of 1952. Tenor singer Huskey had just left the Blackwood Brothers. He moved from Memphis to Atlanta join the new quartet. Jim Waits had been singing with the Chuck Wagon Gang, but his gruff bass voice wasn't suited to their family harmony. Bobby Shaw was a former lead singer for another Atlanta-based group, the Homeland Harmony Quartet, and was serving his country in the Air Force when plans for the new quartet were being made. Huskey and Waits kept in close contact with Shaw's wife, and the Revelaires Quartet was formed when he returned from his stay in Japan. The three founders hired Tommy Rainer to sing baritone and Jerry Briggs to play the piano.

The lineup remained intact for several months until Briggs was drafted. Atlas Howard replaced him at the piano. Not long after that, Tommy Rainer was replaced at baritone by Larry Taylor. This configuration didn't last long so Taylor moved from baritone to piano. Cat Freeman became the baritone singer. This was a very unusual configuration: Two former first tenors from the Blackwood Brothers were singing together in the same quartet.

When Jim Waits left the Atlanta area and moved to Tampa, FL for health reasons, Johnny Atkinson replaced him in the bass slot for the Revelaires Quartet. Atkinson was another Atlanta resident who had recently left the Homeland Harmony Quartet. He sang with the Revelaires for only a short time before replacing J. D. Sumner in the Sunshine Boys. Gordon Hill then took over as bass singer for the Revelaires, and Wally Varner came on board as pianist. By now, the group consisted of Dan Huskey (tenor), Bobby Shaw (lead), Cat Freeman (baritone), Gordon Hill (bass), and Wally Varner (pianist). This particular group was the most stable version of the quartet, and is heard on the majority of their Bibletone recordings. This aggregation also appeared on the *Arthur Godfrey Talent Scouts* program in 1955.

The group had a very solid sound. Huskey and Freeman had great tenor voices, but Freeman could also blend quite well as a baritone. Bob Shaw had a very commanding lead voice. Varner and Hill were seasoned quartet veterans as well. During the 1950s, the "quartet team" concept was becoming popular. In early 1955, the Revelaires Quartet and Harmoneers Quartet began appearing regularly at concerts together. Later that year,

Bobby Shaw announced that he was retiring from the road. Wally Varner and Gordon Hill also left the group at this time. Dan Huskey and Cat Freeman were left to rebuild the quartet. Jim Hamill was hired to replace Bobby, but he didn't stay long and was replaced by Roy McNeil. Soon thereafter, Cat Freeman left to join the Oak Ridge Quartet. The last version of the Revelaires was Dan Huskey, Don Butler, Bill Ballew, Bill Huie, and Larry Taylor. This was one of Don Butler's first professional quartets. After the Revelaires disbanded, Butler went on to form the Sons of Song.
---John Crenshaw contributed to this entry.

Rex Nelon Singers
See **Nelon, Rex**

Richman, Milton "Ace"
See **Sunshine Boys**

Riley, Tim
(August 29, 1945-)
Tim Riley is a native of Gadsden, AL. He began performing at an early age and joined his high school's F.F.A. Quartet as a teen. As a young adult, Riley joined the Dixie Echoes in 1966. This position did not last long as he was drafted for military service a month later. Riley served as a medic in Vietnam for 13 months. By 1970, he had completed his service and again joined the Dixie Echoes, remaining with that group for three years. Riley formed the Southmen in 1974 along with Jack Toney, Jim Hefner, and Larry Beck. He performed with the Southmen for five years.

Riley joined Gold City in July of 1980. The group had been singing as Gold City since the previous January. They had been known as the Christianairs previously, but adopted the new name while planning to relocate to the mining town of Dahlonega, GA. Riley ultimately became the owner of the group. He was blessed with a bright toned bass voice that cut through the mix whenever he hit a note in his lower register. Riley soon surrounded himself with a strong talent pool that included pianist Garry Jones, lead singer Ivan Parker, and tenor Brian Free.

With this group, Riley oversaw the rise of Gold City to the top of the Southern Gospel industry during the 1980s with songs like "In My Robe Of White," "I Think I'll Read It Again" (Gold City's first number one on the *Singing News* chart), and "John Saw." The group also introduced an inspirational ballad style song called "Midnight Cry" that would later be recorded by numerous artists. Riley retired from traveling with Gold City in

2004, but continues to maintain ownership and work for the group behind the scenes.

Roberson, Carroll

Carroll Roberson is based in the town of Ripley, Mississippi and began his solo singing ministry in 1987. Since then he has recorded more than 25 full-length music projects. He has also written more than 100 songs.

Roberson's project titled *His Hand In Mine* has sold more than 100,000 copies. He is best known for the song "Wilt Thou Be Made Whole," which held the number one position on the *Singing News* charts for three months during 1995. In addition to singing, Roberson is known for his evangelistic speaking ministry. He regularly conducts Holy Land tours as well.

Rodeheaver, Homer Alvan
(1880 - 1955)

Homer Rodeheaver was a noted singer and evangelist. He began his career as a member of the Billy Sunday evangelism team, a position he held from 1909 to 1931. Next, he formed the Rodeheaver-Ackley music publishing company, where he subsequently acquired the copyrights to hundreds of songs. Between 1913 and 1942, Rodeheaver recorded for a number of different record labels and founded one of his own, which he called Rainbow Records. It is said that his recording of "The Old Rugged Cross" sold more than a million copies, no small feat for an artist today and remarkable for the early 20th century. Rodeheaver also wrote a number of books and published a monthly choral journal called *The Gospel Choir*.

The SGMA recognized Rodeheaver for his accomplishments in 2003 when he was inducted into the Hall Of Fame.

Roper, Joseph "Smilin' Joe"

Smilin' Joe Roper is best remembered for his tenure with the Melody Boys and the Stamps. He played first with the Stamps-Baxter Melody Boys Quartet in the 1940s. They regrouped again after World War II with bass singer Hershal Foshee and Roper as the key leaders of the group. The group was relocated to Little Rock, AR in 1947 and they began performing on radio station KARK. After Foshee passed away in 1949, the group came to be billed as "Smilin' Joe and the Stamps-Baxter Melody Boys Quartet." Roper was a gifted arranger, but the Stamps-Baxter Publishing Company stressed that its groups perform songs as written in their songbooks. For this reason, the group soon dropped their affiliation with the Stamps-Baxter publishing company, and their billing was adjusted to "Smilin' Joe and the Melody Boys Quartet."

It was around this time that James Blackwood approached Roper and suggested the two groups team up and do performances together so as to dominate the industry. Roper did not agree to the idea, but Blackwood went on to implement his idea successfully with the Blackwood Brothers and Statesmen team over the next decade. In time, the financial pressures became too great for the Melody Boys to continue, and Roper retired the group. Gerald Williams would later revive the name.

Roper played for the Prophets next. He was only with them for a short while, but his arranging skills left a mark on their sound. He left the Prophets to join the Stamps Quartet around 1962, which was several years before James Blackwood and J. D. Sumner purchased the group.

The SGMA inducted Joe Roper into the Hall of Fame in 2005.

Rowe, James
(1865-1933)
James Rowe wrote thousands of song lyrics in the late nineteenth century. He is best remembered for the hymn "Love Lifted Me." Other songs written by Rowe include "If I Could Hear My Mother Pray Again," "I'm Going That Way," and "I Would Be Like Jesus."

Rozell, Roland Dwayne "Rosie"
(August 29, 1928 - 1995)
Rosie Rozell was a native of Hardy, Oklahoma. After singing tenor with the Tulsa Trumpeteers, he joined the Statesmen Quartet in 1958. His most memorable performances with the group were slower numbers that allowed him to showcase his voice. Statesmen fans remember him well for songs like "Hide Thou Me," "Leave It There," and "Oh What a Savior." Rozell remained with the Statesmen for more than a decade. He left to form Rosie Rozell and the Searchers in 1970. In the mid-1970s, he returned to sing with the Statesmen briefly and also sang tenor for the Masters V alongside J. D. Sumner, Jake Hess, James Blackwood and Hovie Lister during the early 1980s.

The SGMA inducted Rozell into the Hall Of Fame in 1999.

Ruebush, Ephraim
Ephraim Ruebush formed a friendship with Aldine Kieffer when the two were young men working in Joseph Funk's printing firm in the 1850s. By the end of the decade, the two had established themselves as a music teaching team. Ruebush, who was seven years older than Kieffer, had married

Kieffer's older sister by this point. The Civil War disrupted family harmony and strained the friendship in the 1860s when Ruebush opposed the secession of Virginia and Kieffer supported the South. They fought on opposite sides.

By 1870, Kieffer was back in the music business and Ruebush ultimately rejoined him in 1872 to form Ruebush, Kieffer and Company. The company went on to standardize the shapes used for shape note singing method, setting the stage for music publishing companies that would come later, such as Vaughan and Stamps-Baxter.

The Ruppes

The Ruppes formed in 1974 as a family trio consisting of mother Brenda Ruppe and her daughters Kim (age nine) and Heather (age eight). The group's first recording was released the following year, titled *The Way, The Truth, The Life*. When Kim took a break from the group in 1986, her younger sister Valerie replaced her. The group got national exposure that same year with their Benson release *Put That On My Account*.

Heather Ruppe left the group in 1990 to form a ministry with her husband Greg Day (co-writer of "Midnight Cry"), so Kim returned to sing with the Ruppes at that time. They recorded for Horizon Records, and then for Makkedah. "Under His Wings" was their first song to break into the Top Five on the *Singing News* chart in 1995 and was a smash success at the National Quartet Convention. The popularity of the song led to the group being signed with Spring Hill records.

In 1998, the Ruppes became the first female trio to have a number one song on the *Singing News* chart with "Angels In The Room." When Kim left the Ruppes in 2000 to form the group Lordsong with her husband Michael Lord, her sister Heather Ruppe Day again returned to sing with the Ruppes. Since that change, the trio of Brenda, Heather and Valerie has released several projects including *Something In The Air* and *Sweet Forever*.

Sanders, Ann
See **The Downings**

Sego Brothers and Naomi
See **Reader, Naomi Easters Sego**

Shaw, Bill
(June 22, 1924-)
Bill Shaw began singing at the age of 14. He is best remembered for the 22 years he performed with the legendary Blackwood Brothers. He joined the group in 1952, two years before the plane crash that took the lives of Bill Lyles and R W Blackwood. Shaw continued to sing during the group's heyday as they teamed up with the Statesmen to form a team that was paid more than any other pair of groups in gospel music. He left the Blackwood Brothers in the early 1970s.

Shaw has continued performing into his 80s. He released a recording at the age of 76 called *Calv'ry In His Eyes*. A recording by Elglebert Humperdink, the Jordanaires, Shaw, and several other Blackwood Brothers alumni was nominated for a Grammy in 2004. The recording was titled *Always Hear The Harmony: The Gospel Sessions*. In honor of Bill Shaw's 80th birthday, the governor of South Carolina proclaimed June 22, 2004 "Bill Shaw Day" in the state. Shaw is also a crowd favorite each year at the Grand Ole Gospel Reunion.

Shape Note Method (Solfege)

Jesse Aikin's seven-shape scale, as used in *The Christian Minstrel*

Musical notation with shape notes has been an integral element of Southern Gospel. With specific shapes defining the scale, singers with little formal music training could quickly learn to sing the four quartet parts. Beginning in 1846 with his publication of a songbook called *The Christian Minstrel*, Jesse Aikin popularized the seven-shape notation system. Employing seven unique shapes to correspond with the musical scale, Aikin's notation system was based on a more primitive four-shape system originated by John Tufts in the early 18th century. Popular early American songbooks like the *Sacred Harp* and *Southern Harmony* employed Tufts' system.

In the years following the Civil War, Aldine Kieffer of the Ruebush-Kieffer Company promoted a competing seven-shape system devised by his grandfather Joseph Funk, a noted publisher in the mid-1800s. At least five other publishers also employed different shapes for the three notes in the scale that were modified from the Tufts four-shape system. By 1876, Kieffer switched to Aikin's original system in the spirit of standardization. Since Ruebush-Kieffer was one of the largest publishers of shape note songbooks at the time, the Aikin system became the de facto standard in the 20th century.

Singing schools were a popular social event in the following years. Groups were trained not only to sing using shape notes, but to teach the system as well. As a precursor to companies like Vaughan and Stamps-Baxter that employed quartets as traveling salesmen, Kieffer and other publishers in the late 1800s paid singing school instructors to peddle their songbooks.

The syllables "do," "re," "mi," "fa," "so," "la," and "ti" are not limited to Gospel music. The practice of singing the syllables has been used for almost a full millennium, dating back to the Benedictine monk who also invented music staff notation, Guido of Arezzo (995-1050), also known as Guido Monaco. The proper term for this practice is "solfege." A similar practice of assigning syllables to the scale was used in India prior to Guido, and is called "sargam." The classic musical film *The Sound Of Music* (1965) directed by Robert Wise and starring Julie Andrews popularized the solfege syllables in song..."Doe a deer, a female deer; ray, a drop of golden sun;" etc.

Shelnut, Dale Lawrence
(July 29, 1935 - 1983)
Dale Shelnut is remembered for his comedic abilities on stage as well as his singing. A native of Guin, Alabama, Shelnut helped form the Rhythm Masters in 1951. He joined the Tennesseans Quartet in 1960. He is best known for his 20-plus years stint as the lead singer for the Dixie Echoes. Shelnut's tenure with the group began in the early 1960s after he replaced their original lead singer Jack Toney.

While with the Dixie Echoes, Shelnut often delighted fans with his interpretations of Negro spirituals. Some of his antics at the time would probably be considered politically incorrect by modern society standards. Shelnut became the manager of the Dixie Echoes in the late 1960s, and was a popular lead singer in the industry until his unexpected death in 1983. He was in his late 40s at the time of his death.

The SGMA inducted Shelnut into the Hall Of Fame in 2001.

Shelnut, Randy
See **Dixie Echoes**

Signature Sound Quartet
See: **Haase, Ernie**

Showalter, Anthony Johnson "A. J."
(1858 - 1924)
A. J. Showalter's efforts with shape note music in the late 1800s influenced numerous performers who followed him. Showalter studied at the Ruebush-Kieffer School of Music in Virginia, and began teaching in singing schools when he was just 14. He got his start in music publishing and instruction a few years later. The Showalter Music Company was formed in 1884 in Dalton, Georgia. It soon became one of the largest shape-note companies in the nation. Showalter also oversaw the Southern Normal Musical Institute and published a monthly journal titled *The Music Teacher.* His company bridged the gap between the singing school traditions and professional quartet sponsorship. By 1918, the Showalter Music Company had four men traveling on the road billed as The Big Quartet.

Like many other music publishers, Showalter also wrote a number of songs. "Leaning on the Everlasting," co-written with Elisha Hoffman, is probably the tune for which he's best remembered.

Showalter was recognized by the SGMA in 2000 when they inducted him into the Hall Of Fame.

Sing A Song For Heaven's Sake
In 1966, Marathon Pictures released a feature length film starring Merle Kilgore titled *Sing A Song For Heaven's Sake.* It has a relatively undeveloped plot about a young boy who thinks attending a gospel music concert will hamper his reputation. He changes his mind after attending a concert in a small rural church.

The movie is essentially a showcase for the top gospel acts of the mid-1960s with more than 30 songs included. The Stamps, Chuck Wagon Gang, Red Foley, Rangers Trio, Swanee River Boys, Blue Ridge Quartet, Lewis Family and others are featured during the course of the film. *Sing A Song For Heaven's Sake* premiered at the 1966 National Quartet Convention, but failed to attract attention at the secular box office.

Pierce LeFevre hated it so much that he wrote a scathing editorial in the LeFevre Family's newsletter. He said all the copies should be bought up and destroyed. The LeFevre Family did not appear in the film. In recent years, the concert portions of the film have been repackaged and offered for sale at reunion events. The full-length film is difficult to find in a modern video format, however.

Singing Americans

The Singing Americans sang for several years during the 1970s as a regional group. Wayne Maynard is probably the most recognized name from the early version of the group. Around 1980, Charles Burke bought the name and the group soon became a major contender on the national level.

The original lineup of the Burke owned group included Mark Flaker (tenor), Ed Crawford (lead), Charles Surratt (baritone), and Dwayne Burke (bass). The group sang together for 14 years. Only five members were ever with the group for more than three years in a row. Those five were Dwayne Burke, Ed Hill, Clayton Inman, Scott Whitener and Larry Stewart. The other positions were like revolving doors at times.

Several Singing Americans members went on to become well known with other groups. Danny Funderburke (Cathedrals), Michael English (Gaither Vocal Band), Rick Strickland (Stamps), Ivan Parker (Gold City), and David Sutton (Kingdom Heirs/Triumphant) are just a few of the names current Southern Gospel fans should recognize. Many of the group's musicians also found fame after cutting their teeth with the Singing Americans. Jerry Kelso, Jeff Easter, Mark Fain, Milton Smith, Jason Clark and Roger Fortner were in the group's band at various times.

The Singing Americans peaked in popularity during English's tenure from 1983 to 1985. Their recording *Live And Alive* included "I Bowed On My Knees And Cried Holy," which held the number one position on the *Singing News* chart for the first three months of 1985. The group is also remembered for songs like "Welcome To Heaven," "Love MIA," "Shadow Of The Steeple," and "Over There."

A PARTIAL SINGING AMERICANS DISCOGRAPHY: *Live* (1975), *Tell The Angels* (1980), *Live And Alive* (1984), *Black And White* (1985), *Sing Out* (1988), *Watch And Pray* (1990), *Live From Chicago* (1993)

The Singing News

Inspired by the Gospel Music Association's newsletter (*Good News*) first published in January 1969, J. G. Whitfield started his own publication called *The Singing News* just five months later. The print run of the May 1969 issue was 100,000 copies, and it was given away for free. Within a few years, Whitfield was offering subscriptions for the magazine at $3.00 per year, but the vast majority of the 300,000 copies printed each month were mailed free to potential concert goers in exchange for advertising by major concert promoters. As time went by, this trend changed and the magazine developed a large base of paid subscribers.

One of the more significant accomplishments of the *Singing News* was the establishment of a monthly airplay chart in January of 1970. The chart ranked the most popular songs for each month based on reports from radio stations. Although the chart would be criticized in later years for lagging behind actual airplay trends by several months, it was an innovative move for the industry in the 1970s in that it placed a stronger emphasis on the popularity of individual songs.

Under the guidance of chief editor Jerry Kirksey and publisher Maurice Templeton in later years, the *Singing News* grew from a basic newsletter format to a full-fledged professional magazine. With colorful ads from all aspects of Southern Gospel music, the content included articles about artists, concert schedules, editorials and opinion columns. The magazine now bears "The Printed Voice Of Gospel Music" as a sub-heading, and by 1998, the *Singing News* had more than 200,000 subscribers.

Over the years, the magazine has become deeply cross-marketed within the Southern Gospel industry. The Crossroads family of record labels introduced a series of soundtracks during the 1990s bearing the *Singing News* name and logo. Most major recording artists in Southern Gospel sell subscriptions to the magazine at their concert events.

The most discussed recurring topic for *Singing News* subscribers is probably their annual Fan Awards. The voting process goes through three rounds each year, beginning with the March issue. Only subscribers can vote. One night of the National Quartet Convention is then devoted to the presentation of the awards. In addition to the presentations, the nominees for Favorite Song typically perform their nominated songs during the event.

Smith, Arthur

Arthur Smith was a popular radio announcer in the Charlotte, NC area in the 1960s and 1970s. Radio station WBT (advertising itself as the "colossus of the South") was the home for Smith's group, the Crossroads Quartet. The group consisted of Smith, his brothers Ralph and Sonny, and Tommy Faile. The group also appeared regularly on WBT's television affiliate, WBTV. In addition to his work with his quartet, Arthur Smith was a songwriter who also owned a successful recording studio in Charlotte.

Snider, Marion B.

(1914 -)

Marion B. Snider took piano lessons from Gene Autry's band member Freddy Martin. He became well known in 1936 playing piano for the original Stamps Quartet on KRLD Radio Station in Dallas, Texas. He then formed the original Imperial Quartet in 1946. The group's sponsor was the Imperial Sugar Company.

After working with the Imperials, Snider was involved in television, producing a program called *Songs of Inspiration* in Dallas. He was also a frequent emcee for *Battle Of Songs* events promoted by W. B. Nowlin. Snider's name was added to the Southern Gospel Piano Roll of Honor in 1996. He was inducted into the SGMA Hall Of Fame in 2003.

SoGospelNews.com

Deon and Susan Unthank launched a website called Sogospelnews.com in 1999 as an online community for Southern Gospel enthusiasts. Over the next few years, it grew to become the largest and most trafficked Southern Gospel website of its kind.

The website originated as place for members of a Southern Gospel email discussion list to post photos of themselves. As Southern Gospel news items were brought to her attention by members on the list, Susan, who is a computer programmer and website designer by trade, began adding those to the website as well. Within three years, the Unthanks were coordinating a staff of writers who were contributing monthly articles ranging from CD reviews to features, devotional, instructional, and opinion articles. SoGospelNews.com also began publishing a weekly radio airplay chart to give fans feedback on what songs are popular more quickly than the industry's traditional monthly charts.

By 2003, SoGospelNews.com had become so popular it was receiving three million page views per month. The site owners also began hosting an annual Fan Festival and recognizing artists each year with a special awards event. Meanwhile, daily news items are still a vital part of the website, as is an active discussion forum where fans can express opinions and exchange information with other Southern Gospel music fans.

Sons of Song

The Sons of Song were formed in 1957 and consisted of Calvin Newton (tenor), Bob Robinson (lead/piano), and Don Butler (baritone). By performing creative arrangements in a trio format, the group developed a unique sound. Trios are now quite commonplace in gospel music, but in the 1950s, they weren't the norm.

They decided to display their newly formed group at an all-night singing in Birmingham, AL. Wally Fowler was the promoter of the event which featured the top groups of 1957. The Sons of Song were not booked for the program, but showed up dressed to the nines in matching tuxedos. Newton persuaded Fowler to put them on the program. From all accounts, they were allowed to sing through the intermission of the program, and set the audience on their ear. They left the concert with a date book full of engagements.

A young and then unknown producer named Ralph Carmichael produced their early recordings. The orchestrations and arrangements they preserved on vinyl with Carmichael were very innovative for the time.

While at the top of their game musically speaking, tragedy struck the trio in the form of a truck full of watermelons. On a rainy summer night in Florida, the Sons of Song struck the rear of a tractor-trailer. In the ensuing crunch of metal, the Sons were sent flying around their vehicle. Bob Robinson was left for dead in the local hospital. Were it not for the help of their friend and future Sons of Song member, Lee Kitchens, Robinson would have likely perished. Butler and Newton were also injured in the crash, but Robinson's injuries were the worst. It was feared that the Sons of Song would never perform again.

Although they did sing again, they never regained the magic they held prior to the accident. Jimi Hall filled in as pianist and tenor for several dates. During Robinson's recovery, Butler and Newton also called on David Young to fill Robinson's role. By the time Robinson returned to the group, Butler had decided to leave due in part to the injuries he suffered in the accident. Butler worked for the Statesmen organization for several years after that and also formed a short-lived group called the Ambassadors.

Newton later reorganized the Sons of Song with Jimi Hall and Les Roberson. Roberson had previously sung with Newton in the Oak Ridge Quartet. This group soon disbanded. After some time had passed, he formed the group again with Bob Robinson and Lee Kitchens. The Sons of Song became quite active on the gospel music circuit with this configuration, and recorded the popular "Wasted Years."

Don Butler returned to the group for a short time in an attempt to revive the magic that had been lost when he vacated the baritone spot. They once again gained popularity and even recorded a number of fine albums on Wally Fowler's Songs of Faith label. Unfortunately, personal turmoil again led to the breakup of this fine trio.

The Sons of Song later emerged at the request of Jake Hess. Hess had become somewhat of a renegade in gospel music having formed the

Imperials Quartet by recruiting vocalists from other top groups. He welcomed the Sons of Song to Nashville, and began to promote the two groups as a team. Kitchens and Robinson were anxious to again be on the concert trail, but promoters and fans weren't as willing to accept the prodigals back into the fold. Again, the group disbanded and Kitchens, Newton, and Robinson went their separate ways.

In the late 1980s, Charles Burke joined Newton and Robinson to revive the Sons of Song. A new, updated recording was released and the Sons worked several major dates before Burke left the group. Roy Pauley sang with the group for a while, but soon the voices of the Sons were again stilled.

Bob Robinson passed away several years ago, seemingly unnoticed by most in the gospel music industry. Calvin Newton has replaced the demons in his life with a newfound joy of singing for God. He is often seen on the Gaither Homecoming videos and maintains an active solo ministry. He has performed Sons of Song classics in recent years with Wallace Nelms and Ken Turner. Newton's life story was recounted in the book *Bad Boy of Gospel Music*, which was written by Russ Cheatham.
---John Crenshaw contributed to this entry.

Southern Gospel Music Association (SGMA)

The idea for an organization called the Southern Gospel Music Association initially grew out of an increasing displeasure in the Southern Gospel industry regarding the direction of the Gospel Music Association as it expanded to include all forms of Christian music. Charlie Waller organized the initial version of the SGMA in 1982. It was ultimately purchased from Waller and more or less dissolved by 1986 to pave the way for the Southern Gospel Music Guild. The guild did not present awards annually as the SGMA had done, and was generally viewed as an organization that was working with the GMA rather than competing.

Singing News publisher Maurice Templeton and other industry leaders formed the second version of the SGMA in 1995. This time, the primary emphasis was to establish a brick and mortar Hall of Fame for the industry. They ultimately reached an agreement with the theme park Dollywood. Under this agreement, the theme park would provide the physical building and the industry would be responsible for the exhibits. The Southern Gospel Hall Of Fame and Museum was opened to the public in 1999. The final location of the building drew some criticism from fans over the fact that a Dollywood ticket was a pre-requisite for a Hall of Fame visit, but previous efforts to raise money to build an adequate freestanding building had failed.

In recent years, Charlie Waller has been named Executive Director of the current SGMA, bringing him full circle. The SGMA annually holds an induction ceremony to bring new members into the Hall of Fame.

Speck, Mike

Mike Speck has a church music background that dates back to the early 1970s. From 1984 to 1987, Speck was the music director for the Freddie Gage Evangelistic Association. He worked for evangelist Bailey Smith in the same capacity from 1987 to 1991.

In 1986, Speck published his first choral music collection titled *Go Tell*. By 2004, eight of Speck's choral collections had been nominated for Dove Awards. Individuals like Lari Goss and Cliff Duren have orchestrated his choral arrangements, and top choral companies like Word Music and Lillenas have published them.

Speck has also been a Southern Gospel artist since the early 1990s, typically performing with his wife Faye and another female vocalist as the Mike Speck Trio. Milena Parks, Katy Van Horn, and Stacie Caraway have provided the third vocal part among others over the years since the trio began. Speck served two years as minister of music at Thomas Road Baptist Church where he was seen on the *Old Time Gospel Hour* each week with Rev. Jerry Falwell. He also conducts a choral showcase each year at the National Quartet Convention.

Speer, Ben Lacy Speer
(1930 -)

Ben Speer was born in Double Springs, AL in 1930 and began performing with his family group at the age of two. The youngest of the four Speer siblings, Ben eventually made "The King Is Coming" his signature song. He also arranged music for the group and developed a reputation as a comic emcee for the group. Ben retired from the Speer Family in 1992, but continued to appear with them at select dates until the group itself retired in the late 1990s. The Speers still appear from time to time on reunion events.

In addition to performing, Ben Speer established the Ben Speer Music Company in 1946, the first major publisher of sheet music. In more recent years, he has been active as a record producer in the Southern Gospel music industry, most notably for the Homeland label and the Gaither Homecoming videos where he's also frequently a featured performer and functions as Gaither's music director. In addition to artist projects, Speer has produced numerous accompaniment tracks for Homeland's EZ Key series and sang with the Homeland Quartet alongside label owner Bill Traylor. Speer has also operated Ben Speer's Stamps-Baxter School Of

Music, a two-week summer program on the campus of Trivecca Nazarene University, for a number of years.

Speer, George Thomas "Dad"
(1891 - 1966)
G. T. Speer was born in Fayette County, Georgia in 1891 and was raised near the town of Double Springs, Alabama. He taught in singing schools for the Vaughan and Stamps-Baxter based schools and had a reputation for being a stickler when it came to proper singing.

In 1921, Speer and his new wife, Lena, organized The Speer Quartet along with G. T.'s sister and brother-in-law, Pearl and Logan Claborn. The Claborn's left the group in 1925. As G. T. and Lena's children Brock, Mary Tom, Rosa Nell, and Ben matured, they were trained and developed into the Singing Speer Family, a group that continued traveling into the 1990s.

Dad Speer also wrote over 600 gospel songs. Many are standard repertoire for groups today. Some of his more popular tunes include "Heaven's Jubilee," "I Never Shall Forget the Day," and "The Dearest Friend I Ever Had."

Speer, Jackson Brock
(Dec. 28, 1920 – Mar. 29, 1999)
Brock Speer began singing professionally with his parent's quartet while still a small boy in the 1920s. Aside from a stint as a soldier in World War II, Speer sang with his family group his entire life. Ultimately moving to the bass position, Speer became the leader of the group after the death of his parents in the mid-1960s.

Under Speer's direction, the group was one of the top draws in the industry until their retirement, recording on the RCA, Benson, and Homeland labels among others. The group had three songs that reached the top of the *Singing News* charts. These were "What Sins Are You Talking About?" (March-August 1979), "Saved To The Uttermost" (June-July 1989), and "He's Still In The Fire" (March-April 1991).

In 1972, Brock Speer served as president of the GMA. He also served the organization as chairman of the board and was a permanent board member. He was inducted into the GMA Hall Of Fame in 1975. The SGMA inducted Brock into their Hall Of Fame in 1997, also inducting his parents that same year.

Speer, Lena Brock "Mom"
(1900 - 1967)
Lena Brock grew up in a musical family. Her father, Charles A. Brock, taught music in the South and trained his children to sing at an early age. Her brother Dwight Moody Brock was one of the more innovative piano players of his day, introducing instrumental turnarounds between verses and being one of the first to establish the five man "quartet," four singers plus a piano player. He was with some of the earliest versions of the Stamps Quartets.

After marrying G. T. Speer in 1920, Lena joined him in forming the Speer Quartet the following year. She was the group's original soprano and continued to perform alongside her husband and with their four children as the Speer Family until her death in 1967. She was best known for her moving renditions of songs like "Heaven Will Surely Be Worth It All" and "Time Has Made A Change In Me."

In 1997, Speer and her husband were inducted into the SGMA Hall Of Fame.

The Spencers
The Spencers released their first recording in 1972. The family group originally consisted of husband and wife J. B. and Barbara Spencer, their daughter Geniece, and sons Wade and Kevin. Geniece wrote the hit song "In My Robe Of White" which catapulted Gold City to popularity in 1982. The Spencers' recording of the same song also made it to the Top 20 of the *Singing News* chart. Geniece would leave the road in 1987 to raise a family, but she returned singing with her husband billed as The Ingolds in 1991.

The Spencers have had two songs reach number one on the *Singing News* chart. "Coming Soon" was the first (August-October, 1989). "Let's Meet By The River" held the top spot in April and May of 1990.

Kevin Spencer left to form his own group (the Kevin Spencer Family) in 1992. He also established a record label called Some Dawning Music. J. B. and Barbara cut their travel schedule back and Wade established himself as a solo artist. The Kevin Spencer Family had a number one song on the *Singing News* chart in March of 1996 with "The Blood Is Still There."

Stamps, Frank Howard
(1896 - 1965)
Frank Stamps was a native of Upshur County, Texas. He served in World War I, and then attended the Vaughan School of Music. When his brother, V. O. Stamps, formed a music company in 1924, Frank organized the Frank

Stamps Quartet as a promotional group to represent the company's songbooks.

In 1927, the Frank Stamps Quartet became the first to sign with a major record label, Victor Records. They had the first Southern Gospel hit record with "Give the World a Smile." When V. O. Stamps died in 1940, Stamps took over his brother's duties at Stamps-Baxter for a few years. Ultimately, Stamps decided to leave Stamps-Baxter in the hands of J. R. Baxter and form his own publishing company, the Stamps Quartet Music Company.

With the backing of Stamps both at Stamps-Baxter and Stamps Quartet Music, many groups traveled under the Stamps name and promoted songbook sales. Frank continued to sing with various Stamps groups, including the company's flagship group, the Frank Stamps All-Stars. This group ultimately became known simply as the Stamps Quartet, and when Frank Stamps retired from singing with the group in 1950 to focus exclusively on songbook publishing, the group continued to record for the next seven years as the Stamps Quartet. They changed the group name to the Plainsmen Quartet in 1957 and severed ties with the publishing company. A few years later, another Stamps Quartet was formed out of the publishing company, but Frank Stamps did not sing with them. He ultimately sold the company and the Stamps Quartet name to James Blackwood and J. D. Sumner.

In 1997, the SGMA Hall Of Fame posthumously inducted Frank Stamps and his brother.

Stamps, Virgil Oliver "V. O."
(1892 - 1940)
V. O. Stamps was a pioneer of Southern Gospel on multiple fronts. Taking advantage of radio when it was first introduced, V. O. took music to the masses.

He got his start in the Vaughan Music Company between 1915 and the early 1920s. In 1924, he formed the V. O. Stamps Music Company, and subsequently merged it with J. R. Baxter in 1926 to form the Stamps-Baxter Music And Printing Company. It was also in the 1920s that Stamps and Baxter started the Stamps-Baxter School Of Music. More than 100 quartets eventually became Stamps affiliates. V. O. also sang with some of the Stamps related groups. Thanks to the promotion of Stamps-Baxter songbooks by their affiliated groups, the company became the largest publisher of shape note hymnbooks by the height of the Depression in the mid-1930s.

In 1997, the SGMA Hall Of Fame posthumously inducted V. O. Stamps and his brother.

Stamps Quartet
(1924-present)
Two Stamps and A Baxter

A series of significant events in the 1920s launched a legendary name in gospel music. It all started in 1924 when V. O. Stamps formed the V. O. Stamps School Of Music. His brother Frank formed the first Stamps Quartet around the same time. Then in 1926, V. O. partnered with J. R. Baxter to form the Stamps-Baxter Music and Printing Company. They would become the most successful publisher of shape note hymnbooks in the United States. V. O. also formed a quartet of his own.

In 1927, the Frank Stamps Quartet signed a recording contract with Victor records, making them the first Southern Gospel quartet to sign on a major label. They also had the first ever Southern Gospel hit single with "Give The World A Smile." In addition to their recordings, they were introducing innovative practices for the time. When Dwight Brock (brother to Lena "Mom" Speer) joined the group at the piano, he was one of the first to introduce instrumental "turnarounds" between the verses. The move to hire a person to just play piano also established the standard "four guys and a piano" configuration for male quartet singing, elevating the importance of the pianist in the process. Previously, one of the singers had typically pulled double duty as a singer and accompanist, either on piano or guitar.

Groups using various versions of the Stamps name were active until V. O.'s death in 1940. At one point, he even sued his brother Frank for using a duplicate (or nearly duplicate) name. The groups served a purpose that ultimately benefited from all the sharing, though. The Stamps-Baxter Company published songbooks, and selling them was a key source of revenue for the groups and for the company in turn.

Stamps Name Multiplied

After V. O. Stamps' death, Frank Stamps became Baxter's partner and took over his brother's duties in the company. He also left his own group, the Stamps All Stars, to sing in the group his brother had owned, the Old Original Stamps Quartet. Under Frank's influence, the publishing company began to arrange deals with many popular quartets of the day to sell Stamps-Baxter songbooks. In exchange, groups were allowed to use "Stamps" or "Stamps-Baxter" as part of their own name. The company also launched a number of groups with the Stamps name. This practice led to more than 100 groups using the word "Stamps" in their name at various times. The partnership lasted five years until Frank Stamps left his position with Stamps-Baxter and began a new company called Stamps Quartet Music Company.

The division did not bring about the end of the various Stamps Quartets, however. Members of groups owned by the Stamps company were swapped around like modern sports stars, only more frequently. The Frank

Stamps All Stars were promoted as the top group in the Stamps family, so any time a member would quit, the next best man was immediately moved up into his place. Ultimately, the "All Stars" designation was dropped and the group that had been the Stamps All Stars came to be known simply as the Stamps Quartet.

Frank Stamps decided to narrow his attention to publishing songbooks around 1950. The remaining group members recorded as the Stamps Quartet for a few years after this. They ultimately decided to end their affiliation with the publishing company and changed the group name to the Plainsmen Quartet. And so, the Stamps Quartet came to its first end.

First Rebirth (1962)
A few years later in the early 1960s, the Stamps Quartet was reborn, again as an outreach of the publishing company. Terry Blackwood, Smilin' Joe Roper, Jerry Redd, Big Jim Waits, and Roger McDuff were members of the new Stamps around 1962. Ready for retirement, Frank Stamps sold his business to James Blackwood and J. D. Sumner a year or two later. By that point, the group included Big John Hall, Jim Hill, and Mylon Lefevre. Donnie Sumner became the group's piano player in 1966 and moved to the baritone slot when it opened up later. The most significant change in the group came in 1967, when J. D. Sumner and James Blackwood "swapped" bass singers. Sumner left the Blackwood Brothers and went to the Stamps. The former Stamps bass John Hall replaced Sumner in the Blackwood Brothers. Part of the deal also consisted of Sumner giving up his ownership of the Blackwood Brothers and James giving up his ownership of the Stamps. Jimmy Blackwood went to work for Sumner in the Stamps at the same time.

Although the Stamps would become one of the most popular gospel acts in the world in the coming years due to their association with Elvis Presley, their only number one song on the *Singing News* chart came in March of 1970 before they joined Presley's entourage. The song was titled "The Night Before Easter" and was written by J. D. Sumner's nephew Donnie Sumner.

Working for Elvis (1971-1977)
As the 1970s rolled around, the Stamps saw a number of changes. Most notable was their launch into global stardom as the key backup group for Elvis Presley. Ed Enoch came on board in 1969. Bill Baize was soon singing tenor, and Ed Hill later came to the Stamps from the Prophets. During their years backing Elvis, Sumner had some health issues, so Richard Sterban and others were used to sing bass at times. It was also during this period that the Stamps had their only female vocalists, first Sandra Steele, followed by Jennifer O'Brien later.

After Elvis' death in 1977, a number of members passed through the Stamps. By 1980, JD was filling in with Hovie Lister and the Statesmen. It was then that he and Lister hatched the idea for the Masters V, and the Stamps name was once again retired.

Second Rebirth (1988)
After James Blackwood, Jake Hess, and Steve Warren exited the Masters V, the underlying concept of the group was significantly diluted. Sumner and Lister carried on for a while with Shaun/Sherrill Nielsen, Jack Toney, and Ed Hill, but ultimately JD decided to revive the Stamps name. Warren returned to sing tenor while Toney and Hill remained with the group during the name change. When Ed Enoch returned to sing lead, the core members of the Stamps from the glory days of the 1970s were reunited . . . Sumner, Hill, and Enoch. Ultimately, Rick Strickland replaced Warren on tenor and Jerry Kelso became the pianist. Before Sumner's death in 1998, the group appeared at numerous Elvis tribute events as well headlining for gospel concerts.

Third Rebirth (2003)
Forbidden by the Sumner estate to continue using the Stamps name after Sumner's death, the group became known as Golden Covenant and carried on after 1998. Tom Graham was hired to sing bass after a year or so of performing as a trio. Not to be outdone by the restrictions on the name, concert promoters often billed Golden Covenant as "The Former Stamps" during this period. Future Dove Brothers bass singer David Hester was with the group for a year or so before being replaced by Butch Owens. In 2003, the group secured the rights to use the name Stamps Quartet again. Royce Taylor joined the group at tenor and former pianist Jerry Kelso returned to the group as well. Longtime baritone Ed Hill parted ways with the group in 2005 and was soon followed by Kelso, who moved to the Dove Brothers later in 2005.

A PARTIAL STAMPS QUARTET DISCOGRAPHY: *Live In Nashville* (1971), *Live at Murray State* (1975), *I Believe in the Old Time Way* (1980), *Peace in the Valley* (1991), *Elvis Gospel Favorites* (1994), *Let's Have Church* (1995), *The Final Sessions* (1999)

Stamps Trio
Numerous "Stamps" groups sang and promoted gospel music for many years. Most of these were quartets. The Stamps Trio is one of the few trios to have used the name.

The members of the Stamps Trio were young, but all had made a mark in gospel music prior to forming the group. They began their career around 1964, and it lasted less than a year. Donnie Sumner was the baritone singer and pianist for the group. The unique sound of the Stamps Trio focused around his interesting arrangements and original compositions. Sumner is the nephew of the late J.D. Sumner.

Byron Burgess sang lead. Burgess had previously spent time singing with the Harmoneers Quartet and was also a member of the Rhythm Masters Quartet. He and Donnie often switched parts, so the title "lead singer" may be a bit misleading. Burgess possessed a very smooth voice, and was a noted vocal instructor at the Stamps Quartet School of Music.

Jim Murray was the tenor singer for the Stamps Trio. Murray's name would later become a household word among gospel music fans when he joined Jake Hess and the Imperials. Prior to joining the Stamps Trio, Jim had traveled the country with the Orrell Quartet.

This group was not full time. All the members had "day jobs" at the Stamps Quartet Music Company in Dallas, TX and were "weekend warriors" as the Stamps Trio representing the company. While the big groups of the day were singing in air conditioned auditoriums, the trio typically appeared at singing conventions promoting the latest Stamps Quartet Music Company songbooks. Instead of giving full concerts, they were often relegated to hot schoolrooms singing one or two "special" songs after several hours of class singing.

Temple Records, a division of Stamps Quartet Music, Inc. released two recordings by this short-lived group. *Temple Records Presents the Stamps Trio* and *Command Performance Featuring the Stamps Trio* are considered collector's items. Some of the arrangements contained on these albums were used almost note for note by other groups in later years.

The gospel music community did not overlook the talents of these men. Donnie Sumner joined his uncle J. D. Sumner as pianist for the Stamps Quartet and later became their lead singer. Jim Murray replaced Sherill Nielsen in the Imperials Quartet. Lee Gann and Dean Brown joined the Stampes Trio for a short time before it disbanded.
---John Crenshaw contributed to this entry.

Stanphill, Ira Forest
(February 14, 1914 - 1993)
Ira Stanphill was a native of Bellview, New Mexico. He was first recognized for his work as an Assemblies of God singer and evangelist. In this role, he preached and sang in 40 nations outside the United States. He wrote more than 400 gospel songs, including many that are now considered to be standards. Some of Stanphill's songs include "Mansion Over the Hilltop", "Room at the Cross", "Suppertime", "Follow Me", and "I Know Who Holds Tomorrow."

The SGMA Hall Of Fame inducted Stanphill in 2001.

The Statesmen Quartet

Hovie Lister was known as the first gospel music disc jockey. When Lister learned that Major Howell, Chairman of the Board of the Atlanta Constitution, planned to start radio station WCON in Atlanta, he requested airtime for his his new quartet. Howell gave Lister the airtime and the Statesmen Quartet debuted on WCON radio in October of 1948 with Mosie Lister (lead), Bobby Strickland (tenor), Bervin Kendricks (baritone), and Gordon Hill (bass). In time, transcribed radio programs featuring the Statemen were distributed to more than twenty radio stations throughout the Southeast.

Early Personnel Changes

Mosie Lister was the first to depart the quartet. He continued to write and arranged songs for the group. The man chosen to replace Lister was the same person that had replaced him in the Melody Masters Quartet, Jake Hess. Aycel Soward also replaced Gordon Hill. Soward had been Lister's first choice for the bass singing role when he was forming the group, but circumstances prevented him joining the group in the beginning (even though he was in the first publicity picture of the quartet). The group signed a recording contract with Capitol Records just before James Wetherington was hired to replace Soward.

After a few weeks with the quartet, Lee Roy Abernathy gave Wetherington the nickname "Big Chief." The quartet composed of Strickland, Hess, Kendricks, Big Chief, and Lister remained intact through the summer of 1950. Bobby Strickland left on September 1, 1950 to form the Crusaders Quartet. Three members of the Melody Masters Quartet were then reunited when Lister hired Cat Freeman to replace Bobby Strickland. Freeman, brother of Vestal Goodman, was a seasoned quartet veteran. Freeman had a strong voice and soon became the clown of the Statesmen Quartet.

When Uncle Sam came calling for Hovie Lister, Big Chief took over the management of the quartet. The most notable change during Chief's tenure as group manager took place when Doy Ott was hired to play piano. Also during this period, Kendricks left the Statesmen to join Strickland's Crusaders Quartet. Once Lister returned from military service, he resumed the pianist position and Doy Ott became the baritone for the group. This was a position Ott would hold for many years.

The 1950s: Glory Days

The Statesmen spent countless hours perfecting their craft and molding the sound that would take them to the top of the gospel music world. Several of their more popular renditions were patterned after black gospel arrangements. Hits such as "You Sho Do Need Him Now," "Talk About Jesus," and "Get Away Jordan" all came from black artists of the day. Once the group stabilized with Cat Freeman, Jake Hess, Doy Ott, Big Chief

Wetherington, and Hovie Lister, they formed an alliance with the Blackwood Brothers to tour as a team. By the end of the decade, the team was collecting as much as $1500 per performance, an amount unheard of previously. Due to their popularity, the team was able to exercise considerable clout with concert promoters, more or less dictating if, where and when other groups could appear. This lasted until the rise of gospel television shows in the late 1960s gave competing groups wider exposure.

Cat Freeman left the Statesmen as they were reaching the height of their popularity. Lister had always dreamed of having tenor Denver Crumpler in the group. He was able to convince Crumpler to join the Statesmen in 1953. Crumpler's clear voice and good looks made him a natural for the group. The precision attained by this lineup led many music authorities to dub them "The Perfect Quartet."

Shortly after Denver Crumpler joined the quartet, they signed a recording contract with RCA Victor records. The quality of their recordings improved with the addition of noted studio musicians like guitarist Chet Atkins, who also produced many of their early RCA recordings. This marriage with RCA Victor lasted for nearly fifteen years. They also recorded a number of songs for the RCA Thesaurus transcription service.

Food giant Nabisco began sponsoring the syndication of the quartet's TV program to other markets. The Statesmen had elaborate sets built for the program and hired the Wade Creager Orchestra, house band for the Biltmore Hotel Ballroom. The group was the first quartet to regularly use an orchestra. Songs were prerecorded in advance. They would then lip-sync the lyrics while being filmed for the program. Lister sold Nabisco saltine crackers and vanilla wafers as the Statesmen sang "merry melodies coming your way, songs of happiness to brighten up your day."

The national media took notice of gospel music in the mid-1950s. On September 6, 1954, the Statesmen Quartet traveled to New York City to make their live national television debut on *Arthur Godfrey's Talent Scouts*. They performed their recording, "This Ole House," and won the competition.

Jake Hess left the quartet in late 1956 to start a new business venture. Les Roberson, formerly a member of the Weatherfords and the Oak Ridge Quartet replaced Hess. Roberson was a natural baritone, but he tried valiantly to fill the lead singer's role. This change in personnel was a big blow to the Statesmen, but nothing on the scale of what would happen on March 21, 1957. As the Statesmen were preparing to leave for a trip, Lister received a call from Denver Crumpler's wife reporting that Crumpler was quite ill. Although Lister quickly summoned an ambulance, Crumpler passed away at the age of 44.

The death of Denver Crumpler brought about a distinct change in the sound of the Statesmen Quartet. Cat Freeman returned to fill in with the quartet until a permanent replacement could be hired. Freeman ended up staying with the group for over a year. Meanwhile, Les Roberson began experiencing vocal problems, so Jake Hess returned to sing lead, making the Statesmen as they were in 1953. Rosie Rozell from Tulsa, OK was hired to fill the tenor role. Rozell brought an emotional vocal style to the quartet.

After Rozell joined the group, the Statesmen produced an album for their own Statesmen label titled *Get Away Jordan*, which quickly became one of their biggest sellers. It was also one of the first to be released on the new Skylite record label, which was a company that the Statesmen and Blackwood Brothers owned jointly.

The 1960s: Lead Singer Roulette and More TV Shows

During the 1960s, songs like "I've Found a New Way," "I Shall Not Be Moved," "Without Him" and "Oh What A Savior" were popular songs for the Statesmen. In 1963 Jake Hess left the Statesmen to form a new group, Jake Hess and the Imperials. Hess had been the cornerstone around which the Statesmen sound had been formed for 15 years. Jack Toney was the man ultimately hired to replace the popular Hess. Although Toney was a young man, he had years of gospel music experience and an excellent voice. Toney did well singing Statesmen classics originally made popular by Hess, but his forte was the new songs he brought to the group such as "Ship Ahoy" and "Beyond the Gates."

In the mid-1960s, the Statesmen began appearing with the Blackwood Brothers on a syndicated gospel music television program called *Singing Time in Dixie*. This program featured the two quartets along with many other top groups. Most of the featured groups on the program recorded for the Skylite label, which was owned by Statesmen-Blackwood Enterprises.

The Statesmen released a number of recordings on the RCA Victor label during the 1960s. One of their biggest recordings was actually released on RCA's budget label, RCA Camden. The project was titled *All Day Singing and Dinner on the Ground*. The Goss Brothers were hired to provide background instrumentation, and the recording was nominated for a Grammy Award.

Roy McNeil followed in Toney's footsteps with the Statesmen. McNeil had formerly sung first tenor with the Rangers Trio and would later assumed that position with the Stamps Quartet. During his tenure with the Statesmen, the quartet was able to pitch their harmonies higher due to McNeil and Rozell's similar vocal ranges. After several months, McNeil returned to his former position as lead singer with the Prophets and Jack Toney returned to the Statesmen.

After Toney returned to the fold, the group launched another television program. The new show called *Glory Road* was recorded in color, which was an emerging innovation at the time. The program featured the Statesmen and the Blackwood Brothers with one guest group on each 30-minute show. Toney continued to sing lead with the Statesmen until 1968. After that, Don Butler filled in until Jim Hill, another established first tenor, was hired to fill the lead singer position.

Much like the situation when Jack Toney joined the Statesmen, Hill developed his style to suit the old Statesmen standards such as "Oh My Lord What a Time," and "Faith Unlocks the Door." He joined Rozell, Ott, Big Chief and Lister and recorded one of their most popular albums, *Thanks to Calvary*. Included on that album was one of Hill's most popular songs, "For God So Loved."

Soon after Hill joined the Statesmen, Rosie Rozell left the quartet to join the Searchers. The Statesmen Quartet hired Sherrill Nielsen to replace Rozell. Nielsen had been the original first tenor with the Imperials. His Irish tenor voice allowed the Statesmen to recreate some of the sounds from the Crumpler years. Nielsen also brought new songs to the group including "The Impossible Dream" and "Gonna Shout Hallelujah."

The 1970s: New Trends and Ultimate Disbanding
The Statesmen Quartet adopted a more youthful sound in the 1970s with the addition of Nielsen and bass guitarist Tim Baty. Their appearance changed as well as they began to dress in polyester suits with open collars. Gary Timbs joined the Statesmen to play organ. He would sometimes leave the organ bench to join Nielsen and Baty as they performed a few numbers on the Statesmen programs. Timbs later replaced Hill in the lead vocalist position. His version of "That's Enough" became a hit for the group, and his boogie-woogie piano style and repartee with Lister thrilled audiences. Nielsen and Baty left the Statesmen and joined forces with Donnie Sumner to form Voice, which became part of Elvis Presley's entourage.

After Nielsen left, Rosie Rozell returned to the Statesmen for a short time. This aggregation revived several Rozell classics including "Oh What a Savior" and "You Gotta Walk that Lonesome Road," but they never made any commercial recordings.

Big Chief Wetherington developed a few medical problems in the early 1970s that required him to miss several months of touring. He was with the group on Tuesday night, October 2, 1973 in Nashville at the National Quartet Convention. The crowd reacted with enthusiasm as the Statesmen performed and Big Chief was featured on the song "Why Me Lord." He also performed a recitation during "The Lighthouse." The following day while the group was still in town for the convention, Wetherington suffered a massive heart attack and did not recover. He passed away on October 3, 1973

The death of Big Chief Wetherington was a devastating blow, and the group never truly recovered. Wetherington had been the foundation of the group's sound for two decades. Soon after Wetherington passed away, Rozell left the Statesmen Quartet for the second time. Willie Wynn of the Oak Ridge Boys was hired to replace Rozell and Ray Burdette joined the group to sing bass. Kenny Hicks, formerly of the Stamps and Rebels, joined the group as bass guitarist. They also employed a drummer, a lead guitarist, and a steel guitarist in hopes of updating their sound. Noted songwriter Elmer Cole joined the group for a few months, as did Wayne Hilton and David Will. With all the changes in personnel and musical styles, Hovie Lister ultimately made the decision to disband the Statesmen Quartet around 1980.

The 1990s: The Return Of The Statesmen
Hovie Lister, Jake Hess, J. D. Sumner, James Blackwood, and Rosie Rozell formed the Masters V during the 1980s and sang together for several years. Lister also spent some time with the Palmetto State Quartet.

In 1992, Hovie Lister and Jake Hess returned with a new version of the Statesmen that included Biney English (lead/baritone), Johnny Cook (tenor), and Bob Caldwell (bass). This group made three recordings (*Revival, Oh What A Savior,* and *O My Lord, What A Time*). Lister credits Bill Gaither with inspiring him to bring the Statesmen back in 1992.

Hess was only with the group a short time before health concerns forced him to retire from the road. As he had done years before, Jack Toney replaced Hess. Toney remained with the Statesmen until the group name was retired at Lister's death in 2001. Other members of the Statesmen during their final decade included Mike Loprinzi, Rick Fair, Wallace Nelms, and Doug Young. Although they weren't particularly successful on radio, the group continued to thrill audiences across the country with their classic style and Lister's charm as the group's emcee and pianist. Lister and the Statesmen were frequent guests on the Gaither Homecoming videos and regularly appeared at events like the National Quartet Convention and the Grand Ole Gospel Reunion.
---John Crenshaw contributed to this entry.

The Steeles
Jeff and Sherry Steele started their group in the early 1990s. The vocal sound of the Steeles is defined by Jeff's distinctive baritone voice. A number of vocalists have sung with the couple over the years including Troy Peach and Karen Akemon. When Akemon departed, the Steele's daughter Christy was promoted to a vocal position. After Peach left to form First Love, the group became a true family group, with all the members related.

The Steeles were particularly successful on Southern Gospel radio in the mid-1990s. Their first number one hit on the *Singing News* chart came in 1994 with "I Must Tell Somebody." The following year, "God Kept His Promise" held the number one position for three months. "I Got Up And Went" gave them their third number one in as many years in 1996.

The group is best remembered for their fourth number one song "We Want America Back," which held the top position for four months in 1997. The song, which includes a captivating narrated passage by Jeff Steele about the decline of modern society, caught the attention of *New York Times* writer R. W. Apple at a Grand Ole Opry performance. Apple sharply labeled the song as "sexist, rabidly homophobic, stunningly anti-government" in an article printed in the *Times*. Jeff Steele responded that it was "a commentary on the decline of moral values in our society and a statement on how people in key positions in media, entertainment and political leadership have let us down."

On September 11, 2001, when terrorists attacked America, the Steeles performed a hastily re-written version of the song for the National Quartet Convention audience that night called "We Want America Free." They repeated the performance the following year on September 11.

In more recent years, Jeff Steele has begun an evangelistic emphasis. The preaching/singing events are promoted as "Revival America" concerts. He has also published a book outlining his method for losing weight. Steele, who had weighed as much as 330 pounds, shed 80 pounds over the course of a few months. He has also written a book titled *We Want America Back: A Call To Action* that addresses the controversy surrounding the song.

Stewart, Derrell
(October 6, 1934 -)
Known for his characteristic choppy style of piano playing, an ever-present smile, and wearing red socks, Derrell Stewart has been a constant favorite of Southern Gospel fans. A native of Brunswick, Georgia, Stewart's father worked as a concert promoter. Stewart began taking piano lessons at the age of five and joined the Dixie Rhythm Quartet in 1953. Three years later, he moved to the Florida Boys Quartet and stayed with them into the next century.

Stewart became known nationally when the Florida Boys began appearing on the *Gospel Singing Jubilee* television program. In 1970, he became the first to be honored as the Favorite Pianist in *Singing News Magazine* Fan Awards. Also known for his comedic skills (he has appeared in some comedy sketches dressed up as a woman), Stewart was inducted into the SGMA Hall Of Fame in 2004.

Strickland, Bobby
(1920 - 1953)
Bobby Strickland is a native of Sand Mountain, Alabama. He was a popular Southern Gospel singer from the late 1930s through his tragic death in an automobile accident in 1953. He first became known for his work with the Harmoneers Quartet. He also sang with the Sand Mountain Quartet and was the original tenor for the Statesmen Quartet in 1948. Strickland went on to form the Crusaders Quartet in 1950, and served as a music advisor to Elvis Presley as he was beginning to rise to popularity.

Strickland was inducted into the SGMA Hall Of Fame in 2003.

Sumner, John Daniel "J. D."
(Nov. 19, 1924-Nov. 16, 1998)
John Daniel "J.D." Sumner was born in Lakeland, Florida. Sumner was inspired to become a bass singer at the age of eight after hearing Frank Stamps perform. He began developing his talent from that moment. Sumner was in the military from 1942 until his discharge in 1945. He began to pursue his dream of being a bass singer when he formed the Sunny Side Quartet. His popularity grew after joining the Sunshine Boys in 1948.

Sumner/Blackwood Partnership
In 1954, Blackwood Brothers members R. W. Blackwood and Bill Lyles lost their lives in a plane crash. James Blackwood asked Sumner to replace Lyles in the bass slot. Sumner and James Blackwood soon became partners in a number of business ventures that took on a life of their own. In 1957, they held the first National Quartet Convention, an event that continues to be the largest event in gospel music. Sumner dubbed it "the Granddaddy of them all." Sumner and Blackwood also formed the Gospel Music Association, which recognizes achievement annually in all forms of gospel music through the Dove Awards. Sumner and Blackwood are also known for adapting the first bus to be used by a group for touring purposes.

In addition to his other accomplishments, Sumner wrote more than 700 songs. Many of these tunes were written while he was a member of the Blackwood Brothers. Some Blackwood Brothers recordings feature Sumner's songwriting exclusively. James Blackwood and Sumner purchased the Stamps Quartet in 1963. Sumner continued to sing with the Blackwood Brothers for a few years, but ultimately decided to switch to the Stamps so he could manage them directly. In time they came to be billed as "J. D. Sumner and the Stamps."

Elvis Presley
In November of 1971, J. D. Sumner and the Stamps were invited to tour with Elvis Presley. The group became a regular fixture with Presley until his last concert on June 26th, 1977. The Stamps were also featured on most of Presley's studio recordings between 1972 and 1977. Following Presley's death, Sumner was put in charge of coordinating the funeral.

In the midst of their popularity while performing with Presley, the Stamps released what is probably their most critically acclaimed recording, a double LP titled *Live At Murray State*. The singers joining J.D. Sumner on that recording were Ed Hill, Ed Enoch, and Bill Baize.

Masters V
Sumner disbanded the Stamps in 1980 after a series of personel changes. He then joined with Hovie Lister, Jake Hess, James Blackwood, and Rosie Rozell to form the Masters V. This group of "living legends" toured until 1988. Lister served as the group's emcee while Sumner injected his brand of dry humor into their performances.

Guinness Book Of World Records
In 1983, the *Guinness Book Of World Records* recognized Sumner's 1966 solo recording of the hymn "Blessed Assurance." According to Guinness, the song contained the lowest recorded note ever produced by a human voice, a "double low" C. The recording was re-issued in 1984 as part of Sumner's solo project *Thank God For Kids* and again in 1999 posthumously on *The Wait Is Over*.

Stamps Reborn
By 1988, Jake Hess and James Blackwood had left the Masters V. Realizing the conceptual idea behind the group name had lost its appeal with fans, Sumner renamed them the Stamps. Sumner brought back former members Ed Hill and Ed Enoch to recreate the sound of the 1970s Stamps. Masters V tenor Steve Warren sang with the Stamps for a few years as well. During the 1990s, the Stamps were active participants in the Gaither Homecoming videos. They also enjoyed a great deal of success performing at Elvis Presley tribute events, both domestically and overseas. In addition to the two Eds, tenor Rick Strickland and piano player Jerry Kelso were members of the group during Sumner's final years.

Sumner passed away on November 16, 1998 in Myrtle Beach, SC. He was on tour at the time of his death.

The Sunliters
See: **Bagwell, Wendell Lee "Wendy"**

The Sunshine Boys
(circa 1938-present)

The Sunshine Boys were formed in Macon, GA during the late 1930s as a Country and Western band. Original group members included John "Tennessee" Smith (tenor), his brother A. L. "Smitty" Smith (lead), Milton "Ace" Richman (bass), and Pat Patterson (baritone). Each member played a variety of instruments. The group initially performed on radio station WMAZ before moving to Atlanta, GA where they were on WAGA and WSB. Pat Patterson was the first to leave the group when he was drafted into military service in 1942. Eddie Wallace, a young musician who was attending Georgia Tech at the time, replaced Patterson. Wallace brought a gospel musical heritage to the group, so they expanded their repertoire to include gospel music.

The Sunshine Boys demonstrated their versatility at this time by performing as two different groups on radio station WAGA. The station needed a Western swing band, so the Sunshine Boys became the Light Crust Dough Boys. They performed a 15-minute radio program as the Light Crust Dough Boys with guitar, bass, fiddle, and an accordion as accompaniment. During a thirty-second commercial break, the group would transform themselves into the Sunshine Boys. Eddie Wallace would move to the piano, swing the microphones around, and the Sunshine Boys would sing a 15-minute gospel program. This lasted for several years, and very few listeners realized they were listening to the same group. The group was always billed as the Sunshine Boys at concerts.

In 1945 the Sunshine Boys traveled to California to begin a career in motion pictures. They appeared in a series of Western films with stars like Eddie Dean, Lash Larue, Smiley Burnette, Charles Starrett, and the Durango Kid. In these films, the Sunshine Boys would sing Western songs and spirituals in the context of the movie.

The Sunshine Boys recorded a few gospel songs for the Village label in 1945 and some secular numbers for the Pan-American label in 1947. The Smith brothers were more interested in pursuing country and western music, so in 1949 they left the Sunshine Boys. This was their first personnel change in nearly seven years. Ace Richman and Eddie Wallace performed for a short time billed as the Travelers Quartet, hiring Horace Floyd (tenor) and J. D. Sumner (bass). Fred Daniel of Covington, GA. soon replaced Floyd. The group then relocated to Wheeling, WV to sing at radio station WWVA.

Wallace, Richman, Daniel, and Sumner divided their time between Wheeling and Atlanta with occasional trips to Hollywood to pursue their movie career. In the early 1950s, the Sunshine Boys signed a major record contract with Decca Records. Their affiliation with Decca led to them to take part in one of the biggest selling recordings in gospel music history when they sang backing vocals on Red Foley's hit "Peace in the Valley".

In 1954 the Blackwood Brothers hired J. D. Sumner to sing bass. This brought about the first personnel change for the Sunshine Boys in several years. Johnny Atkinson was chosen to replace Sumner. During this time, the Sunshine Boys began a network program for Minute Rice. The Sunshine Boys also did commercials for other products such as General Foods, Prince Albert pipe tobacco, and Tube Rose Snuff.

Burl Strevel left the Blue Ridge Quartet and joined the Sunshine Boys in 1956 replacing Johnny Atkinson. The Sunshine Boys became the first gospel artist to headline in major hotels on the Nevada circuit. They moved to Nevada in 1960 to work venues such as the Golden Nugget in Las Vegas and the Nevada Lodge in Lake Tahoe. Their blend of gospel and western music made them favorites on the Nevada circuit. Strevel rejoined the Blue Ridge Quartet in 1964 replacing George Younce. At that point, Jim Boatman joined the Sunshine Boys as bass singer.

Although the Sunshine Boys ceased traveling full time years ago, they still performed on a limited basis. They typically enlisted the services of the late J. D. Sumner or the late Johnny Atkinson to fill the bass slot. The group sang at "Old Timers Night" at the National Quartet Convention for several years. They have been regular performers at the Grand Ole Gospel Reunion since it started in 1988. Fred Daniel, Bob Shaw, Jimmy Jones, and Ed Wallace have performed on a limited basis around the Atlanta area. They sing many Sunshine Boys classics just as they did in years past. This group has also released a video and CD.
---John Crenshaw contributed to this entry.

Swaggart, Jimmy
(March 15, 1935-)
Jimmy Swaggart has been one of the most controversial figures in modern Christianity. A cousin to popular musicians Jerry Lee Lewis and Mickey Gilley, Swaggart's piano playing and singing made him a force in Southern Gospel music during the 1970s and 1980s. His first song to reach number one on the Singing News chart was "There Is A River," appearing in July of 1972. It returned to the top position for February 1973 and July-August 1973. Swaggart also had a number one song over a decade later with "Gone At Last" (January 1986).

During the 1980s, Swaggart's popularity as a televangelist rose to new heights. Singer John Starnes was featured performing with Swaggart on a popular live recording. Although it was never a number one song, their version of "I've Never Been This Homesick Before" was forever etched in the minds of Southern Gospel fans as Swaggart would call out, "Sing it, John" and encore it several times.

In the mid-1980s when the downfall of Jim Bakker was big news, Swaggart was viewed as a favored alternative by the mainstream media. Larry King invited him to appear on his show to comment on the Bakker situation in 1987. In 1988, the Christian world was shocked to learn Swaggart had been caught with a prostitute in 1987. His weeping confession and "I have sinned against you" statement was regularly lampooned by *Saturday Night Live* and other comedians.

In 1991, Swaggart was stopped for speeding and found to have a known prostitute in the car. The second revelation led to Swaggart's dismissal from the Assemblies of God denomination. The pattern repeated in 1995 when he was again pulled over for speeding and a prostitute was discovered to be in his car. Since that time, Swaggart has continued to preach at his church, but his influence on Southern Gospel music has virtually disappeared.

Swanee River Boys

The Swanee River Boys embraced soft harmonies and a spiritual sound that resembled a black gospel quartet. Their sound was remarkably similar to early recordings of the Mills Brothers. Even their stage mannerisms were different from other groups as they crouched down toward the microphones and swayed in time to their soft refrains.

The roots of the Swanee River Boys can be traced to the Vaughan Four based in Lawrenceburg, TN. Bill Carrier and Stacy Abner formed the group in October of 1938 soon after they graduated from the Vaughan School of Music. In late 1938, Stacy invited his nephews, Buford and Merle Abner, to join the quartet. They made their income from personal appearances and songbook sales for the Vaughan Music Company. The group appeared regularly on radio station WNOX in Knoxville, TN.

In late 1939, Buford and Merle Abner along with Bill Carrier moved to radio station WDOD in Chattanooga, TN where they joined forces with former Rangers Quartet tenor George Hughes to form the Swanee River Boys. Much like other groups of the day, the group did a mixed bag of songs including western, swing, and popular music in addition to their gospel fare. Buford Abner was the lead vocalist, Hughes sang the tenor, and Carrier was the baritone. Merle Abner provided a soft, subtle bass line that laid a perfect foundation for their smooth spiritual sound. For many years, the gentle strum of Bill Carrier's acoustic guitar was the only accompaniment used by the quartet. During this time, the Swanee River Boys appeared on programs frequently in Tennessee, Georgia, and Alabama. A typical program for this group encompassed a wide variety of musical styles along with comedic relief.

Buford Abner was responsible for vocal arrangements, and he composed many of their songs. The Swanee River Boys added variety to their programs by including folk songs and Negro spirituals with their gospel and popular repertoire. This varied repertoire allowed the Boys to perform entire sacred concerts for churches or give a musical variety reviews in school auditoriums or for civic organizations. According to a logbook kept by the late Bill Carrier, by 1941 the Swanee River Boys had an extensive repertoire of 186 titles. A little over half of their songs were gospel numbers.

The quartet accepted a position at WSB radio in Atlanta, GA in 1941 and soon became a regular fixture on the famous *WSB Barn Dance*. Their own program, *The Little Country Church,* was a regular feature of WSB radio for more than four years.

Both Abner brothers entered military service during World War II. Fleming Culberson, Lee Roy Abernathy and Bill Lyles temporarily filled their positions. At the completion of their armed forces tours of duty, the Abner brothers reunited with Carrier and Hughes in Atlanta. They soon moved to WBT radio in Charlotte, NC where they performed on the CBS radio network. When the Mills Brothers decided to take their act to Las Vegas, the Swanee River Boys moved to radio station WLW in Cincinnati, OH where they replaced this famous quartet. In 1947, the Swanee River Boys took second place on the NBC Radio talent show *The Big Break*.

The group had been without a permanent change in personnel for twelve years when Bill Carrier left the group in 1952. Horace Floyd, formerly with the Sunny South Quartet and Sunshine Boys, joined the group as tenor singer and George Hughes moved to the baritone slot. By 1954, George Hughes had also departed and the quartet consisted of Joe Thomas, Horace Floyd, and the Abner brothers. Don Stringfellow, formerly of the Stamps-Baxter Quartet, soon joined the group as baritone and remained in that position for many years.

During the 1960s, they spent a lot of time overseas performing for the troops in USO programs. After recording many gospel songs for the predominately secular King label, the Swanee River Boys turned their recording talents to several sacred labels. An early 1960s recording titled *Swanee River Boys Finest* introduced Bill Carver as the new tenor of the group. Gordon Stoker, lead singer of the Jordanaires Quartet, wrote the liner notes for this Zondervan album, stating, "The Quartet is now doing only Gospel singing and Buford Abner, the leader, is writing some very fine Gospel songs."

Many top groups including the Rebels Quartet, Statesmen Quartet, Sunshine Boys, Rangers Quartet and others, recorded Abner's songs. Jake Hess and the Imperials used the Abner classic, "He Was a Preachin' Man" for the title song of one of their best-selling albums. The Swanee River Boys were included in the gospel music movie *Sing a Song for Heaven's Sake* performing "Up To The House Of The Lord."

The quartet released a number of albums on the Skylite label. Buford Abner retired in 1970 and the others followed suit shortly thereafter. A resurrection of the group performed at the 1989 Grand Ole Gospel Reunion. The reunited group consisted of Bill Carrier, Buford Abner, Bill Carver, Lem Kinslow, and Don Stringfellow.
---John Crenshaw contributed to this entry.

The Talleys

Roger and Debra Talley were married in 1978. They traveled with the Hoppers for several years after their marriage. Roger's brother Kirk sang tenor with the Cathedrals in the early 1980s. He wrote the song "Step Into The Water," which reached number one on the *Singing News* chart for the Cathedrals in October of 1982 and remained number one for nine months. It was the Cathedrals' first number one, though they had been singing since the 1960s.

In 1984, Roger, Debra, and Kirk formed a vocal trio called The Talleys. This group performed together for almost a decade. Their song "Sweeter As The Days Go By" held the number one position on the *Singing News* chart for three months in 1986. "He Is Here" was also successful for the group. It was recognized with a Dove Award for Southern Gospel Song in 1991. The Talleys popularized a number of worship songs during the 1980s including "Hallelujah, Praise The Lamb."

Talley Trio

In 1993, Roger and Debra Talley retired from the road to raise their daughter Lauren. As Lauren grew older, she expressed a desire to pursue a career in gospel music. She, Roger, and Debra formed the Talley Trio in the late 1990s. They found success on the *Singing News* charts in 2000 when their song "Searchin'" became a number one hit. They would reach the top position five more times in the next five years with "The Healer," "The Answer Is Christ," "I Love The Lord," "Jesus Saves," and "His Life For Mine."

Talley, Kirk

Kirk Talley launched a solo career after The Talleys left the road in 1993. "Joy On The Other Side Of Jordan" was a number one song for Talley on the *Singing News* chart in 1996. Talley has also been the recipient of a number of *Singing News* Fan Awards. The song "Serenaded By Angels"

153

was recognized as the fans' favorite song in 1996. Talley sparked controversy at the National Quartet Convention in the late 1990s during a *Singing News* Fan Awards acceptance speech, by publicly complaining about the organization's policy against using soloists during the evening concerts. The comments were edited out of a video used as a promotional item by the magazine.

A few years later, Kirk Talley was the victim of blackmail when a man named Walbert Farmer threatened to provide evidence that Talley was a homosexual. Talley contacted the FBI, who set up a sting and arrested Farmer. Farmer was later successfully prosecuted for his crime. In the process, Talley's sexual orientation became national news, to the dismay of his fans and concert promoters. After canceling his scheduled concerts and spending several months being counseled by a team of ministers, Talley returned to the concert circuit. He released a live recording in 2005.

Talley, Lauren
In addition to singing with her parents in the Talley Trio, Lauren Talley has released three solo recordings. She remains a full time member of the Talley Trio, but is showcased individually at most concerts where the Talley Trio appears. Her 2005 release was titled *I Live*.

Teddy Huffam and the Gems
See **Huffam, Teddy**

Thrasher Brothers
(1948-1996)
The Thrasher Brothers (Jim, Buddy, and Joe) performed on the *Wally Fowler Gospel Sing* at the Grand Ole Opry when they were children in 1948. Five years later, they won *Ted Mack's National Talent Show* and subsequently toured with Mack's group for two years.

From 1967 to 1976, the Thrasher Brothers produced a television show called *America Sings*. When the *Singing News* magazine began publishing a monthly chart 1970, the Thrasher Brothers were one of the first groups to score a number one song with "Jesus Is Coming Soon." They weren't at the top on the first chart in January, although four other groups shared the honor for the same song, but their version of the song did make it to the top for the February chart. The group had one other number one song on the *Singing* News chart with "One Day At A Time." It was the top song for three months (non-sequentially) in late 1974 and early 1975. A foray into pop and country music on the MCA label garnered the Thrasher Brothers a mainstream hit song ("Still The One") in the early 1980s.

While maintaining their music careers, brothers Jim and Joe Thrasher co-founded the Thrasher Brothers Motor Coach Company in 1969. After the quartet retired in 1986, Jim became the sole owner while Joe went to work in the state highway department. Jim has since served as President of the Alabama Motorcoach Association. Joe's son Neil sang with the Thrasher Brothers and later formed Thrasher Shiver, a country vocal duo act with Kelly Shiver that released a debut recording on the Asylum label in 1996.

In 1996, Ben Speer produced a Thrasher Brothers release on the Homeland label titled *Encore*. This final recording by the three brothers featured an all-star cast of bass singers including George Younce, J. D. Sumner, Brock Speer, and Rex Nelon. A 1971 recording of deceased Thrasher Brothers bass singer John Gresham was also incorporated into the project.

Toney, Jack

Jack Toney began his professional singing career in the 1950s doing evangelistic work with Rev. John Hull. Hull's group, the Joymakers, sometimes featured the young "Jackie" Toney. A few years later, Toney joined a part-time group called the Songmasters. As his fame grew, he took a job singing with the Prophets Quartet, joining forces with Ed Hill, Lew Garrison, Jay Simmons, and Joe Moscheo. Toney didn't remain with the Prophets for very long, but this first taste of professional gospel music whetted his appetite for full time singing. Over the next few years he filled in for Les Beasley with the Florida Boys and traveled with the Speer Family for a short time. J. G. Whitfield then asked Toney to join the Dixie Echoes.

The Dixie Echoes thrived with the talents of George Forbis, Jack Toney, Joe Whitfield, and Sue Whitfield. Toney's success with the Dixie Echoes led to a call from Hovie Lister of the famous Statesmen Quartet. Jake Hess turned in his resignation with the Statesmen in late 1963, and Lister began searching for the man that could aptly fill the role Hess had occupied for nearly fifteen years. Not only did the singer have to be an excellent musician, he would have to look the part of "Statesman." Toney would later comment, "I've had gray hair for a long time. But there was no way Hovie was going to have a gray-headed lead singer! That just didn't fit the part. I used a lot of Clairol to keep Mr. Lister happy."

This would prove to be the first of several times Toney would follow Hess in a quartet. Jake Hess was one of the most popular men in gospel music, so there was a period of transition as the fans became used to Toney's style. Fortunately, he related to fans both on and off the stage, and the Statesmen went on to do some of their finest singing with Jack in the lead spot.

The group continued their long association with RCA Victor, producing some of their finest recordings with the group of Rosie Rozell, Doy Ott, Big

Chief Wetherington, Hovie Lister and Jack Toney. They began *Singing Time in Dixie*, a syndicated television program, during this time. Toney was an accomplished songwriter who brought songs to the group such as "Ship Ahoy" and "Beyond the Gates."

While with the Statesmen, Toney married the former Cheryl McSpadden, and life on the road as a newlywed led to his departure from the Statesmen Quartet in 1966. Roy McNeil, the man that had replaced Toney in the Prophets, replaced him in the Statesmen Quartet. This lineup only lasted for a year or so before Toney returned to the Statesmen and McNeil returned to the Prophets. He remained with the group for another year before again resigning. In the book *Happy Rhythm* Toney related, "I had some family problems. Just to make it plain, my wife didn't want me on the road. I have never been a good road person. That was probably my downfall in the singing business. I love to be at home."

Not long after Toney left the Statesmen for the second time, tenor Rosie Rozell also departed to form Rosie Rozell and the Searchers. He wanted Toney to sing lead, and before Jack could turn down the offer, Rosie informed him that he'd already purchased new suits. Toney spent about a year on the road singing with the Searchers.

During some of Jack's down time from full time gospel singing, he worked as a choir director and sang in several part-time groups in Alabama. One group was the Southmen, where he sang with a young Tim Riley. Another was the Gadsden Ambassadors. Jack and Gail Toney were married November 14, 1984. He and Gail began writing songs together, and turned out more than 500 songs. Some of their songs that were recorded by top groups include "I Will Rise Up From My Grave" (a number one for the Kingsmen), "Some Dawning" (Kevin Spencer Family), "Ridin' High" (Kingsmen), and "Jesus Is Coming for Me" (Inspirations).

Full time work called again in the 1980s when Toney replaced Jake Hess with the Masters V. After Hovie Lister's departure from the Masters V, the group name was changed to the Stamps Quartet with Jack Toney continuing as the lead singer. He performed with the Stamps Quartet for about three years before again retiring from full-time singing.

Hovie Lister and Jake Hess joined forces again in 1992 to bring back the Statesmen. Life on the road soon took its toll on Jake's health, and Toney was again called on to replace him. By now, the Statesmen were only singing selected engagements, so the travel wasn't nearly as extensive for these quartet veterans. The personnel of the Statesmen Quartet changed at the other positions over the next few years, but the lead vocals of Jack Toney remained the anchor of their sound. The Statesmen recorded several of Toney's songs on their last few projects including "You Can't Shake the Rock", "Grace Marches On", and "I Wanna Rock My Soul."

Shortly before Hovie Lister's death, Grand Ole Gospel Reunion promoter Charles Waller formed the Grand Ole Gospel Reunion Quartet with Lister, Toney, Roy Pauley, Buddy Burton and tenor John Rulapaugh. This group was originally intended for a one time performance, but Lister wanted the group to make a recording together. The Grand Ole Gospel Reunion Quartet's first recording proved to be the last recording for the Hovie Lister. After Lister's death, Jonathan Sawrie joined the group and they continued to perform at the Grand Ole Gospel Reunion until Toney's death.
---John Crenshaw contributed to this entry.

Unseld, Benjamin Carl
(October 18, 1843 - 1923)
Benjamin Carl Unseld was known as a gospel music teacher in the late 19th and early 20th century. He was originally a professor at the New England Conservatory of Music in Boston. Unseld later instructed at Fisk University in Nashville, leading the famous Fisk Jubilee Singers. He was the first principal of the Virginia Normal School of Music. While there, he insisted that students learn to read round notes as well as shape notes. Although not known as a lyricist, Unseld composed numerous tunes for lyrics written by others, including Fanny Crosby. His most popular tune was for lyrics written by A.S. Kieffer titled "Twilight Is Falling." In his later years Unseld edited the *Family Visitor*, which was published by the Vaughan Music Company. He also served as Principal of the Vaughan School of Music.

The SGMA Hall Of Fame inducted Unseld in 2004.

Varner, Wally
(January 13, 1926-December 28, 2004)
Wally Varner was noted in the Southern Gospel industry for two skills: songwriting and lightning fast fingers. Most remembered as the former pianist for the Blackwood Brothers, Varner also played for several other groups in the 1940s and 1950s including the Homeland Harmony Quartet, the Deep South Quartet, and the Melody Masters (a group that also included Jake Hess and Jim Wetherington at the time). Wetherington typically introduced Varner to radio and concert audiences as the "King of the Keyboard." Some of Varner's better known compositions include "Sing Your Blues Away," "Bells of Joy Keep Ringing," and "Crown Him King."

After his stint with the Blackwood Brothers Quartet (1958 to 1963), Varner engaged in a number of entrepreneurial ventures. At one point, he and his brothers operated a franchise of 23 Kentucky Fried Chicken locations. Varner also owned a tire company and a gas station. He and his wife Polly formed a Southern Gospel music mail order business in 1991.

When Charlie Waller began promoting the annual Grand Ole Gospel Reunion, Varner became a regular fixture at the event. He also participated in a number of Homecoming video tapings where he thrilled a new generation of fans with his up-tempo piano playing abilities. Varner passed away in December 2004 at the age of 78 after a bout with myelofibrosis, a rare bone marrow disease.

In 1996, Varner was honored when he was inducted as a charter member of the Southern Gospel Piano Roll of Honor.

Vaughan, Charles Wesley
(1875 - 1965)
Named after the famous Methodist evangelist, Charles Wesley Vaughan was the original bass singer for the Vaughan Quartet. Vaughan also wrote songs and wrote music for lyrics written by others. After the death of B. C. Unseld, Vaughan took over the editing duties for the company publication, the *Vaughan Family Visitor*, a position he held from 1923 to 1938. He was also the mayor of Lawrenceburg, Tennessee from 1927-1931, and became a State Senator in 1935.

The SGMA recognized Vaughan's achievements in 2004 when they inducted him into the Hall Of Fame.

Vaughan, Glenn Kieffer
(1893 - 1969)
Glenn Kieffer Vaughan managed and sang with the Vaughan Quartet in the early 1920s. He was one of the first to promote Southern Gospel on the radio. Vaughan taught voice at the Vaughan School of Music and wrote several gospel songs He also formed the Tennessee State Singing Convention in 1934. When his father James D. Vaughan passed away in 1941, Vaughan took over the Vaughan Music Publishing Company and ran it for more than 20 years. In 1947, he followed in the footsteps of his father and uncle Charles Vaughan by serving as mayor of Lawrenceburg, TN. The National Singing Convention elected him president in 1949.

The SGMA placed Vaughan's name in their Hall Of Fame in 1997.

Vaughan, James David
(1864 - 1941)
James D. Vaughan is generally regarded as the founder of Southern Gospel Music. He started the James D. Vaughan Music Publishing Company in 1902 and in 1910, he was the first to establish a professional quartet and

put them on the road for the purpose of selling songbooks. The Vaughan School of Music was formed in 1911. Numerous gospel performers would study there in the following years. In 1912, Vaughan began the *Vaughan Family Visitor*, an influential publication across the South during the early 20th century.

In 1922, Vaughan founded one of the first radio stations in Tennessee, WOAN, where he broadcasted Southern Gospel music until 1930. He also founded the first record company based in the South, Vaughan Phonograph Records. Vaughan was involved in local politics, serving as mayor of Lawrenceburg, TN from 1923 to 1927, a position his brother Charles Wesley Vaughan and son Glenn Kieffer Vaughan would hold after him.

Vaughan's induction into the SGMA Hall Of Fame took place in 1997.

Waits, James Parks "Big Jim"
(1899 - 1973)
Big Jim Waits was highly respected both by fans and by other bass singers. Often called "The Dean of the Bass Singers" or "Deacon Big Jim Waits," he set a standard of excellence in the field of bass singers. His was also known by the nickname "Pappy." Waits spent several years on the vaudeville circuit before giving his life to gospel music. One of the first groups he sang with was the "Sunny City Four." He was with this group when he made his first real tour. They were hired to travel to New York and sing for a chain of theaters.

In his early years, Jim sang with groups such as the Electrical Workers Quartet, the John Daniel Quartet, and the Belmont Quartet of Atlanta. He was with several groups in the Stamps organization including the Stamps Baxter Mixed Quartet, and he replaced Frank Stamps in the Stamps Quartet in Dallas, Texas.

Waits excelled not only on the stage, but also in the recording studio and on the radio. He sang with several of the major groups in the Atlanta area, including the LeFevre Trio on at least two different occasions. The group made several recordings for the Bibletone label when Waits was a member. Wally Fowler, a close friend with whom he had sung in the John Daniel Quartet, convinced Waits to move to Nashville and work as a soloist with Fowler's All Night Sings on WSM radio. He remained with Fowler for a while, and later moved to Fort Worth to sing with the Chuck Wagon Gang. This venture was short lived as the desire to sing with a male quartet pulled Waits back to Atlanta. He joined forces with Dan Huskey, Bob Shaw, Tommy Rainer, and Jerry Briggs to form the Revelaires Quartet.

Health concerns necessitated Wait's retirement from the Revelaires, so he moved to Tampa, FL to live near his daughter. The Rebels Quartet of

Tampa soon procured his services, but in 1955, Waits suffered a heart attack and had to leave the Rebels Quartet. Although he was no longer a member of the Rebels, he continued to be their mentor and their biggest fan. After he recovered from his heart problems, the allure of the road once again pulled at the former vaudeville performer. He traveled with the Speer Family as an added attraction at their concerts. Brock and Ben Speer were both quite active in the Skylite-Sing recording company, so they had Waits record four of his classic songs with the Speer Family.

According to the old timers, Jim Waits never appeared at a concert without perfectly shined shoes and a perfectly ironed suit. His voice could cut through an auditorium. Jim's vaudeville career helped him overcome any obstacles he might meet on stage. He was a premier showman and the first bass singer to perform the "trombone" routine that was made popular by Billy Todd and later revived by Ken Turner. He would cup his fist and make his voice sound like a trombone as he performed crowd pleasers such as "On the Jericho Road."

Many gospel music legends give credit to Jim Waits for teaching them the quartet business. Hovie Lister worked with Waits both in the LeFevres and the Homeland Harmony Quartet. In the book *Happy Rhythm*, Hovie Lister is quoted, "Big Jim taught me more about quartet work and how important it is to love people more that anyone else I've ever known...Big Jim was my mentor. What I know about showmanship, I learned from him. When I was with the Homeland Harmony Quartet, he would slide down to get the low notes and he taught me how to go down the keyboard like I was trying to find the note, and I would end up falling off the piano bench. If it was a grand piano, then I would crawl under the piano like I was embarrassed and they would have to coax me out."

Waits' last stint in a full time quartet was again with the Rebels in the mid-1960s. London Parris had taken a leave of absence, and Waits spent several months with the Rebels. He recorded the album *Good News* with the quartet before Parris returned.

Waits was the first living member to be inducted into the GMA Hall Of Fame in 1971. He was also part of the inaugural class inducted into the SGMA Hall Of Fame in 1997.
---John Crenshaw contributed to this entry.

Walbert, James D. Walbert
(1918 -)
James D. Walbert is a classically trained musician who was given the title "wizard of the keyboard" by his fans and cohorts in Southern Gospel. Walbert has a rich heritage in gospel music with William Walbert as his father and James D. Vaughan as his maternal grandfather. In the 1930s,

Walbert first became known for his work as pianist for the Vaughan Radio Quartet. Since that time, Walbert has appeared on stage with many popular secular artists including Liberace, Jerry Lee Lewis, Red Skelton, and Judy Garland. He is often noted for his flamboyant style. Once he surprised an audience and shocked his more conservative father (W. B. Walbert) by turning around playing a piano backwards during a concert.

The SGMA inducted Walbert into their Hall Of Fame in 2004.

Walbert, William Burton "W. B."
(May 18, 1886 - 1959)
W. B. Walbert was a native of Barren County, Kentucky. He attended the Vaughan School, and subsequently began to work for them in 1912 as a representative. In 1915, Walbert married James Vaughan's daughter Mable Grace Vaughan. Along with Vaughan's son, Keiffer, Walbert was very instrumental in the success of the Vaughan Music Company over the next 50 years.

Walbert was both a band director and staff artist for Vaughan's radio station, WOAN, in Lawrenceburg, TN. Beginning in 1923, Walbert managed the Vaughan Radio Quartet. Walbert was also an editor of the Vaughan *Family Visitor* in the 1930s and began running the Vaughan School Of Music after James Vaughan's death in 1941. Walbert wrote more than 100 gospel songs, including "Peace Like A River," and "Tell It Everywhere You Go."

Walbert was inducted into the SGMA Hall Of Fame in 1999.

Weatherford, Earl Henderson
(1922 - 1992)
Earl Weatherford formed his first group in southern California in the mid-1940s. The greatest success of Earl's group came when Glen Payne, Henry Slaughter and Armond Morales joined him and his wife Lily Fern. Noted for their smooth blend, the Weatherfords were often the envy of their Southern Gospel counterparts.

In 2000, the SGMA inducted Weatherford into the Hall Of Fame.

Weatherford, Lily Fern Goble
(November 25, 1928 -)
Lily Fern Weatherford was born in Bethany, Oklahoma. By the 1940s, her talent as an alto singer had become so compelling that her husband Earl decided to changed the format of his traditional all-male quartet to include his wife. When Lily Fern Weatherford replaced the tenor singer with the

Weatherford Quartet, the group's sound was dramatically redefined. Her inclusion in what had been a traditionally all-male world paved the way for the modern mixed quartet. It did not hurt that she was a master of harmony and blend. Since Earl Weatherford's death in 1992, Lily Fern Weatherford has continued to travel and sing with her son Steve.

In 1999, the SGMA inducted her into their Hall Of Fame.

Wetherington, James Stephen "Big Chief"
(1922 - 1973)
James Wetherington emerged in the 1940s as a bass singer with the Sunny South Quartet. In the late 1940s, he joined with Mosie Lister to form the Melody Masters in Georgia. He spent a year or two with the group, moving them to Lincoln, Nebraska for a period of time where Wally Varner and Jake Hess also performed with the group.

In 1949, Wetherington joined Hovie Lister and the Statesmen Quartet where his fame grew to new heights. Hovie Lister and Lee Roy Abernathy felt he should have a nickname, so Wetherington became known as "Big Chief," out of respect to his Native American heritage. He was the foundation of the Statesmen sound for 24 years and a continuous fan favorite until his death in 1973 while attending the National Quartet Convention.

In 1997, the SGMA inducted Wetherington into their Hall Of Fame.

Whitfield, Jesse Gillis "J. G."/"Whit"
(September 8, 1915 -)
J. G. Whitfield has been one of the most influential personalities in Southern Gospel music. After serving in the Air Force during World War II, he formed the Gospel Melody Quartet in 1947. Glen Allred joined the group in 1952, with Les Beasley coming on board the following year. In 1954, Whitfield changed the group name to the Florida Boys. After his first wife died in a car wreck, Whitfield remarried in 1958. He quit singing with the Florida Boys the same year, but continued to own the group for several years.

Whitfield formed the Dixie Echoes Quartet (originally calling them the Messengers) in 1960. He helped launch the black and white *Gospel Song Shop* program on television as well as the highly popular color *Gospel Singing Jubilee* program that followed. During this time period, Whitfield was also getting experience as a concert promoter across the South, helping launch the careers of many up and coming groups at the time. He formed Jubilee Enterprises in 1966, selling records, songbooks, and sheet music. In May of 1969, he published the first edition of *The Singing News*, a publication originally used to promote his concerts.

In 1970, Whitfield launched the International Gospel Song Festival. In 1979, he purchased the National Quartet Convention from J. D. Sumner and James Blackwood. Whitfield ran the convention for two years, and then sold stock to quartet owners. A board of directors has overseen the convention since 1982. Whitfield also joined forces with fellow concert promoters W. B. Nowlin and Lloyd Orrell to form the Skylite Talent Agency.

In 1997, the SGMA recognized Whitfield by adding him to their Hall Of Fame. He celebrated his 90th birthday in 2005 and still makes appearances singing bass with a Florida based group called the Workmen Quartet.

Winsett, Robert Emmett "R. E."
(January 15, 1876 - 1952)

R. E. Winsett was an early promoter of shape note singing. A native of Bledsoe County, Tennessee, Winsett taught in singing schools, promoted his own publishing company based in Dayton, Ohio, and wrote more than 1000 gospel songs. His most popular song is probably "Jesus Is Coming Soon," which won a Dove Award in 1969 for Song Of The Year.

The SGMA inducted Winsett into their Hall Of Fame in 2002.

Younce, George Wilson
(Feb. 22, 1930 – Apr. 11, 2005)

George Younce was a native of Lenoir, North Carolina. He studied shape note singing and performed with the Spiritualaires when he was still a teenager. He sang with several groups over the next 20 years including the Watchmen, the Homeland Harmony Quartet, the Weatherfords, the Florida Boys, and the Blue Ridge Quartet. In 1964, he joined what was then called the Cathedral Trio, so named after Rex Humbard's Cathedral Of Tomorrow in Akron, OH where the group was based. With the addition of Younce's bass voice, they became the Cathedral Quartet.

For the next 35 years, Younce and Glen Payne moved the Cathedrals to the top ranks of Southern Gospel. By the 1990s, the Cathedrals were universally acclaimed by fans and the Southern Gospel industry. A farewell tour prompted by Younce's gradually declining health and the death of Glen Payne ended the Cathedrals' run in 1999.

In 2000, Younce formed the Old Friends Quartet with his son-in-law Ernie Haase, the legendary Jake Hess, and Wesley Pritchard. This group released two recordings and appeared on limited dates until Hess' death in 2004. Younce and the Cathedrals are members of the GMA Hall Of Fame, and Younce was inducted into the SGMA Hall Of Fame in 1998. Most remembered for his singing and mastery as a concert emcee, Younce also wrote several gospel songs including "Yesterday."

Acknowledgements

Special words of thanks are due to all the individuals who contributed to the content found in this book. I won't attempt to name them all, but I'll mention a few key sources.

James Hales and John Crenshaw contributed several entries when I was first getting started on this project. Crenshaw in particular gave me permission to adapt several articles he had written to my encyclopedia format. The bulk of the writing and research ultimately turned out to be a one-man job, but I probably would have never started at all had it not been for their help in the beginning.

Several historical books written by Bob Terrell (particularly *The Music Men*) were a great source of information. Another book I referenced frequently while compiling this material was *Close Harmony*, by James R. Goff, Jr. This book is meticulously researched with nearly 80 pages of supporting notes. If you prefer reading about Southern Gospel history in a continuous narrative format, I highly recommend these books and authors.

The Internet was another source of information. Special thanks is due to all who answered my questions, particularly the posters on the Usenet group alt.music.gospel.southern (AMGS) and those who participate on the forums at Sogospelnews.com and the Southern Gospel Nuts website. I also appreciate all information provided by the artists and their families. Many of these entries were initially posted on my weblog. Thanks to all who pointed me in the right direction when I had a detail incorrect.

If this book whets your appetite for more Southern Gospel facts, see my website at www.musicscribe.com. There I have posted additional information that fell outside the scope of this encyclopedia such as complete album discographies for various groups and dated lists of group members. The site is typically updated on a weekly basis.

5277399R0

Made in the USA
Lexington, KY
22 April 2010